T0195618

WEST-BLOC DISSIDENT
a cold war memoir

WILLIAM BLUM

soft skull press
2002

West-Bloc Dissident: A Cold War Memoir
ISBN: 1-887128-72-7
©2002 William Blum
First Edition

The author can be reached via email at BBlum6@aol.com.

The cover photo was taken by Robert Parent and appeared on the bottom of page 38 in "In The Teeth Of War," a photographic documentary of the March 26th, 1966, New York City demonstration against the war in Vietnam, published by The Fifth Avenue Vietnam Peace Parade Committee.

Book Design by David Janik

Soft Skull Press, Inc
107 Norfolk Street
New York, NY 10002
www.softskull.com

distriuted to the trade by:
Publishers Group West
1 800 788 3123
www.pgw.com

TABLE OF CONTENTS

CHAPTER ONE
EXPOSING THE CIA

The fourth day of August, 1969, 7:30 of a warm, clear Monday morning, Route 123, Langley, Virginia. Before the week is out, the sociopathic followers of Charles Manson will carry out their gruesome murders. Strangely enough, though what I'm about to do is completely non-violent, many Americans would regard it with equal abhorrence.

I park my red Volkswagen bug along the shoulder of the road, about 50 feet before the turnoff. The exit is marked "Bureau of Public Roads," but everyone knows that this is where you turn right to approach the entrance to the headquarters of the Central Intelligence Agency.

I take out my spare tire, which I had deflated the day before, lay it on the ground near the right rear tire, crouch down and pretend to be changing a flat. Sal stands a few feet to my right casually looking over that morning's *Washington Post* spread open before him on the top of the car. As cars pass by us and turn off toward the CIA, Sal furtively reads as many license-plate numbers as he can into a microphone. The microphone lies hidden under his shirt, taped to his chest, its cord trailing out to a portable cassette recorder inside a brown paper bag lying on the front seat.

How long can we get away with this, I wonder as I jack up the rear wheel and remove the inflated tire. What would they do to us? The law was quite ambiguous on the matter, but then the CIA was quite ambiguous on matters of law.

I stand a tire up, turn it around, put it down, move it a bit, same with the other one, then put the good tire back onto the wheel. If someone's watching, they can't be certain I've put the same tire back, particularly with my back blocking their view.

There's only so much time one can spend dallying over a tire change. I pick up the back hood and earnestly look over the engine, handling wires, spark plugs, wires again; a VW engine doesn't offer many possibilities. Every once in a while I stand up and stretch, like any hard working man is entitled to do.

An hour and a half has passed, we've used both sides of a 90-minute tape, and recorded several hundred plate numbers. It is remarkable indeed that perhaps a thousand people trained in exacting security procedures have passed right by us without their spy noses smelling anything fishy.

We've already decided to pack up and leave when a car pulls up behind us. It is marked "Central Intelligence Agency" something-or-other. Two men step out, one in a police-type uniform, the other in civilian clothes.

"Can we give you a hand?" the uniform asks, though not in a tone generally associated with heartfelt concern.

"No thanks," I say. "We had a flat and a loose spark plug (an odd combination, it occurs to me later), but it's okay now."

As I begin putting things away, the suit walks slowly around the car, on the side opposite Sal, looking it over, glancing inside. There is nothing in the car except a tennis racket (a reassuring touch in these ultra polarized times, I had thought), and a brown paper bag and newspaper lying on the front seat. Sal has already painfully ripped the microphone and wire from his chest, stuck them in the folded up newspaper, and placed it all on the front seat of the car.

My CIA file, received years later under the Freedom of Information Act, while in little doubt as to our purpose, states: "There were no recorders, cameras, or other technical equipment noted in use or present in the vehicle." They were under the impression that Sal was writing the plate numbers on the newspaper. The same document describes me as 6 feet 2 inches tall, weighing 220 pounds, when I was actually 5 feet 10, about 160 pounds.

"Shit, look at my hands," I say to Sal, displaying two grimy paws. Now who would suspect someone of anything devious who's concerned only with his hygiene? The CIA would. My file states: "The man had a slight amount of grease on one hand but this appeared to have been 'smeared on' more than 'worked in'." How, I wonder, did we (i.e. "they") win the Cold War?

"So long," I nod to the two men with all the relaxed friendliness I can muster. As Sal and I start to get into the car, I'm absolutely convinced that I'm about to hear: "Hold it there, please!"

But nothing. We take off and don't exhale for at least half a mile. I would later read in the CIA file: "Due to lack of jurisdiction in the area, no attempt was made to confiscate the newspaper from the car." Funny, this obeisance to the law thing. The CIA, in the same period, was bugging and breaking into embassies in Washington and destabilizing governments and plotting assassinations abroad with impunity, but they were reluctant to contravene Virginia legal niceties.

As I'm driving, Sal plays the tape back. A mess of static fills the air, then a period of silence which seems much too long, then more static. I turn to look at him, our hearts are in our throats. Is it all fucked up? All for nought? We can't go back again, they'd never believe the coincidence. . . Then, lovely Washington license-plate numbers, melodious Virginia and Maryland numbers. We give out a whoop and drive back to the District to a well-earned breakfast on Connecticut Avenue.

We were like kids at play over the next couple of weeks, spy film, detective story, cops and robbers, all rolled into one game. After painstakingly transcribing the tape—it would have been inexcusable to implicate wholly innocent people—we traveled out to the Motor Vehicle Departments in Baltimore, Richmond and downtown Washington. (We didn't have regular jobs of course, the natural state of things in those days.)

Washington made it easy for you: several fat books of computer printouts lying on a table right out in the open; just look up the license-plate number and there's the name and address of some poor sap with no idea he's about to become famous, the last thing someone in his job wants. But a few of the numbers weren't listed, just skipped right over. Strange, and very interesting. We asked some clerks behind the windows if they could explain this. They didn't know, were not allowed to say, couldn't care less, please don't hold up the line. The arm of the CIA stretched everywhere. . . is that guy over there watching us?

In honored bureaucratic fashion, Maryland guarded its motor vehicle information like the proverbial national security was at stake. (Ironically, in this case they may have been right.) If you mentioned to a clerk that in Washington, D.C., only 40 miles away, the capital of his country, the very same information was freely available to the public, he found this news as relevant to his job, his mind, and his life as if you had been reciting the local train schedule between Nairobi and Addis Ababa.

Back in Washington, I decided that this was a job which called for. . . I stepped into a phone booth and became Sergeant Johnson of the Washington Police Department. The young woman at the other end of the line in Baltimore immediately snapped to attention at the sound of authority, and unresistingly gave the deep, deep voice whatever it commanded of her. Yet, as I waited on the phone for her to return with the information on ten license numbers, I could not help but picture my call being traced and a police officer suddenly appearing at my shoulder with me still clutching the receiver.

The system in Virginia naturally bore no resemblance at all to those in Washington or Maryland. In Richmond it seems that they would give you a fixed number (varying according to which clerk you spoke to) of names and addresses, if you paid a fixed-variable fee, and if, further, you gave a good reason for needing the information. Sal and I and our friend Leslie spent several hours there (she soiled neither hands nor soul with a regular job either), dressed in our bourgeois best, trying out different stories with different clerks, usually some variation on the theme of a bunch of cars illegally parked in the parking lot of our uncle's or father's apartment house in Arlington or Alexandria to whom we wanted to send a warning. "No, we've tried notes on the windshields; now we'd like to send a letter to their homes."

It was a long day. None of us would have spent so much time and energy on a normal paying job, nor would I have arisen at six a.m. to park on a highway and change a flat tire as a condition of employment.

The anxiety that we couldn't possibly get away with this was my constant companion. But struggling for primacy was an intensity that could pass for being high. I remembered reading Sartre on his work in the French underground resistance during the war. It was then, he wrote, when in constant danger of betrayal and death, that he felt most free and alive. The previous four years that I had been working in the American resistance, not yet underground, such feelings had been brought home to me, though death hardly ever lurked. Betrayal was another matter.

Leslie was cut from very different cloth than Sal Ferrera and I were. At 24, this vivacious brunette was Sal's age and 12 years my junior. Composing and playing music so dominated her passion and her life as to enclose her in a tight little box with no windows; mention of the name of any political figure, with the exception of the President, drew a blank stare from her. The likes of she and I could never get romantically involved, but we got along splendidly because of a shared New York City-Jewish sense of humor, very fine tuned. Leslie was typical of many people in the '60s—they didn't look out at the world through ideological eyes, though some could mechanically spout the rhetoric; but rather from long and painful experience with Authority, experts, parents, teachers, ministers, hypocrisy, rules and regulations, and just plain "shit," they knew which side their emotional and existential bread was buttered on.

The Quicksilver Times was a newspaper in Washington which could spout the rhetoric with the best of them—each issue was a new chapter of the exciting melodrama, "The People vs The Pigs"—but the reader who made the effort to look behind the heavy prose could occasionally be rewarded with an intriguing factoid or insight, or a slice of irony not to be found in the daily press. The Quicksilver was one of the "underground" papers of the day, a weekly which appeared each ten days to two weeks, and we used it to publish our list of 215 names and addresses because it was the only show in town for such an exposé.

There was no need to make fools of ourselves by asking the *Washington Post* if they'd be interested, though we'd have loved the greater coverage. Trying to throw a monkey wrench into the delicate covert circuitry of the Central Intelligence Agency was the kind of thing we did for a living, whereas the *Post* would have been on the phone with the Agency before we were out the door.

The list was not presented "in-your-face;" it was innocuously laid out and entitled, with a small-size font, "Know Thy Neighbor" because we didn't want the story to catch the eye of the printer, who, like many other commercial printers of the time, might be seized by a rush of patriotism and refuse to print the paper. My own weekly newspaper, the *Washington Free Press*, had suffered just such a fate on several occasions before it went belly up.

We prefaced the list with a strong indictment of the CIA and a recounting of their covert illegal and immoral activities over the years. Little did we know then that our catalog of CIA misdeeds was scarcely even the tip of the iceberg.

The preface also contained the following note:

> These names were provided the *Quicksilver Times* by a person closely associated with the CIA. Due to the position of our informant and the unorthodox methods employed in obtaining the information, the list is a combination of: employees (primarily), spouses of employees, and persons doing associate and consultant work for the CIA. Should any person listed wish to correct or clarify his inclusion we will gladly print any correspondence we receive.

Not surprisingly, no one on the list communicated with us, and our attempt to camouflage the origin of the names proved quite futile. A *Washington Daily News* article made it clear that the CIA knew how it was all carried out. *The Daily News* also telephoned a number of the individuals on the list, and, while some apparently admitted their employment with the Agency, most denied it or declined to comment. One man responded: "I don't even know what CIA stands for. . . all I know is that they are a bunch of spooks who run around the city."

"I don't work at all, much less for the CIA," said a Virginia woman, presumably the wife of an employee, with the car in her name.[1]

I've often wondered about the people on the list. Were there melodramatic confrontations with shocked friends, or was there newly-won admiration? The ironies must have abounded. A reporter with *Newsday* confided to us that the CIA had informed him that some of those on the list had been slated for overseas covert assignments which had to be canceled because of their covers being blown.

I look over the list every few years or so to see if there's anyone I've come upon in my travels or research. I'm taken with the idea of meeting one of them and just seeing what kind of human encounter would take place. Undoubtedly, most of them felt deep contempt for the anonymous authors of the exposé, wondering how people living in the United States, presumably Americans, could furnish such "aid and comfort to the enemy." For the next couple of months or so I was not without your basic paranoia.

I took to stringing a very thin piece of cotton across the hallway, a few feet from the front door, inside my apartment at 17th and Swann. The green cotton, about two inches above the green carpet, was virtually invisible to a person standing up. Unfortunately, suffering from chronic absent-mindedness as I do, I often forgot about its presence when I came home, and finding it broken later I had no way of knowing whether I or an intruder was responsible. But once when I remembered to check it as soon as I walked in, I found the cotton broken. Aha! cried Sherlock in triumph, with heart sinking nonetheless at this rape of his privacy. How the hell do they do these things? Do they have a key for every fucking door in the world?

Then Holmes had to stop and think whether he had taped the string in place again after finding it broken the previous time. Such was the battle: the CIA's arsenal of state-of-the-art technology versus my piece of green thread.

Although our preface to the published list of names unambiguously spelled out, in clearly moral terms, the authors' contempt for what the CIA had done, the Agency, perhaps unable to shake off its capitalistic upbringing, referred to the action (in a document in the file sent to me) as an "attempted exposure of CIA connected persons as a means of harassment and sensationalism calculated to 'sell papers' and to establish the paper's own image."

Shortly afterward, I happened to place a classified ad in the *Quicksilver Times* offering various personal articles for sale, one of my occasional survival techniques. A guy came by to look at a pair of binoculars. He was about 35 and said that he was a lawyer for a congressional committee. In those polarized days, when everyone was acutely conscious and self-conscious of their supposed categories, one look at my longish-hair and beard, one glance at my wall-to-wall Che, Ho, Mao and Fidel, and the guy could be left with no doubt that I was one of "them."

"If I didn't have this job," he assured me, in response to absolutely nothing at all, "I'd sure like to join you guys and help out, maybe live in a commune or something, ha-ha."

I managed a weak smile, when I'd rather have told him that he had no need whatever to explain or defend his life to me, that I was not making any sweeping assumptions about him. It was an awkwardness of a kind I was to experience often in those years.

"If you have an extra thousand girls, gimme a call, ha-ha," were his parting words. I mumbled something inane, annoyed at his swallowing such media hype whole, and wondering whether he really thought that by asking for a thousand he had cleverly disguised his longing for one.

He bought the binoculars, and I never heard from him again. I concluded that he was not other than what he purported to be.

Marie-Paule I was not so sure about. She called, and in a heavy French accent asked about a few of the items I had advertised, jumping from one thing to another before I could explain anything, and then suddenly abandoning the subject altogether and asking me personal questions laced with sexual innuendos.

She was, she said, a governess for two children of an American family in Chevy Chase. The next day she called again; buying something was not mentioned at all, the sexual talk became franker; and again the next day, and about five times the first week. The conversations usually bordered on the juvenile, yet I was intrigued for more than one reason.

Each time I suggested that we get together she spoke of a jealous boyfriend with a terrible temper. And sure enough, as we spoke one day I suddenly heard an angry male voice in the background and she said she had to hang up. Two days later she called to tell me that her boyfriend had roughed her up and she was through with him forever, and, yes, we could get together.

Saturday night found me driving through Chevy Chase, the prosperous suburb hugging Washington's northwest side, passing one lovely home after another, homes of GS-17s, politicians, all manner of lobbyists, agents and foreigners, many grown fat off of intrigue. . . perhaps what would have been my own home had I continued playing the game. The thought struck me that I was 36 and had never lived in a house.

I was on the right street but still a couple of blocks or so from Marie-Paule's house. When I stopped to check a house number I noticed a woman across the street walking in the other direction. Before I could say a word, she crossed the street toward me. When I asked her if she knew where the number was, she responded with something I couldn't make out, continued walking around my car, opened up the passenger door, got in, and shut the door.

It was Marie-Paule. Where was she going, I asked. Why wasn't she at home waiting for me? How did she know it was me? She lapsed into what was to be a pattern for the evening in the face of pertinent questions: her English was very poor it seemed, she did not quite understand the question; she offered half-answers and non-sequiturs. It was possible, I thought; there were difficulties over the phone for which my high-school French was wholly inadequate.

The woman sitting next to me was in her late 20s, I judged. Her features had a hard edge to them, the kind I tended to associate with bitterness, with having been through the mill. But it was not an unattractive face, and the figure in tight sweater, short skirt and boots made me think that someone had been studying my sexual appetites.

This was the first "blind date" I'd had in years, not since my former incarnation in New York where a team of highly trained and dedicated sisters, aunts and cousins labored to provide me with at least one every few weeks, notwithstanding the fact that none of them had the slightest idea of what I liked in a female; my efforts to explain my tastes were incomprehensible to them because I was, in effect, asking for someone very much unlike them.

In the mini-world in which I now lived, where social and sexual contact arising naturally from shared political endeavors was commonplace, a blind date was a practice placed on a par with primitive tribal rituals. Younger friends were genuinely astonished to learn that on many occasions in the past I had actually telephoned a woman I had never met before, for the purpose of meeting her in her apartment alone, and that she had neither panicked nor called the police.

Marie-Paule and I had not made any particular plans. As if I were still a Bright Young Systems Engineer at IBM, I suggested the cocktail lounge at the Shoreham Hotel, where we could sit and have a quiet talk. For reasons unclear to me, she rejected this and made no counter suggestion. I asked if she was hungry; perhaps we could have a bite to eat somewhere, although I certainly didn't have the Shoreham in mind for this.

No, that wasn't right either. She seemed troubled, unhappy. Perhaps I was a disappointment to her. The specter of blind dates past flashed through my mind.

Well, would she want to go back to my apartment and have a drink? She managed to convey to me in a mixture of English, French, facial expression and body language that this would be acceptable. She clearly did not mean to appear lewd, but that was the only thing that *was* clear to me.

"Movement" friends tended to look askance at my living in my own apartment, but I spent a lot of time in communal houses and I never grew fond of giant dust balls, footprints on my phonograph records, an army of nomads wandering zombie-like through the living room at all times of day or night, endless house meetings, or meals where the only meat to be found was in spaghetti sauce or chili. Besides, I could not do without the peace of my own place to do my writing. To others this smacked of "bourgeois individualism" or something. In truth, many of them, suffering from communal "burnout," would have dearly loved to have their own apartment if they could afford it, as I could with my savings from my previous bourgeois embodiment.

Though I was not invulnerable to being made to feel self-conscious about living alone, I generally shrugged it off as more image than substance. What, really, did such stuff have to do with working for fundamental social and political change in the United States? Yet this was one of the types of issues which could lead to movement organizations splitting into factions.

With Marie-Paule I was self-conscious in the other direction. My apartment was but a studio; small, and furnished with plastic-looking (not to mention genuine plastic) furniture—I was sure she had never seen the likes of it in Chevy Chase or Paris—located in a somewhat downscale neighborhood, a block or so on the white side of Washington's white-black divide.

There was an ex-husband in London, she told me as we sat drinking Canadian Club and ginger ale on what passed for my sofa. And there had been another governess job in Bethesda with an Indian family, but the husband couldn't keep his hands off of her and the wife was too intimidated by the husband to intervene, a tale told many times in the Washington area by governesses, au pairs, and nannies: the man of the house thinking that he had imported a desirable piece of property, who would not complain to any authorities for fear of losing her visa.

I leaned toward Marie-Paule, put my lips on hers, and received half kiss, half bite. Was this her usual way? I tried again, and got bit again; this time it really hurt. I sat back and looked at her staring at me with an expression I could only describe as wild-eyed. What was I to make of her? I had really found me a space case. Or had she found me?

Yet, the next moment my hand was all over her without any resistance; within minutes we were lying in bed making love. Or at least I was. Marie-Paule carried on with all the passion of a hooker staring at the ceiling over her john's shoulder; it was as if she had no alternative. Normally, her firm shapely body would have triggered an erotic meltdown in me, but my passion was sharply cooled by her odd behavior and the mysteriousness of the whole affair. What was this strange French woman doing in my bed?

At one point in the evening, I disappeared into the bathroom for a few minutes. If she had been sent into my life to try and get the remaining CIA employee names—we had told a reporter that there would be more names in a forthcoming issue—it was futile, for I had burned my notes a few days before, as well as the tape which the CIA didn't even know about. But perhaps the CIA was after certain documents, because they, like the FBI, were a victim of their own propaganda—that "foreign" influences were at work in the anti-war movement. Both agencies had been given explicit instructions by Presidents Johnson and Nixon to uncover the black Red hand of Moscow or Peking or Havana, if not Satan. On the one hand, the CIA had to put forth this line to try to justify, under its own charter, its incursions into domestic affairs if such became known. On the other hand, they needed to believe it because the alternative was to accept the notion that there was something so grievously wrong in American society and foreign policy that the protesters did not need any specific outside incitement to demonstrate their condemnation.

The time came to take Marie-Paule home. It had not been the most charming date of my life, nor of hers I dare say, and I did not exactly take her home. I took her to Chevy Chase, drove along at her direction, and stopped when she told me to. I had no idea where we were. The evening was not to be prolonged: she said goodnight, I said *au revoir* in my best continental style, and she got out and began to walk. In the still, deserted street there was no way to follow her covertly. My gaze picked up a lighted living-room window that framed several people in animated conversation, liquor glasses in hand. I suddenly felt very sorry for Marie-Paule, and for myself as well. I drove off, turned the first corner I came to without looking back, and found my way home.

She called me two or three times after this, but I never saw Marie-Paule again. She had made up with her boyfriend, she said. I did not take to drink.

Who was Marie-Paule? This little tale bears the fingerprints of the CIA. My guess is that she was in the Agency's employ unwillingly, being eminently vulnerable to pressure as a foreigner. The FBI has long intimidated aliens to do their bidding, using the threat of deportation. She well may have worked for the CIA before in Europe. The Agency likes to keep track of such "assets." But on this assignment she was a painfully torn person. How else explain her erratic behavior?

It's unlikely that she was assigned to seduce her way (though I was not exactly a tough lay) into my apartment to find particular papers. That was bound to take much more time than her handlers could count on her having while I was preoccupied. My guess is—and this, oddly enough, is a thought I'm having for the first time as I write this many years later—my guess is that she may have planted a bugging device in my apartment, perhaps a little self-sticking apparatus that she pressed into place in an instant.

In any event, the focus of my suspicions was wildly misdirected. Years later I was to discover that my partner in crime, Salvatore Ferrera, had been working for the CIA all along.

CHAPTER TWO
PASSING THROUGH STATE
DEPARTMENT SECURITY

Such were the times. Sal worked for the CIA, a girlfriend of mine worked for Vice President Hubert Humphrey, the father of the woman I lived with (not simultaneously with the girlfriend) worked at the White House, and I worked at the State Department.

And before the State Department I had worked at the Norfolk Naval Base, sent there by my Washington employer, Planning Research Corporation. by name, one of the many consulting firms that dotted the District landscape and sucked on the big government teat. I was sent there as an "anti-submarine warfare expert," which credential I had earned solely by means of attending a three-hour briefing in PRC's office given by a legitimate anti-submarine warfare expert to computer programmers like myself. I had literally slept through a portion of the early-morning briefing, including some of the "secret" information that was supposed to titillate us, I think. (I had at this time, 1964, a Secret security clearance.) All I can remember of the briefing is that he told us how many submarines of each type the United States had. This, we were informed, was a secret from the Russians and other bad guys. If I remembered any of it, dear reader, I'd gladly tell you, whether you have a "need to know" or not. But you can always ask your friendly neighborhood still-active Russian spy. I'm sure he can provide you with (yawn) all the latest figures.

Every Monday morning for three months I took a plane to Norfolk, Virginia; each Friday afternoon I flew back to Washington. It was the closest I ever came to military service and I never got accustomed in the least to all the young sailors snapping briskly to attention and saluting me each time I entered or left the base. I tried to explain to various of them that the United States was a democracy and that in any case I was not of royal birth, but they didn't know they had the right to listen to me. Before long I could not bear to look any of them in the eye, so uncomfortable did their reduction to automaton make me. What conceivably could it mean, as one often heard, that such men were defending freedom?

Many an afternoon I sat with commanders and captains in the Officers' Club during Happy Hour as they downed their scotch at 25 cents a shot, their steak plates at 50 cents, talked about their housing (free) and their medical care (free) and complained about "people on welfare lookin' for government hand-outs. . . what's this country comin' to, everyone wantin' somethin' for nothin', damn lazy coloreds."

Has it not been the same with military men since Napoleon was a corporal?

Though I felt scant personal affinity for these smug men, my quasi-liberal politics found surprisingly little quarrel with their views. I liked to think of myself as being engaged in a bitter war with conservatives, but at root it was often no more than a pillow fight; for we shared a fundamental acceptance of the logic of, and the pressing need for, our capitalist system, which perforce led us to believe that those on the bottom of society's heap were there, deservedly, as a result of their own defects; albeit conservatives reposed peacefully with this conviction, while I derived little pleasure from it, and could not always shake off the nagging doubts.

Even less quarrel did I have with the officers on matters of foreign policy, good little anti-communist, loyal and true, that I was.

Near the end of my stay in Norfolk, I found myself in the curious position of lecturing to groups of naval officers on what kinds of information to collect during simulated anti-submarine warfare and how to record the information in a manner acceptable to a computer. Through the magic of electronics, these earnest warriors could then determine, amongst other wonders, how many enemy subs and how many of the good guys' subs had been destroyed in the for-adults-only games of war they played. At the time, I didn't actually know what to make of what I was doing—either it was really much more complicated that it appeared, or much more simple. Eventually I decided that it was just more bullshit, like so many other uses computers were being put to. I formulated a new Parkinson's Law: Computer output expands so as to fill the time available for producing computer output. But that didn't keep me from writing a manual on the subject, put out by my firm and sent to naval bases throughout the world. I imagine that a bent-out-of-shape, unread copy of this pseudo book can still be discovered wedged behind a filing drawer in some remote outpost of the U.S. naval empire. Later, when I left the job, I asked for a copy of the manual—it was, after all, my only published work—but I was told I couldn't have one. It was classified.

And for this *opus magnum*, which I doubt ever saw the light of a useful day, the United States Department of the Navy shelled out maybe $100,000 of our nation's wealth, including all my expenses. I had traveled on business before, but never in full dress like this: airplanes, rented cars, hotels, telephone credit card, free-flowing booze, overeating, expense-account padding. . . the good life, I really had it made. But what had I made? I had been given an elegant blue-velvet tuxedo to wear, and sent to clean out the chicken coop.

Meanwhile, the wheels of the State Department bureaucracy had stopped spinning, a full five months after I applied there. To the question: "Do you have any reason to doubt William Blum's loyalty to the United States?" the FBI had received only "no" answers from friends, neighbors, and former colleagues. What else? The FBI conducts security interviews on the premise that if you ask enough people enough questions in enough different forms, if the person being investigated has ever displayed a "dark side," at least a hint of it will slip out from at least one interviewee. But those interviewed could only speak of the William Blum they had known up to the present time—for many years, but only up to the present. No one, not even Blum himself, could have predicted his dark future.

The newest line on my already crowded resumé now read: State Department, computer programmer. This was not because I had any particular desire to be a computer programmer at the State Department, but only as a means to a new end. Although programming made the puzzle-solving lobe of my brain happy, after five years in the computer field—the first four with the grandaddy of them all, IBM—the novelty and the "glamour" had begun to wear thin, and I was left with the prospect of only higher and higher salaries to look forward to, as well as a basic conflict I had carried with me for several years: I could never take seriously the idea that IBM, for example, should sell more computers than Remington Rand or RCA. The fact that IBM paid me a salary was irrelevant to me. I lived in a society, not a company, and what difference did it make to the society in which I lived which of several basically similar computers was most predominant? I don't think I realized for a moment how subversive an idea that was.

It was marvelously simple. I was going to become a Foreign Service Officer. I was going to serve my country and plunge myself into something of real substance. Plus—deep breath here—travel! adventure! foreign intrigue! a cast of thousands! That sort of thing. I had it all planned. I would use the programming position as an "in" into the State Department, pass the exams, and be appointed an FSO without the large cut in salary I would have sustained had I come in from the outside. But I never even checked whether this was actually kosher personnel policy, so eager was I not to deface the perfect picture of my new future.

It was during this period that American diplomats were kidnapped in Venezuela and the Congo, a U.S. Information Service office broken into and the American flag burned in Bolivia, and similar anti-American outrages committed in other parts of the world. These actions incensed me and contributed to my decision. Like all good Americans, I could not fathom the behavior of these Third World people. I never wondered whether they—from their point of view—had a rational, bona fide reason for doing what they did. I only wondered why they couldn't see what was so plain to me: that the United States had been a kind of Salvation Army to the rest of the world, disbursing freedom, democracy and material goodies to all the poor, ignorant and diseased peoples, and keeping communist darkness from descending upon them. In some manner, not yet defined in my mind, I—Super FSO—was going to teach those benighted foreigners a lesson!

And I was gonna do this with the help of the good ol' U.S. military if need be, and I was gonna make the world safe for our good ol' U.S. companies, teach those furriners to keep their cotton-pickin' nationalizin' hands off, and I was ...Wait a minute...I couldn't care less about the prosperity of corporations in the United States; what was I doing worrying about their fate overseas? Was I now their protector? And the military, did I now love and admire them? Whatever was I thinking?

I wasn't. Not one thought about such matters crossed my mind, no such connections were made, no warning bells sounded to slow down my plans.

> Subject indicated that he had never been arrested, charged, or held by any law enforcement agency; that he does not use intoxicants to an excessive degree; had never used narcotics nor associated with anyone who used narcotics; had never been fired from any job; had never been sued for the collection of any debt nor refused credit at any time; that he had never visited nor been visited by a psychiatrist or a psychoanalyst, and that to his knowledge, there is no history of mental or emotional disorder in his immediate family; that he never took part in a sexual act with another male; that he does not now nor has he ever belonged to the Communist Party or any Communist front or Communist dominated organization, or any organization which could be subversive in nature, and he also added that he knows of no one whom he considers as a Communist.

A snapshot from my State Department file, my pre-employment security interview, a catalog of middle-America's heresies at the close of the year 1964. In actuality, I had used a narcotic (marijuana was so labeled at the time); had been asked to leave more than one accounting job (another of my former incarnations) for being too methodical when time is money; and had taken part in a sexual act with another male. This had been an experiment to bring out the latent homosexuality that my old friend Martin insisted resides in all men, a notion I didn't share. I think I did my best not to fight any feelings that might come over me, but none came.

The high spot of the interview came when the totem-faced security officer asked me if I'd ever been in jail.

"No," I replied.

"Do you have any relatives who have ever been in jail?"

"No, I come from a very dull family."

"Well! If you think that not being in jail is dull. . ."

Forget it Jack, I felt like saying, I lost my head, it won't happen again.

But I was eventually hired, and was rewarded with a lengthy security briefing. They showed us various kinds of clever bugging devices, including the one discovered behind the United States Seal at the American Embassy in Warsaw, and the famous bug in the famous martini olive, ideal for diplomatic functions. The two speakers were properly grim; fighting Communism was Serious Business (from all appearances, they had gone to the same school as my friend Jack), and closed with ominous warnings about being befriended by mysterious foreigners, especially Russians. No matter how lowly your job at the Department, you probably know something that some foreigner would also like to know. And, as is well known, foreigners will stop at nothing to get what they want, even stooping so low as to become your friend.

Little did I know that one day soon I too would be totally paranoid.

Soviet Life was a slick picture-oriented magazine put out by the Soviet embassy in Washington, the opposite number of the magazine *Amerika* published by the U.S. embassy in Moscow. I had been a subscriber for several months when, in January 1965, I received a card which read: "The Embassy of the U.S.S.R. cordially invites the readers of 'Soviet Life' to attend a gathering at the embassy." There was no question that I wanted to go, to walk into the Western Headquarters of the Enemy.

When I showed the invitation around my office, only one person was less than suitably impressed—Al R., a stocky, crew-cut programmer who had spent eight years with the CIA. "You can't just go to the Russian embassy whenever you feel like it," he snapped. "You have to inform Security. . . and you oughta tell them about your pen-pal too."

I should have just gone, not even mentioned it; that would have been more my way. Security probably couldn't care less. But now the insidious bug had been planted in my head. I thought of the warning given at the security briefing, and then I remembered Washington's worst-kept secret—the FBI in the building opposite the Russian embassy photographing everyone who went in or out. Tourist bus guides passing down 16th Street reportedly would point out the embassy on one side, "and on our right, the FBI." Obviously it was better to tell them beforehand than have them find out on their own, so off went a memo to Security. The next day a call came asking me if I wouldn't like to pop up to the second floor for a little chat.

I allowed a small feeling of self-importance to creep over me as I walked into the Office of Security. In a life of anonymity, being called in by The State to explain one's behavior is an occasion, even when the behavior is trivial. Yet the sight of the two men I encountered was not reassuring. To others they were friend or colleague, husband or daddy—real people—but all I, still fresh from my Brooklyn-Jewish-ghetto lifetime, all I could see were two cookie-cutter Norman Rockwell gentile guys, probably named John and Jim. I figured we didn't have an ancestor in common apart from Adam, or some ape.

I was directed to a seat on one side of a table as big as Texas, which served to emphasize the gap between us, lest human intimacy subvert the business at hand. Stealing a glance around the nondescript room, I spied a couple of metal bookcases housing neat stacks of standard GPO reports of congressional hearings, likely dealing with internal security, perhaps other immortal classics as well; several filing cabinets with those good combination locks to keep Statesecrets from Noseycitizens; the artificial flowers for the aesthetic touch; and the ubiquitous official portrait of Lyndon Baines Johnson peering down and giving his blessing to these right nice folks, y'heah now?

A couple of minutes of human-like chit-chat disarmed me; this clearly wasn't going to be any heel-on-windpipe dialogue. Silly boy, that's what they learn in their first lesson in interrogation school. I was hit with lesson two when the conversation abruptly turned, not to why I subscribed to a Soviet magazine, not to why I corresponded with someone in a Communist country. . .

"How many girls do you know in Washington?"

I was genuinely startled. . . "I don't know. . . a few."

"How many would you say?"

"Well it depends on what you mean by *know*. Do you mean how many do I go out with?"

"That'll do."

"Well. . . about two or three I'd say."

"How often do you see them?"

My mind raced to make sense of this line of questioning. "About once a week maybe, I don't date that often."

"Why not? Don't you like girls?"

I flinched. "Of course I like girls, it's just that there are other things in my life too."

"When you take them home, do you stay late?" the voice continued.

"What do you mean by late? It depends."

"Let's take one of them. Who do you see the most often?"

"You mean you want to know her name?"

"Yes."

"Why? I mean what does that have to do with anything?"

"You don't have to answer if you don't want to."

I shifted in the hard seat, took a drag on my cigarette. . . It was funny, they knew they had me over a barrel because I was an employee who presumably wished to remain an employee, but the barrel was even bigger than they suspected—I could find a job a programmer anywhere, but where else could I become a Foreign Service Officer?

"Well, there's one I go out with named Arlene."

"What's her last name?"

"R_____."

"Who does she live with?"

"She lives alone."

"Do you stay late when you take her home?"

"Sometimes."

"How late? Do you ever stay until the morning?"

"Sometimes."

"Do any girls ever stay overnight at your apartment?"

"Once in a while." My voice sounded resigned. I lit another cigarette.

"Can you give us the address and phone number of this Arlene R_____?"

I paused a few moments, then reached into my back pocket for my address book, a foolish thing to do.

"Do you mind if we look at that?"

The address book was dutifully handed over.

"By the way, can you bring in the letters you've received from that person in the Soviet Union?"

Why don't you ask me first if I still have them you bastard? "I guess so."

"Bring them in tomorrow. You can pick up your address book at the same time."

I dragged my feet slowly down the long corridor, lighting yet another cigarette. Now what the fuck was that all about? Do they think I'm homosexual? Why the hell couldn't they just come out and ask me if I was getting laid? Why the hell couldn't I just tell them? My god, they aren't gonna call Arlene and ask her, are they? I began to laugh. . . maybe this is their way of finding women.

In any event, the whole idea behind hounding homosexuals out of sensitive government positions was seriously flawed to begin with. If the employer already knows of the employee's homosexuality, that removes the primary, if not the sole, threat that a blackmailer has hanging over the head of the employee. The national security issue here, in fact, may have been little more than a cover for homophobia.

Years later, through the magic of the Freedom of Information Act, I was able to read in my State Department file a snippet of the report on my interview:

> Blum's general activities and associations were discussed at some length, with no significant security information being developed. The names of Blum's friends and associations as contained in this report were checked through the indices of the CIA, SY and SY/SIS with negative results except for _____ as previously mentioned.

Other information in the document clearly indicated that the blank space belonged to one Nikanov, my private Russian teacher in New York, when my ambition of the month was to spend some time in the Soviet Union and observe for myself this phenomenon that crowded 20th-century history. Nikanov was very unique amongst Russian émigrés in that he had a rather positive attitude toward the Russian revolution and communism. I used to argue with him on that score, spouting all the anti-communist clichés and platitudes Americans are carefully taught. We had zero influence upon each other's heart and mind. I wonder what the old rascal was up to.

As it turned out, the embassy party was postponed. On February 7, 1965, a few days before it was to take place, American planes staged their first massive bombing of North Vietnam; this while Soviet Premier Kosygin was visiting there, amid reports that he was seeking to exert a moderating influence on North Vietnam and encourage a summit meeting with President Johnson. The next day thousands of angry Russian, Vietnamese and Chinese students attacked the American embassy in Moscow. All in all it was not deemed to be an altogether felicitous time for a peaceful-coexistence cocktail party. It was never rescheduled.

Soon afterwards, the correspondence with my Russian pen-pal, Valery, also fell victim to the Cold War. It had been a nice arrangement for mutual language study. Each letter was written partly in Russian and partly in English, and I was very pleased when he complimented me on my Russian though I knew it had taken me an hour or more to compose a good paragraph. I also got a kick out of the idea of communicating with someone behind the "Iron Curtain." I wondered how he felt about living there and what he really knew about the United States, but those questions could wait until we got to know each other a little better.

One day a letter arrived from Valery, from Kishinev, in the Moldavian Republic, in which he asked me why the United States had overthrown the governments of Brazil and Guatemala. I was shocked that he would insult my intelligence and disrupt our burgeoning friendship with such flagrant communist propaganda. So *that's* what he "knew" about the United States! As if *he* could know such things and not *me*. I never wrote to him again. Not too long a time was to pass before I wished that I had saved his address so that I could write to him and apologize for my ignorance.

CHAPTER THREE
JUDAISM AND QUAKERS

Early 1965. Winter evenings, standing in the small kitchen of my apartment on Wisconsin Avenue, a few blocks south of the National Cathedral, fixing dinner while I listened to the news on the radio; catching up on the day's Vietnam statistics of American firepower, bombing sorties, and body counts. I was filled with patriotic pride at our massive power to shape history. Words like those of Winston Churchill, upon America's entry into the Second World War, came easily to mind again—"England would live; Britain would live; the Commonwealth of Nations would live." Then, one day—a day like any other day—it suddenly and inexplicably hit me. In those villages with the strange names there were *people* under those falling bombs, *people* running in total desperation from god-awful machine-gun strafing.

This pattern took hold. The news reports would stir in me a self-righteous satisfaction that we were teaching those damn commies that they couldn't get away with whatever it was they were trying to get away with. The very next moment I would be struck by a wave of repulsion at the enormity of it all.

During this period most Americans were taking in the same news reports and seeing the same terrible photos in the papers and experiencing only the first part of what I felt. Still others, a tiny group, felt only the repulsion. (Amongst the latter could be found a number of young people who had arrived at certain conclusions years before the best and the brightest of the *New York Times* did.) The stage was being set for a completely unimaginable eight-year drama of an

America torn and polarized from sea to shining sea as it had not been since the Civil War.

The weight of the ambiguity and confusion I carried around with me was lightened by the anticipation that I, as an FSO, would be in a position to influence my government to avoid such a brutal side to an otherwise admirable goal. Inasmuch as we have seen several Secretaries of State in modern times relegated to junior-partner roles in important foreign-policy decision making, my trust in the clout that could be wielded by a lowly, new FSO was naive to the point of clinical insanity. Not to mention that my non-Plymouth Rock, non-Ivy League, non-gentile pedigree would have portended a pace of advancement in the foreign service leisurely in the extreme.

My ambivalence towards the war did not stem from any kind of pacifism. At this point in time I would have been hard pressed to even define what a pacifist was, or believed in—peace, sure, but who wasn't in favor of peace? I was about to receive an education on the subject from the American Friends, the Quakers.

I had been raised as a Jew. That's like saying the Pope had been raised as a Catholic. Suffice it to say that compared to my mother Mrs. Portnoy was a nun. This woman, who had lived under a Polish government, the Russian Czar, and the German Kaiser, and had experienced anti-Semitism under each one, tried the only way she knew to make her only son a good Jew. She failed because, even at the age of five, for reasons lost forever in the evolutionary mist, I had to know "Why?" And the only answer this woman from the old country had for such a strange question was: "Because you're a Jew."

Yes, this is another dreadful tale of "I was raised by a Jewish mother and lived to tell about it!" But please don't kvetch, it's important to my story.

I tried my best to suspend belief in my disbelief, to make sense of the life being imposed upon me. My mother, whose name was Ruth, told me that each three steps I took wearing my *tzitzis* (a thin shawl worn under the shirt by Orthodox Jewish males) would be a *mitzvah*, a holy act, a blessing in the eyes of God. I can still see that boy of nine or ten walking around his room one evening, wearing his *tzitzis,* earnestly counting his steps and picturing God up in heaven with a giant ledger open to his name and marking down the hundreds of *mitzvahs* he was racking up.

And when I got into a street fight one day and my pink (!) *tzitzis* with its yellow fringes became exposed to my non-religious friends, I was so mortified by their taunts and open-mouth wonderment—"What the fuck is *that*?"—that I refused to ever wear it again. I was able to wrench that concession from my mother, though not without several tearful scenes and much pain for us both.

But I couldn't get out of wearing a yarmulke (skullcap) at home whenever

I ate. The bad part of that was the many times a friend from the block—where we were the only Orthodox family amongst the many Jews—dropped by as I was eating. Like all young people, I dreaded being set distinctly apart from my peers—the reason sects isolate their youth of course—and I was afraid that he would see the yarmulke. I had to keep my head thrown back a little as I talked to my friend, or at a moment when his attention was diverted, quickly remove the yarmulke and stuff it in my pocket. Numerous times over the years did I suffer this humiliation.

Neither could I be freed from going to Hebrew School several times a week, in addition to my regular public school. There I was taught Hebrew, not as one learns a language, but taught in a rote manner only to pronounce the strange alphabet, simply to be able to recite the even stranger prayers in the synagogue. To this day I am able to "read" Hebrew fluently, but I understand the meaning of about as many words as I do of Bulgarian. In some of the prayer books in the synagogue, the English translation was on the page facing the Hebrew, so I could look afterwards and see the meaning of what I had just mechanically pronounced. But the English had scarcely more relevancy to me than the Hebrew—a hundred variations on the theme of "Thou shalt love the Lord thy God with all thy means," and "On the New Year it is written, and on the Day of Atonement it is sealed: Who shall live and who shall die, who shall prosper and who shall live in poverty, who shall die by fire and who by water, who by hunger and who by thirst, who by hanging and who by suffocation. . ." and so on into even nicer ways the Lord thy God would deal with you if you didn't love him with all thy means. In the "reform" synagogues, almost all the praying and singing is in English, but I'm not sure that I find that to be an improvement—they *know* what they're saying at the moment of *saying* it.

And to the synagogue was I forced to go every Saturday and holiday, my bitter pleading to stay home usually beaten down with "You'll send me to an early grave!" (She lived to past 90.) I loathed the feeling of dishonesty and absurdity that came over me as I walked the three blocks to "shul," wishing for no more than to throw off the suit I was wearing and go play punchball or stickball with my friends. For twenty years I watched my father and hundreds of other men recite prayers to an explicitly vain and wrathful god, recite and sing in a foreign language that very few understood though they had memorized scores of long litanies. I watched them fall to their knees, wrap prayer shawls completely around their bodies, shake like Holy Rollers, and pound their hearts with their fists; while I, wrapped in a shawl of suffocating boredom, faked whatever I could get away with.

And from the age of 13, when I was bar mitzvahed, until I left home at the advanced age of 26 (not unusual in the 1950s), every morning except Saturday, of every week, of every year, I put on *tvilin,* a two-part contraption, of which one is a small black wooden box that is held in place on the top of the head by a leather band, with two long leather strands dangling down the sides to the waist; the other, an identical box strapped around the upper left arm, with a long leather strand emanating from it that is coiled around the arm exactly seven times until it reaches the hand where, in a very precise manner, it is intertwined amongst three of the fingers. Thus costumed, my head bobbing up and down, my feet in the right position, my knees bending at the appropriate words in the Hebrew prayer, my right hand thumping my heart at other appropriate words, I might have appeared fully as strange and incomprehensible to most Americans coming upon me as would a young Masai of Kenya performing an initiation rite. And I experienced myself as no less strange.

Imagine, if you would, two decades of a young life. . . wrapped in tzitzis, yarmulkes, and tvilin, force marched to Hebrew School and synagogue, chronically tormented by embarrassment, pretense and tedium. . . the choice facing that child, that young man, was either to succumb—and have all of what he sensed as "himself" swallowed up—or to resist. Who can be surprised if the seeds of a rebellious character and a deep-seated aversion to injustice were sown throughout the inmost parts of his young being? Nonetheless, as the old proverb tells us, the hammer finds the spark in the stone. Why did I rebel to begin with when so many other boys at the synagogue and cousins of mine fell in line unquestioningly? Like nice little Jewish boys.

American society did an incomparably better selling job on my consciousness than my parents or Judaism ever did. It was not until I was past 30 that my basic patriotic and economic beliefs began to explode, along with the bombs over Hanoi. I remember the good warm feeling I used to have whenever I heard good ol' Bob Hope dishing out his good ol' American humor to the good ol' American GIs scattered all over the world. I never gave much thought to what the good ol' American GIs were *doing* all over the world in the first place. But would good ol' Bob Hope be entertaining good ol' American GIs embarked on less than honorable missions? Could the nice, young, clean-cut American boys who laughed so heartily at the same jokes I laughed at be up to no good? Had our soldiers *ever* been up to no good? Nothing I had ever heard in any school had left me with that impression in any firm or lasting way.

Nonetheless, my curiosity showed signs of life, and during the late 1950s and early 1960s in New York, I attended public functions of the Communist Party, the Socialist Workers Party, the Fair Play for Cuba Committee (of Lee Harvey Oswald fame), and other organizations that made the Justice Department Hall of Fame. On a Sunday afternoon in 1963 I was at Town Hall to hear the first group of American students back from Cuba, speaking of their experience and protesting the State Department's attempt to prevent such travel. There were some 1400 people in the audience and the atmosphere was charged. Outside, in the Times Square area, thousands of anti-Castro Cubans swarmed about carrying signs like "America Do Not Believe the Red Liars." At the door a guard ran his hands over my pockets; women's pocketbooks were searched. Inside the auditorium two groups of Cubans were forcibly ejected before the program began, leaving perhaps myself and the FBI agents and informers as the only non-believers still sitting there.

Adding to the tension was the news of that morning of September 15 that was to write a page in civil rights history: In Birmingham, Alabama a bomb had exploded in the 16th Street Baptist Church, killing four young black girls. There were mutterings among the Town Hall audience about insufficient police protection; people were very apprehensive about the scene outside.

I sat there with a mind steeled against "commie propaganda," of which there likely was some, but I was not into making distinctions—here was a group of young people enthusiastically describing an attempt to create a new kind of society, but all I could see and hear was a bunch of brainwashed jerks defending The Bad Guys.

As we filed out of Town Hall we were separated from the demonstrators by a line of mounted police and other helmeted officers. "Let us just get one or two beards!" implored some of the Cubans, straining against the police barricade. Suddenly, some of them broke through and fights erupted amidst rearing horses. I ducked my head, threw my hands up, and kept yelling, "I'm not with them! I'm not one of them!"

I went to these meetings not only to learn what made these strange people tick, but also because I enjoyed arguing with them (some ancient Talmudic gene floating in my blood?). Yet it still puzzles. It was as if an unconscious struggle was taking place within me between my outward convictions and some inner logic that had already decided that those convictions were just so much walking around with my pink *tzitzis* on, counting the blessings. Obviously I was looking for something not to be found in home or work, nor in school, religion or country, but I didn't dare find it. I was not yet ready to enter the political wilderness of "extremists."

In New York I had done some volunteer work with the Friends, spending a few weekends at the mental hospital on Randalls Island trying to bring some reminders of the (by definition: sane) outside world into the patients' lives. In Washington, with the Foreign Service exams still months off, I turned to the Friends again, to satisfy my craving for involvement in something larger than the routine strivings which insist on passing for life. It could be said that I was existentially horny. My confusion about Vietnam, too, undoubtedly led me to the stately old building on Florida Avenue near Dupont Circle which served as the Friends Meeting House. Thus began a long friendship and deep admiration for a community of people who are universally as trusted today as they were by the American Indians in the 17th century; trusted and respected for their belief in the inherent goodness and perfectibility of every person, and—what separates them from most other religions—their unhypocritical *practice* of that belief.

On a couple of occasions I was drawn to their Sunday "meetings," where I participated in the hour-long meditation, a silence broken only when someone, anyone, felt moved to relate an experience or thought he or she wished to share with the others. It was all in English, there were no rabbis, no sermons, no prayers, no strange vestments, no jerky body movements; at the conclusion we each shook hands with our neighbors and I felt a closeness to the people in that simple room that I could not remember ever feeling inside any synagogue. If my mother had observed me thus, she would have *plotzed*. She hadn't raised her son to be a Quaker. (Neither, as it turned out, had Richard Nixon's mother.)

Somewhere in all the Jewish ritual, ceremony and incantation that circumscribed my life in New York, I presume there lay, at least historically, a spirit of how people should better relate to each other and form a more perfect union; but the message never got through to me, neither at home, in Hebrew School, nor in the synagogue. The rabbi's sermons were too much like, well, sermons—predicated on the unshakable belief that nothing good was possible without a life filled with Judaism—and I learned to tune out at an early age. I was never inspired in my youth, nor later, to investigate beyond these external trappings, not only because of my own unhappy experience, but because the "religious" men I observed about me appeared to be no less mercenary, intolerant, uncompassionate, authoritarian, and boring than their impious brethren.

Although the idea did (incredibly) cross my mind, I was not to become a Quaker. Religion—not to be confused with being kind, peaceful or ethical, nor with experiencing a host of pleasurable feelings, from well-being to ecstasy—now boiled down to one question, and one question only, for me: Is God in control over what takes place in people's lives, or do people, individually and collectively, have the "free will" and the power to fashion their world? If the latter, God is utterly irrelevant and we can still cling to some hope. Whereas if God is responsible for the witches' brew of unspeakable horrors inflicted round the clock upon the body and spirit of an endless number of poor souls—has any kind of suffering been overlooked?—He-She-It is plainly evil, should be indicted by the International Court of Justice at The Hague for crimes against humanity, and is certainly not worthy of our worship. End of sermon. A sermon that will undoubtedly not sway in the least the countless millions for whom religion serves as a therapeutic device to feel good about themselves, to fill their emotional holes, to pacify a gang of inner demons, to counterbalance the unethical scramble for money that's their daily lot, to turn pain into meaning. Or to keep at bay Pascal's well-known nightmare. . . "When I survey Man, lost in this corner of the universe without knowing who put him there, what he has come to do, what will become of him when he dies, I am moved to terror."

"It's God's plan," said a young man in India, viewing the earthquake damage that killed 30,000 in 1993, including his entire family. "Some walls are standing. Some have fallen down. It's all God's creation. This is all God's game. But what it means, I don't know."[2]

If it's any consolation to Jewish readers who may be dismayed by my unflattering words about Judaism, herewith is a capsule view of Christianity as seen by Havelock Ellis:

> Had there been a lunatic asylum in the suburbs of Jerusalem, Jesus Christ would infallibly have been shut up in it at the outset of his public career. The interview with Satan on a pinnacle of the temple would alone have damned him, and everything that happened after could but have confirmed the diagnosis. The whole religious complexion of the modern world is due to the absence from Jerusalem of a lunatic asylum.

At the Washington Peace Center, located in the Friends Meeting House, I spent more time studying the material than I did filing it away or stuffing it into envelopes. The Friends' parish was the world; their service was humanitarian and peace-seeking projects. I was very intrigued to come across a statement made in 1954 by their political-action arm, which began: "The American Friends Service Committee is profoundly disturbed with the pressures for United States military intervention in Indo-China. On the basis of long Quaker experience in international service we are convinced that nothing but disaster lies down this road."

I read reports from AFSC people who had been working in Indochina for years, and other literature dealing with the conflict in Vietnam, which began to put things more in perspective for me, in a way that the *Washington Post* never did, and never could, because of its commitment to official Cold-War ideology. (No, that's not just a left-wing cliché.) I was brought to appreciate that the Vietnamese people, who had fought the Chinese occupiers for centuries, then the French, then the Japanese, followed by the French again, could not fail to see the Americans as yet another foreign invader.

I went through the entire Geneva Agreement of 1954 and other material that made it plain that it was a civil war going on in Vietnam that the United States was intervening in, one that had been ignited in large measure by the conspicuous cancellation—by South Vietnam and the United States—of the election aimed at unifying the country. I read for the first time what was to become a standard feature of anti-Vietnam flyers and leaflets over the next few years: Eisenhower's ingenuous admission in his memoirs that the election had been canceled because of the certainty that the communists would easily win. Good ol' sweet Ike, it was like he just didn't know how the ol' propaganda ball game was supposed to be played.

Well, so what! Could communists be trusted to keep to an honest election?

Oh come on, Bill, you can do better than that. After the election is the time to point that kind of finger, not before. You read that the UN and the International Control Commission were both ready to supervise the election.

So we just let the commies take over another country, and we abandon our allies, right?

Our allies? You mean that bunch of venal and brutal gangsters who stage elections so phoney that our own advisers have to tell them to announce 60 percent and not 98 percent? Hey, what principle are you coming from?

Yeah, I know, I know, but that doesn't change the very basic fact you seem to ignore that we have to fight the damn commies wherever they raise their ugly heads if the free world is gonna survive, and we can't always use kid gloves or play by nice little rules. Isn't that right?. . . Hey, where'dya go? Isn't that right?. . . Hey, buddy, where are you?

There came the day when the skinny old guy who ran the Peace Center, Gelston McNeil, asked me to hand out flyers in front of the White House to protest American actions in Vietnam. He asked me in the same manner he would ask me to file some papers away; for him it was that simple—you perceive a serious threat to world peace, your own government is precipitating the situation, you petition the government to turn away from such a policy—why, he'd been doing it all his life!

Whereas I was flabbergasted by the very idea. Hand out leaflets to strangers in the street? Right in front of the White House? In moments, a lifetime of social conditioning made the only decision it was capable of making: "Uh, no, I'm sorry Gelston, I can't, I'm, uh, going away for the weekend. Maybe some other time."

Now what the heck did he think I was? Some kind of exhibitionist nut? I worked for the State Department. I was going to be a Foreign Service Officer! And he knew that.

At home later that evening, sunk deep into an old armchair, legs stretched out easy on the hassock, glass of smooth bourbon in one hand, cigarette in the other, my upbringing began to relax its choke hold. . . Protest had a long tradition in America, a noble one. . . But what was I doing working with the Quakers—looking for something larger than myself, or rebelling against my Jewish upbringing?. . . Was the Peace Center just another oddball meeting to go to?. . . But how could I face the Quakers again? They would know! I wasn't exactly sure what it was they would know, but it wasn't something nice. . . What indeed *was* the principle I was coming from? Sure we had to fight communism (whatever *that* meant) but was this the way?

A chilly Saturday morning, the first week of March. I'm standing in front of the famous White House (smile, snap). I'm all alone and I'm holding a pile of flyers, burying one hand and then the other into a pocket to keep warm, not having learned yet that gloves had been invented. The flyers are headed: "Vietnam: Another Korea?," with quotations from Senator Church, Senator McGovern and others warning about the danger and futility of escalating the war, and calling for a political settlement; with a coupon to be sent to President Johnson asking him to end the conflict. Nothing I couldn't feel comfortable with at that time. It was not too long though before I found it totally ridiculous to appeal to the President as if he were some unaware innocent bystander who needed only to be "enlightened" before he would see the error of his ways.

So there I stand, handing out these flyers, the first of countless thousands in a glorious career that was to earn for me a spot amongst the top ten for "most times protesting in front of the White House by a right-handed batter." Needless to say, I'm feeling self-conscious as hell and fearful that someone I know will pass by, prepared—if it's someone from the State Department—to disappear like a snail poked with a stick. Without actually having checked into it, something deep inside tells me that State Department officials would not look charitably upon an employee with a Top Secret clearance handing out flyers attacking American foreign policy in the midst of a war, albeit an undeclared one.

Half the passers-by hardly look up. Others pause in their stride only long enough to catch the drift of the flyer and throw me a wisecrack—"Shove it!" appears to be especially popular. "Where? Into your open mind?" is usually all I have time to shout at their retreating backs. "Why don't you get a job?" is another favorite of the insult crowd. When I respond, "I have one, I work for the State Department," their smirk is broad enough to make me doubt my own words. Altogether a most stimulating intellectual atmosphere. Democracy in action.

A few people do stop to ask me just what *is* going on in Vietnam *anyhow?* The Great American Bear is beginning to stir from hibernation and rub its eyes. Fortunately, no one confronts me with anything too complex or esoteric, for I am not yet the bona fide expert on the subject, the veritable wonderland of knowledge, I am destined to become.

How long has it been since the pudgy little guard at the West Gate of the White House had any excitement? When he finally spies me, he bounces right over in his Mickey Mouse uniform and demands to see a copy of the flyer and my "permit." I don't know anything about a permit, but I suspect that he does-n't either. (Guards the world over seldom know what laws they're supposed to be enforcing.) I tell him that I don't think I need one, whereupon he switches to demanding my name and address and which organization I'm representing. When I reply that I don't have to tell him that (I'm guessing again), he asks me to come with him.

Something is beginning to stir around in the pit of my stomach as I follow him back to his booth, his little kingdom wherein he reigns supreme. He proceeds to telephone someone in a higher kingdom, speaks for a few minutes (while I seriously consider making a dash for it; Mickey Mouse here could never keep up with me), then turns to me and regretfully informs me that I can go. I may be stretching my luck, but I return to my spot. I've just learned a few things.

Enter the Bolshevik, stage left. . . black horn-rimmed eyeglasses rest on a face of Dostoyevskian despair under a full head of black curly hair, a cigarette dangling from thick lips. He squints sorrowfully through the thick lenses and the smoke as in an opium den. I'm surprised to see that he's holding the very same flyers as mine. It turns out he'd been handing them out a block away and has come over for a chat. No more than two minutes pass before he tells me, very matter-of-factly, that he is "a communist." I am literally speechless. In my 32 years on the planet never before has anyone come right out and said that to me. But I do not panic. He gives every indication of being of the same species as myself. He even comes complete with human-sounding name: Arnold; and respectable job: Russian translator at the Library of Congress.

Over the next few months, Arnie B. and I formed a close friendship, although his days revolved around exhausting bouts of deep depression. The long, drawn-out cycle of this psychoanalysis and that psycho-whatnot he had endured over the years certified him as another living example that psychotherapy was in over its head, no pun intended. Yet it may be that he could not have brought his mind to bear upon his work nor function otherwise without the aid of the various tranquilizers prescribed by a psychiatrist. The bottles of pills were everywhere to be found in his dark and disheveled apartment across from the zoo on Connecticut Avenue. I spent many an hour sitting there with him so that he could hear a voice other than his own. His manner was always gentle and subdued. How much of this was due to the tranquilizers and how much was his "normal" manner, I had no way of knowing.

The book of Arnie's life read like the proverbial Greek tragedy. When he was 11 or 12 back in Boston, he told me, his mother was a prostitute and she obliged him to have intercourse with her on many occasions. Somehow he grew up and got married. I don't recall how long the marriage lasted, but shortly after he and his wife separated, she developed a serious case of multiple sclerosis. He insisted that, despite certain symptoms, he hadn't suspected the oncoming of the disease before they parted, but his feelings of guilt were plainly evident. He still had occasional contact with her, but carried too much of his own burden to be able to help her bear hers. And if that weren't enough for one of God's children, shortly before I met Arnie, a young woman whom he had met at a halfway house and whom he cared for a lot, laid herself down on the tracks of the Pennsylvania Railroad and found her way out. I remembered having read about it in the *Post*.

His psychiatrist would argue with him about his politics. When all else failed, the good doctor would take refuge in diagnosing Arnie's communism as pathological. Arnie told me that things reached the point where the psychiatrist was screaming at him and finally ordered him out of his office, never to come back. I found the story hilarious, but poor Arnie was at loose ends with one of his security blankets wrenched away.

I, of course, was not going to let slide the opportunity to argue politics with the only admitted communist I knew in the entire world. Over a pint of beer, or walking around Dupont Circle, or in his bleak rooms, we tripped a hundred dances around that question that will not go away: private ownership or social ownership of the means of production, and all the immense implications contained therein. In one form or another it had occupied the mind of Plato and the early Christians, had remained on history's agenda throughout the centuries, confronted the industrial revolution with renewed urgency, and today was still irresistibly upon us. Sad to relate, the discussions between Arnie and myself did nothing to advance the state of the art.

Like a windup toy, I could do no more than reach into my little bag of standard American arguments against socialism: people will not work without the incentive of profit. . . centralized government planning can only produce a monster bureaucracy that stifles initiative, efficiency, freedom, and god-knows what else, maybe sex. . . socialism is impossible because you can't change human nature. . . the Soviet Union is nothing more than state capitalism anyhow. . . the people in the United States are better off than the people in the Soviet Union in every way, and this proves that capitalism is superior to socialism. . . etc., etc., etc. (I had at least graduated to the point where I no longer repeated that under socialism everyone thinks, acts and looks alike, or that personal property like houses and cars is not allowed.)

Why did I so earnestly believe these clichés when only a moment's relaxed reflection would have told me that *I* worked without the incentive of profit? I worked for a salary and always had, and furthermore I had no desire to join the ranks of entrepreneurs. As for "human nature," did I see myself as genetically greedy or competitive? Was I impervious to any ideals loftier than narrow self interest? That certainly didn't sound like me. And what of the Quakers? Were we all some kind of mutation? All of us freaks?

Arnie was more learned on the subject than I, but his words sounded no

31

less platitudinous to me than mine did to him. Whatever penetrating insights may have lain in his mind poised to strike, whatever passion he carried to his cause—in his drugged, lethargic state, thoughts came too slow, emphasis fell too soft, fervor was rendered tranquil. He was unable to maintain the quality of polemic which might have influenced a know-it-all like me; although I was not to be influenced too easily it would seem, not about to wrap a leather strap seven times around my arm and stick a little black box on top of my head.

My allegiance to American foreign policy was meanwhile reeling from another body blow. During the last few days of April, over 20,000 U.S. Marines landed on the shores of the Dominican Republic to put down a "communist" rebellion. Nineteen months earlier, when the democratically-elected liberal president, Juan Bosch, had been overthrown in a military coup, the United States had stood by and left him twisting in the wind. Now, when the right-wing military regime was threatened, the people of the Dominican Republic awoke to find their streets being "guarded by the United States Marines." What was an aspiring Foreign Service Officer to make of this? What was an *American* to make of this? What, actually, did my government believe in?

Not long after, I could be found standing in front of the Pentagon with hundreds of other people in an "interfaith vigil" organized by the Friends and other religious and pacifist groups. We had walked four miles from Capitol Hill, over the Memorial Bridge, to the other side of the Potomac, to stand in the blazing midday sun and "bear witness." We stood facing the Pentagon shoulder to shoulder in a line that stretched around more than half of the fortress-like building; motionless and silent, veterans of "Ban the Bomb" and Korean war protests alongside men who had sat out World War II in prison, and now their children.

One of the men was Norman Morrison, a 31-year-old Quaker from Baltimore. Six months later he was to return to the Pentagon, to a spot not far from Defense Secretary Robert McNamara's office window, where he doused himself in gasoline, lit a match, and became a martyr for the ages.

As we stood there, the utter peacefulness of it all seemed unreal to me, the broad expanse of open space, the manicured lawns and flower beds, the sycamores and the elms, a stillness disturbed only by the chopping motor of a helicopter that might have been a tractor in a distant field. . . a bizarre deception, but soon dispelled by the sight of military officers on the front steps, waiting for their chauffeured rides into the city to confab with their civilian counterparts on *Which remote people shall we bomb and napalm into submission today?*

Strangely, I also sensed a certain alienation from my fellow protestors, one not easily dispelled. I was moved by the Quaker plea of "If not now, when? If not here, where? If not you, who?" That was why I was there, then. But at the same time, I felt "unworthy" to be amongst them, as if I were there under false pretenses. I thought of them as "saintly," which of course they weren't and never pretended to be. I thought of their "brotherhood of man" and their "non-violence," and all I could find inside myself was anger—anger at the people a hundred yards away casually going about their business as usual. And when a young woman on our line succumbed to the heat and fainted, and a soldier rushed over with a first-aid kit, I felt more resentment than kindness toward him—what kind of "game" was this we were playing at? And later, when we broke for lunch in the Pentagon cafeteria, I felt ridiculous to be eating there. It seemed that the military was closer to my sentiments than the Quakers were, for the Pentagon had sectioned off a special area for us, to prevent any fraternization between the peaceniks and the warniks.

But I was stereotyping myself unjustly. I later came to define more precisely what at that time I had sensed only intuitively. What separates the Friends and other pacifists from those like myself is not compassion as opposed to hate or anger. Where our paths diverge is along the more prosaic road of *tactics*. Whatever any one of us may or may not feel in his "heart," non-violence, and all that that implies, is, ultimately, a tactic—and I do not say this cynically—used by pacifists for achieving social change, and, like all tactics, to be judged only by its results. Pacifists of course insist that tactics and results are inseparable—the means determine the ends, "the way to peace is peace" and so on. It's all very seductive, would that it were so, but it remained for my own study and experience to carve out a philosophy and tactics I found more historically sound and which I could feel more at home with personally.

The Friends' approach to taming *l'enfant terrible,* Congressman Mendel Rivers of South Carolina—the Newt Gingrich and Jesse Helms of his day—would have been to put him on a secluded farm with a few dozen Quakers for a year of daily living together. That method may well have brought out the best possible Mendel Rivers. But there were a million Mendel Rivers in the country, and we had neither enough time, enough secluded farms, nor enough Quakers. And I don't think I would have been crazy about even the best Mendel Rivers.

Though the great majority of those in the anti-war movement were not pacifists, the media throughout the '60s often insisted on referring to them as such. I think this was the easy way out for journalists' intellect and conscience. When they affixed the label "pacifist," they were saying in effect that it really wasn't the war in Vietnam that the protestors were against, it was *all* wars. Thus they and their audience didn't have to think about what the United States was doing in Vietnam, they only had to ponder the abstraction "war," a much less threatening subject. The fact was, most of the protestors would gladly have fought for what they saw as a just cause.

CHAPTER FOUR
COMMIE DUPE

"A Marxist study group." Now what images did *that* old *bête noire* flash in my American mind in the year 1965? A dark subterranean room; a clandestine Communist Party cell; cunning, experienced men whose eyes would knowingly turn toward me, the newest sheep, as I walked in. . . or will they shrewdly feign disinterest to lull me into a false sense of security?

When I arrived with Arnie at the house on Lamont Street, I smiled to see that we were going down into a basement apartment which shut out the light of the early May evening. The place was actually one large room partitioned by curtains into a living room with little furniture and even less pretension, an uninviting sleeping alcove, and a decrepit old kitchen which would never move a soul to prepare a Thanksgiving dinner for a dozen people. The floor of the apartment was earthen covered by linoleum, except where it was not covered. As poor as my origins had been, I had never before come upon so Spartan a habitat, although I'm sure there were enough in Greenwich Village, where they were called bohemian, and in Harlem, where they were called tenements.

The young couple who lived there, Patrick and Dianne Cawood, were still eating dinner; two or three others were sitting around on cushions reading pamphlets. Pat—slim, spectacled, dark-haired, and bearded—was a computer programmer at the U.S. Geological Survey of the Interior Department; Dianne, a pretty, long-haired blond, was an aspiring opera singer who worked as a secretary at the embassy of Thailand. They plainly could have afforded a grander style of home, but these two transplants from a San Francisco beatnik circle, which had included an unknown Janis Joplin, had a principle about paying high rent to some landlord. They preferred to take their luxury from dining out, filmgoing, buying books, and traveling. Pat and I became instant good friends, a friendship that has lasted to the present day. Although he was six years younger than me, he became my political guru.

Others drifted in, a few students from George Washington University and American University, a geologist friend of Pat's from Interior, a Washington cab driver, a woman who worked as an editor for the government, another woman who was the daughter of a brigadier general (this woman, Linda Wetter, ran as the Socialist Workers Party candidate for President of the United States in 1972). I had thought, with some pixy satisfaction, that my employment at the State Department would at least raise a few eyebrows, but this, after all, was Washington, and one had to work *somewhere.*

Using various source materials, the group had been discussing "the Cuban experiment" for a few weeks: What was the nature of the revolution there? Which were the social forces that had fought against Batista? Was it a "united front" of workers, peasants and socialists of one stripe or another, or was it a "popular front" which cut across class lines and had a nationalist, anti-Yankee-imperialism base to it? In what ways could Cuba be called a socialist society? How was democracy manifested there? Had Castro been a Marxist, or even a socialist, from the outset, or had popular demands and other circumstances impelled him in that direction?

I could only listen. It had never sunk in before that politics could be dissected in such a manner. Was I naive? Of course. Remarkably so. And I was of that tiny segment of the population interested enough in foreign affairs to want to make a career of it. Yet I had gone all the way through college without once being confronted with a discussion of socialism or Marxism, nor even a presentation of capitalism which did not presume it to be a timelessly valid institution and not one created to satisfy a certain historical need.

Ironically, I had been to Cuba. In August 1958, while vacationing in Miami, a friend and I took the one-hour flight to Havana, $36 round-trip. We passed a few days there in the grand manner of decadent running-dog-of-capitalism gringos, amusing ourselves with nightclubs, gambling casinos, prostitutes, beaches, and a tour of the beautiful estates of the rich in the suburbs with our own English-speaking cab driver. It was about four years later that it dawned on me one day that I had been in Cuba in the midst of the revolution, less than five months before Castro took over. I had wondered about all the soldiers in the street, but this being my first time abroad, I had assumed that that must be the way it was in foreign countries. I wonder what our friendly cab driver really thought of us.

At times, during the discussion, Arnie would begin to develop a line of thought, then halfway through he would start to fade out and slowly slide downhill until we suddenly realized that he was asleep. Ten or fifteen minutes later his eyes and mouth would open simultaneously and he would pick up more or less where he had left off, sublimely oblivious to everything, including the fact that someone else was speaking. Poor Arnie, we didn't want to laugh, but there was no way not to.

One day about a year later, I went to call on Arnie and was shocked to discover that he had vacated his apartment. The resident manager told me that a cab had come for him and Arnie had loaded some luggage into it. He then walked back into the building, saying that he had forgotten something. . . and apparently walked out the back, never to be seen again. For months after, I checked with the city department that was holding Arnie's "unclaimed property" to see if anyone had claimed it. No one had. And no one at the Library of Congress knew of his whereabouts. I could not be optimistic about Arnie's prospects. Doom had a 30-year head start over hope in the footrace for his future.

I was surprised to hear criticism in the group of Cuba for failing to institute certain democratic reforms. I was even more surprised to hear the same said about the Soviet Union. What kind of Marxists, or Communists, or whatever they were, were these?

After these Friday evening meetings, some of us would go over to Connecticut Avenue, north of Dupont Circle, for a drink at Childe Harold or a bite to eat at Rand's diner. The latter is an establishment no longer amongst the living, presumably because it featured the slowest and most incompetent service in the Western Hemisphere. It was not unusual for a customer to finally leave his table, walk behind the counter, and actually prepare the food he had ordered an hour ago. The help couldn't care less. They all looked like down-and-out skid-row types, with grim, despairing faces; one in particular looked as though he'd come fresh from auditioning for the part of Death in *The Seventh Seal*. They seldom spoke and knew little or nothing about the menu; some were unable to write an order and would hand pen and pad to the customer to do the honors. A staff like that couldn't have been assembled by chance. We could only wonder what arrangement the owner had with the flophouses, the jails, or the mental hospitals of Washington.

But the food wasn't bad, it was cheap, there was plenty of time to talk, and the people-watching was first class. Although hippie-man and psychedelic-man had not yet been discovered by that eminent anthropological journal, *Time* magazine, many of the late-night customers displayed drug-induced polymorphous perversity, and the interaction between them and the waiters from hell convulsed us repeatedly in laughter.

"You don't see such lost souls in Cuba," said one of the American University students who had been there the year before. "And no beggars or prostitutes or pimps, and no one lying in the street."

"Why is it that so many Cubans want to come to the United States?" I asked, trying not to sound provocative.

"For the same reasons thousands of Americans went to Canada after the American Revolution, and so many left after the Civil War," replied someone. "And ours was just a bourgeois revolution, not a profound social revolution like in Cuba which has turned everything upside down."

"If you offered the people of any poor country legal residence in the United States, plus all the other benefits the so-called refugees from Cuba get, you'd deplete the Third World of population overnight."

Pat and a few of the others were members of the Young Socialist Alliance, the youth-wing of the Socialist Workers Party. "Trotskyists" was the proper genre, I learned; those who didn't like them—like the Communist Party, from which the SWP had split many years ago—referred to them as "Trotsky*ites*."

After a few of our meetings, I figured they wanted to recruit me into the party, and a montage would sometimes roll across my inner screen. . . of Alger Hiss and the Rosenbergs, of FBI films with Jimmy Stewart and World War II spy tales, of Senator McCarthy and his infamous list of communists in the State Department. . . It's not that I was scared; on the contrary, I was amused to picture myself cast in the central role of some new American public drama. But somehow, intuitively, I knew—even apart from the obvious ideological question—that I didn't want to be joining any such formalized, structured organization.

But they never actually asked me to join the party, never even hinted at it. That was fine by me. I would do the readings and attend the discussions. I had to understand a lot more if I was going to argue with them.

On Monday morning I was back at my desk at the State Department, working on a computer analysis of voting at the United Nations, comparing how the United States had voted vis-à-vis the Soviet Union on various questions, how often unaligned nations had voted with each of the two superpowers, and other statistical breakdowns. Someone in some office upstairs felt a real need for the report. Fine. But for the life of me I couldn't understand why the information was classified. The source data, after all, was public knowledge. I was only rearranging it into a more readable format, trying to squeeze out whatever significance it might hold. Somewhere in the Kremlin, my counterpart was probably busy doing the same. And it was undoubtedly classified there as well.

I was not to leave such a vital state secret exposed on my desk if I left the room; no telling when a commie-fiend-spy might just happen by, rush in, and, completely ignored by the other four people in the room, quickly photograph each and every sheet, thus saving the Kremlin several hours of work, except if they wanted it in Russian. It was not unusual for me to leave my desk a dozen times in the course of a working day. Amongst other reasons, I sometimes took a walk around different floors of the building because I loved to look at the names of the offices along the long hallways, the simple cardboard signs stamped with the likes of: Bureau of European Affairs—France, Benelux (EUR/FBX). . . National Review Board for the Center for Cultural and Technical Interchange between East and West. . . Bureau of Economic Affairs—Office of Fuels and Energy (FSE). . . Bureau of Intelligence and Research—Office of Research and Analysis for East Asia and Pacific (REA). . . Government Advisory Committee on International Book and Library Programs. . . of such stuff was my world going to be. Of course I had to chuckle at some of the names, but it was only a proud father delighting in the way-out vocabulary of his genius child.

I felt very put upon, and kind of mindless, turning a desk full of scattered papers face down each time, and then face up again, and then maybe I'd leave the room five minutes later to discuss something technical with a colleague and not bother. . . Sure enough, someone beat a path to Security, and I was given Naughty-Boy-Lecture No. 18. If I repeated the offense a couple of times more, I'd be fired. I knew it was absolutely futile, even juvenile, but I couldn't resist asking the Security Officer why the United Nations report was classified. He looked at me as if I had just asked him why the sky was blue.

How many Americans know that the United States once invaded the Soviet Union? Suffering thousands of casualties! I was shocked to discover this bit of history in one of the side readings which were suggested to me in the study group. Equally surprising: the horrifically oppressive "Red Scare" in the U.S. in the 1920s, of which the execution of Sacco and Vanzetti was but a footnote; the rejection by the United States and Great Britain of the Soviet Union's desperate appeals for a joint stand against Hitler, which forced the Russians into their infamous pact with the Nazis; and after Germany invaded the Soviet Union, Senator Harry Truman calling for the U.S. to help the Nazis if we saw that Russia was winning. . . I was now a student in adult education remedial history: anti-communism and the origins of the Cold War; supporting the Greek fascists after the World War; the hidden military campaign against Indonesia; the other side to the Korean War; and my Russian pen-pal's claim about Guatemala—sure enough, a CIA operation. The Agency's role in Brazil I had not yet come across.

When I connected all these dots, I found myself looking at a picture that only yesterday had been invisible, if not unthinkable: the government of the United States, *as a matter of course,* scheming to overthrow the governments and popular movements of other countries which had done the U.S. no harm at all. Even the glaring example of the Bay of Pigs of a few years earlier had not successfully penetrated my mind set. In *1984,* Orwell wrote about the conditioned reflex of "stopping short, as though by instinct, at the threshold of any dangerous thought. . . and of being bored or repelled by any train of thought which is capable of leading in a heretical direction." [3]

The material I was studying did not spring from secret sources. The books and the old newspapers were available at any good library. But neither Walter Cronkite, nor James Reston, nor John Gunther, nor any teacher had ever encouraged me to read any of it. Should this evoke surprise? Has any society, past or present, placed a priority upon teaching its citizens the seamier side of its history? The absence of such a priority is called "national security."

Summertime in Washington and the livin' is air-conditioned, but people were marching in protests against the war, outside the White House, Selective Service, and other newsworthy spots. Amongst their number a computer programmer from the State Department could occasionally be observed (and in fact was), though he was not very comfortable with the chanting when it bordered on ritual.

The study group shifted its focus from Cuba to Vietnam, and soon gave birth to a separate group: The Washington Committee to End the War in Vietnam, which people young and old began flocking to after the government added one animal too many to the Official Explanations Zoo, or after looking upon one photo too many of a naked napalmed child.

Meanwhile, back at the office of one of the targets of the protests, I was beginning to work on a project of singular interest. The State Department, it turned out, maintained two large lists of people on magnetic tape. One list was of foreigners—individuals stamped as "leftist" of one shade or variety, others as prostitute, drug dealer, criminal, etc., whose applications for visas to the promised land were to be regarded with prejudice by American embassies everywhere.

I looked through those names many a time, wondering about the stories which lay behind their inclusion. I felt sure that many of them would have been rather surprised to learn that they were part of such a list. Some would not, like Isaac Deutscher and Ernest Mandel, prominent European writers who, though anti-Stalinists were unrepentant Marxists, and had already experienced difficulties in gaining entrance to the United States. I had never read the writings of either man, but it distressed me to think that the ideas expressed in their books were enough to certify them as threats to the American Way of Life. I was inspired to purchase a copy of Deutscher's biography of Leon Trotsky, which revealed the author, as well as his subject, to be eminently civilized and compassionate, not to mention brilliant. Later I was to relate to Deutscher again, for writing that when he became an atheist he was more worried about offending his mother than about offending God.

It was a simple matter to punch an IBM card in the appropriate manner to remove a name from the list. I had the power to flood the United States with all kinds of foreign wrong-thinkers. At this time, the list contained some 175,000 names. By 1996, U.S. consular posts all over the world had electronic access to a database of four million undesirable aliens.

The other list was reserved for Americans, more than 200,000 of them. For some time I was uncertain about what use the list was being put to, but in March 1966 a story broke in the newspapers which appeared to provide an answer. It seems that H. Stuart Hughes, a Harvard history professor and outspoken critic of American policy in Vietnam, was planning to travel in Europe. Frances G. Knight, the Director of the State Department's Passport Office and paranoid anti-communist *par excellence,* cabled the American embassies in Paris and Moscow to institute surveillance on Hughes. The press somehow got wind of this and a minor scandal ensued. In defense of her actions, Knight stated that she had ordered the surveillance at the request of the FBI, and that the practice was routine, dating back at least 20 years. It was estimated that the State Department received hundreds of such requests from the FBI each year. [4]

But how, I wondered, would the FBI know which American no-no's were going where. Only the passport office would know, from the form filled out by persons applying for a passport and checked against the list I was working on. My theory was that Knight regularly furnished this information to the FBI, which in turn "requested" surveillance of certain individuals, thus making the whole operation more kosher and providing Knight with a cover.

As time went by, more and more people I knew, or knew of, from the anti-war movement made the list. I watched with curious fascination for my own name to appear.

One afternoon, as I walked along the corridors of the State Department during a break, I found that I was not getting my usual kick out of the names on the offices. They now appeared to me as euphemisms and cover-ups, they didn't tell the real story. I looked for a Center for the Study of Intervention into Latin American Affairs (CSI/LA). . . Bureau of Intelligence and Research— Office of Disinformation for the American Public (IR/DAP). . . Under Secretary of State for Counter-Revolution and Stifling Rising Expectations. . . Bureau of Imperialism—Office of Protection of American Multinationals. . . I realized with a start that I no longer wanted to be a Foreign Service Officer. The grand design for my future had slipped away in the night. When had my unconscious made the final decision that I couldn't go home again? Perhaps it had been the moment I found myself wishing the Cubans well in their experiment.

CHAPTER FIVE
THE LEGENDARY ANTI-VIETNAM WAR MOVEMENT

It might be called "I Led A Double Life," although that implies more covertness than there was. Throughout the balance of 1965 and all the following year, I continued doing my best for the Automated Data Processing Division of the Department of State, at the same time becoming one of the leading organizers in Washington of the anti-Vietnam War movement, being intimately involved in setting up dozens of rallies, picketings, and educational meetings, and writing many a flyer, even a song. The Washington Committee to End the War in Vietnam was now a member of the National Coordinating Committee to End the War in Vietnam, located in Madison, Wisconsin. The Great Sixties Anti-War, Question-Everything, and Freak-Your-Parents-Out Traveling Show was on the road, marching to a continuous drumbeat. There was no getting in our way.

I wrote the following verse, which appeared in the Coordinating Committee's Newsletter under my name, to be sung to the tune of the Marine Corps Hymn:

> From the Dominican Republic to the shores of Vietnam,
> We suppress all revolutions, to preserve old Uncle Sam.
> Kill for peace, for love and justice; kill for truth and democracy,
> Kill and bomb and burn and torture, so to keep the people free.
> Oh we are honor bound to save the world, to make it safe for democracy.
> We will fight for this in any land, 'cept Alabama and Mississippi.

Kill the men, the women, the children, 'tis a danger for any to be missed,
For you never can be sure who is OK, and who's a dirty old communist.
Now the Reds, they want to enslave the world, to keep it bent under their
whip.
But we have the perfect alternative, a military dictatorship.
Oh we must be right, cause we have the might, and my country right or
wrong,
We shall escalate to a nuclear fate, and you won't have to wait too long.

Neither did I shy away from expressing my political views in the office to
colleagues, or to the head of the division who called me in because I was the
only employee under him who had not signed up for payroll bond deductions
to finance the war effort. It was literally inconceivable to this gentleman that I
could have any reason for not taking part in the program other than a financial
one. He opened our talk with a spiel about how it really wasn't so expensive,
how I could easily afford it, how I could cash in the bonds immediately anyhow,
just as long as the division hit 100 percent.

When he came up for air and I told him that I wasn't buying bonds because
I refused to support the war, he gaped at me as if I had just told him that on the
way to his office I had encountered an extraterrestrial in the hallway.

"But we have a commitment under the SEATO agreement," he finally
sputtered.

Whereupon I proceeded to list the absurd, supra-legal provisions of the
SEATO (Southeast Asia Treaty Organization) agreement, and how this didn't
justify anything.

This near-death experience with knowledge was enough for him to termi-
nate the conversation forthwith. I presume that a memo from him to Security
was not overly long in coming.

In the countless discussions about Vietnam that I had with people I came
across in the '60s, I often thought I was making an impression and moving their
views closer to mine (i.e., to truth, beauty and justice). Eventually, I began to
realize that it was not uncommon for individuals, in all sincerity, to simply
adopt the views of the last person they had spoken to on the subject, until they
met the next person of contrary persuasion.

On several occasions during lunchtime at the State Department I had long
conversations with one of the FSOs, Allen Greenberg by name, who was spending a few months in my division as part of his training. As fellow Brooklyn Jews
with a shared nostalgia for the Dodgers all was harmony between us until one
day I mentioned that I too had planned on entering the diplomatic corps and
explained why I had changed my mind. As I had, Al effortlessly embraced a
belief in the underlying nobility of American motives, and a view of an America
that is always the aggrieved innocent in a treacherous world. If love is blind,

patriotism has lost all five senses. And the effect upon him of my chiseling away at some of his most cherished convictions with chapter and verse was, as he put it to me once, to leave him feeling "like a wet rag."

Recent converts to a belief are typically the most gung-ho, often the most obnoxious, but I didn't much enjoy my attack upon Al's ideological immune system. What made it less than gratifying for me was that he didn't come on like an American who knocks off half a dozen anti-communist clichés before breakfast; he seemed to genuinely want to keep an open mind and understand. Yet the whole thing was incongruous—I, the former accountant and computer programmer, telling a Foreign Service Officer all kinds of things about American foreign policy that are seemingly new to him.

In any event, what could I expect him to do, abandon his career? I had, but would I have done so if I had already been well embarked upon it? Al was past the point of no return, and was soon off to Florence for his first posting.

A decade later, I was to look through the State Department's *Biographic Register*. Sure enough, there was Al Greenberg. He had stuck it out, spent more than four years in Paris after Florence. And then it was on to Warsaw, and then Moscow. As such things are measured, it was a lot more than I or my new little world had to offer him.

In November 1965, Washington was the site of the first national conference of anti-Vietnam organizations, which I helped to organize. At the closing session of the conference, one of the speakers casually mentioned what needed to be worked on and accomplished before the next conference a year hence. My mouth literally fell open—*a year from now?* He expects this disgusting war to be still going on *a year from now?* Is he crazy or something? I often failed to take into account how new I was to this whole dissenter business compared with some of the old left, the red-diaper babies, and many of the new left, who had diligently been doing their homework and had learned to question the state's motivations, assess its long-term plans, and see through the official lies long before my metamorphosis.

At this conference, as elsewhere, I was often at a loss to understand the criticisms made by one individual against another. The remarks seemed excessive, and were not only confusing, they were disheartening. It scarred my image of a unified movement of idealists fighting a noble cause against a single common enemy. It took awhile to sort out the Trotskyists from the Stalinists and the Maoists, the anarchists from the pacifists, as well as those, particularly of the New Left, who pronounced *a plague on all your houses.*

Pat Cawood and I stuck our necks out every few days when we spoke on the phone to arrange to meet for lunch. We figured that given the nature of my employment, and his association with an organization (the Socialist Workers Party) widely known to be in the FBI's Top Ten, there was at least an even chance that our conversations, from one government agency to another, were being shared with complete strangers. Thus motivated, we sometimes spoke in hushed conspiratorial tones, calling each other "comrade," using a coded-sounding language, and dropping heavy hints of secret meetings. Words like "Trotsky," "Lenin," and "Do you have the tape?" crossed our lips.

Several decades down the line, as I write this, it's hard to believe that we had the nerve to do a thing like that. Unlike expressing my views in the office, it served no political purpose; it was only delicious entertainment. In the early 50s, at the height of McCarthyism, if I had been a government employee I might have suffered serious difficulties for a lot less than the things I was engaging in now, which may be why I was not summarily fired—"State Department Employee Fired For Political Views" was not the kind of headline the beleaguered Johnson administration was anxious to revive. That may have also been one reason I had so much nerve. If they fired me, I'd make a super stink in the media, winning points for the anti-war movement. So I told myself.

I was not completely unrestrained. One time, when I walked out of the State Department building, I was surprised to find myself face to face with an anti-war sit-in on the steps; a dozen or so people, of whom I knew two or three. When one of them appeared to be on the verge of greeting me, I threw him a very discreet shake of the head and hurried my way past the protesters and the police. Things were fast getting tight and weird.

Neither did I escape punishment altogether. I had been scheduled for some time to be transferred to Paris to help install a European-wide automated system for the list of foreigners I had worked on, and was sent to take classes in French at the State Department's Foreign Service Institute in Arlington. But I was never sent to Paris, and I could never get a clear answer as to why. I had filled my head with Parisian picture postcards, and now, in one brush stroke, they were all whited out. Did they think I'd team up with Daniel Cohn Bendit in France to storm the American Bastille?

My State Department and FBI files make no mention of the phone conversations between Pat and I, but they're chock full of interviews with my work colleagues about me. One said he felt that my outspoken disagreement about Vietnam "is the result of a disturbed individual who has not as yet found himself." Another was of the opinion that my views were "the result of an inferiority complex and this is his way of being different."

This was a common phenomenon in the '60s. Those who supported the government's policy often felt threatened by the protestors—a threat to that highly emotional and exquisitely vulnerable part of themselves: their patriotism, which frequently exerts a more powerful hold on an individual than religion or family. When they couldn't deal with this threat on an intellectual basis, couldn't respond adequately to the protestor's knowledge or perception, they often liked to convince themselves that there must be something wrong with the person.

We find the same with how people the world over look upon "traitors." Either they're just greedy for money, says conventional wisdom, or they have some very serious character defects. The patriot finds it exceedingly difficult to accept that one of his fellow nationals could believe in "the enemy's brand of patriotism." But virtually all traitors, even those who would not do it if not for the money—Aldrich Ames, for example—have to, at a minimum, break the death grip their own brand of patriotism has on them in order to commit treason; which is to say—there has to be an *absence* of loyalty.

The enemy's traitors are seen in a different light. Soviet defectors (i.e., traitors), once their legitimacy was accepted, were looked upon as courageous and principled men. And after Ames was arrested, the head of the Russian Foreign Intelligence Service, Yevgeny Primakov, said that the American had turned over secrets to Moscow "not only for the sake of money" but also because he saw that the Soviet people were not as "aggressive and hostile" as they had been portrayed by his CIA employers. Russian defectors, however, said Primakov, "are fond of explaining everything by ideological causes. That is rubbish. They all betray exclusively for mercantile considerations, for money."[5]

"To me," wrote philosopher George Santayana, "it seems a dreadful indignity to have a soul controlled by geography."

One of the documents in my FBI file, dated 1966, lists 13 informers the bureau had in play at one time or another against individuals and groups I was associated with. The informers are identified as WF T-1 to WF T-13, with all other information about them blacked out. Blacking out portions of an unending number of documents, however, is a task tedious in the extreme, and the poor unsung souls who do this day after day in their little government cubicles can certainly be excused for slipping up occasionally. Consequently, while information about WF T-5 was obliterated on one page, on another page his name was left uncovered twice. Thus it was that I learned that Jan Tangen, a student at American University, a participant in the study group, and a member of the Young Socialist Alliance, was providing the FBI with information about individuals from his various associations; information that the FBI would probably categorize as vital to—yes, national security—but which I would call mundane details about legitimate political protest with some personal tidbits thrown in so the informer can perhaps lay claim to greater recompense.

Despite a YSA ban on members using drugs—the authorities were just looking for any excuse to bust them, so why make it too easy—Jan, Pat Cawood and I smoked dope together once and had a great laughing time. I wonder now what Jan was laughing about.

In the late 1970s, when Pat and I were both living in Berkeley, we went to see the guitar-playing and singing Jan perform at a local music club. Back in the '60s he had done some singing to the FBI, and now—was this a step forward or backward?—now he was singing for. . . god help us!—yes, Jesus! Good ol' Jan had become a Jesus freak, to Pat and I a condition akin to having a radical frontal lobotomy. So the pleasure of seeing an old "comrade" for the first time in over a decade was diluted considerably, listening to Rock of Ages instead of Rock and Roll. The reunion would have been even more painful, albeit more interesting, if I had already been in possession of the FBI's Tangen document. I'd like to know who good ol' Jan is singing for today.

Another informer, although probably unpaid, if that means anything, was one Mrs. O'Toole, the resident manager of my apartment house on Wisconsin Avenue. She and I lived in the same building, but in different centuries. Her fifteen minutes of fame, my FBI file reports, was spent informing the bureau that:

> the employee has some of the strangest looking people for friends she ever saw, they being the beatnik bearded type whom she described as "kooks," and she considered him the biggest "kook" of all. His friends impressed her as the "banner carrying, demonstration type of people whose pictures are frequently in the newspapers these days, they being the ones who object to any and everything imaginable." She said [Blum] received in the mails some strange kind of publications and boxes. He received a large box, which was broken open [?], and she could see that it contained large buttons which had the words "shoot" and "kill" and other strange words written on the buttons.

This being 1966, relatively early in the era, one can only wonder with trepidation how this woman—with a tolerance for deviation from the norm apparently approaching zero—made it through the rest of the '60s and the equally deviant '70s.

One reason Mrs. O'Toole (I don't think she had a first name), felt less than love for me had to do with my girlfriend Suzanne—whom I had met in the antiwar movement—coming to live with me. O'Toole collared me one day and demanded to know whether I and the young woman were married. I was totally unprepared for the question, and though I presumed that in the capital city of the United States in the second half of the twentieth century there did not exist a legal prohibition against living in sin, I wasn't actually sure what my rights were. I took what I thought was the safe way out. I said "yes."

This tall, skinny, washed-out blonde, who had been denying her juice for lo these many years, was not pacified. She insisted upon knowing the when and the where of the holy nuptials. A month ago, I said, in Silver Spring, which was the Maryland suburb where Suzanne was from. O'Toole and I had a couple more animated exchanges before I finally brought Suzanne to meet her. I subsequently learned from my file that both the FBI and O'Toole—in medieval times she would have been called O'Toole the Terrible—had actually checked with the Circuit Court of Montgomery County to find a record of a marriage under my name, and failed. A person with a security clearance was expected to report the acquisition of a spouse so she or he could be investigated. I imagine that there was less of an official standing procedure regarding unmarried couples living together. Perhaps it was a bit like the story told about Queen Victoria—that she refused to declare female homosexuality a crime only because she couldn't bring herself to believe that it existed.

When my supervisor at work, Henry Hill, called me in one day to ask me whether it was true that I was married, I gave this mild-mannered career civil servant from Mississippi a man-to-man wink, nod, and elbow-in-the-ribs negative answer, all conveying SEX out of wedlock. He smiled in complete understanding. I sometimes wondered about ol' Southern gentleman Hank; he'd been placing various kinds of marks on various kinds of government forms for decades—did he have any dream other than an ample pension, any philosophy more profound than Cover Your Ass?

Living with Suzanne was not anything illegal or subversive that I necessarily had to hide, but the fact that it was now a fit subject for my boss to formally call in and question me about in the office gave me a sinking feeling that the walls were closing in on me a little.

I seemed to lunge between security concerns and tempting the fates. On the one hand, when an NBC reporter called me at home one day about an anti-war demonstration I had helped to organize, I begged him not to use my name, telling him candidly that I worked at the State Department and would lose my job. I surprised myself at how much heart I put into my plea, as if I were leading the life of an underground guerrilla whose exposure meant torture and death. Whether he used my name or not I don't know, but I felt a bit ashamed afterward about placing such a moral burden and guilt trip on the guy.

On the other hand, I went to a party at the home of one of my co-workers, where almost all the guests were from the State Department, and took Suzanne with me. She was a folksinger, who performed at anti-war rallies, and at my suggestion had brought her autoharp with her. At an opportune moment in the evening, she began to play and sing "Where Have All the Flowers Gone?" This piece wasn't exactly "The Internationale," but it was virtually the theme song of the anti-war movement, very well known, and stirring. The response of the other guests was cautiously calibrated: a comment or two about Suzanne's nice voice, but no other expressed interest.

Remarkably, it appears that the FBI never stumbled across the fact that

Suzanne's father, Harry Le Bovit, until shortly before had been working in the Executive Office of the White House, and was now at the State Department. A former diplomat, he was with the Food for Peace program. I played tennis with him a couple of times, and he seemed like a nice enough guy, with no connection to the war effort. Or so I assumed. To this day I'm still learning that the suitcase with which U.S. foreign policy travels the world almost invariably has a false bottom. The Food for Peace program, I later discovered, was used throughout its two decades as a cover for military and other foreign policy objectives.

As time went by and I met more and more people in the anti-war movement from outside Washington, including many of "the old left," I found scarcely any of them who were amused or indifferent to the fact that I was an employee of the United States Department of State. I went from declaring this with a smile on my face, to not mentioning it at all unless directly asked where I worked. I of course didn't want to *hide* it, for that would look very suspicious. But they were right. What the hell *was* I doing working there?

I was saving money to nurture me through my upcoming "dropping out." When I finally decided that the time had come to part company with the object of my protests, the object was already a step ahead of me. My work load had been shrinking, to the point where I had less to do than a bartender at a Mormon wedding. Then, one morning, I was called in by the Office of Security. There was no advance warning. I was told to report immediately. This was it, what I had been expecting for well over a year.

Again two men. New ones. For three hours, they sat there with my file (an anagram of "life") in front of them and slowly turned the pages, letting me know how much they already knew about me, perhaps to impress me with how clever and efficient they were and with how many informers the FBI apparently had on its payroll; which is to say, to impart the message: Who the hell did you think you were fooling?

They knew of many of the specific demonstrations I had attended and how I had helped on the logistics; who some of my friends were; what well-known persons in the anti-war movement I had met; what publications I received in the mail; that I had sent a dozen letters to the *Washington Post* critical of U.S. foreign policy. Inasmuch as only two or three of these had actually been printed, I later wrote to the *Post* , asking for an explanation. I never received an answer. In security work, all is fair, or at least done.

I sat there listening to the two men like the subject of a perverted "This is Your Life," program, fearful that I would somehow be "seen through." "Everyone suspects they are a joke," novelist Martin Amis once wrote, "which other people will one day get."

Of all the demonstrations they cited, I categorically denied being at only one of them—outside the Shrine of the Immaculate Conception while the President's daughter, Luci Baines Johnson, was getting married. They gave me a second chance to admit to this a while later, and again I denied it. When they raised the matter a third time, asking me if I was "sure" that I hadn't been there, I felt ridiculous denying what they obviously knew to be a fact and finally confessed to it. My reluctance to admit to this particular action was a bow to what I imagined was conventional sentiment: a wedding was not an appropriate target of political protest. But the Johnson family had chosen August 6 for the date of this joyous celebration—Hiroshima Day—in the midst of the Vietnam carnage which was already drawing comparisons to the dropping of the A-bomb on other Asian people.

How much, I wondered, did these two security professionals facing me really care about what I had done or what I believed? Were they as passionate about their side as I was about mine? I would have been more amused than shocked to discover that one of them was a closet peacenik. Perhaps they were "just doing their job," and their job at the moment was to ascertain what they did not know—what they were most interested in knowing—to wit: just how far from the flock had this particular sheep wandered, just how extreme were his political views? And, not knowing exactly when those views had been formed, just how much had their pre-employment security investigation of me proven unacceptably fallible, even worthless?

They knew that I had attended a Young Socialist Alliance conference in New York and they found it difficult to believe that I wasn't a member of the organization. I told them that I was over the age limit of 27. And the Socialist Workers Party? Too much factional bickering amongst its members, I replied. Neither answer, of course, indicated a lack of sympathy with the ideology of either group, a fact duly noted in my file.

At one point, tired of their pushiness and my own evasiveness, I declared that I was "a socialist." Did I just say what I just heard, I wondered, as soon as the words left my tongue? They immediately asked me to explain what I meant by the word. According to their notes, I defined it as "one who is in favor of the distribution of wealth amongst the people, but only by lawful means." I don't remember if that's exactly how I put it, but reading it today I find it rather simplistic and uninspiring. To the two men seated in front of me, however, my definition may well have sounded one of their selective alarm bells. American society is much more tolerant of a dissenter who claims "individualism" as his motivation for doing something—the cherished "maverick" fighting city hall— than it is of the dissenter who is part of a movement which aims to rearrange some of the basic building blocks of the economic system on behalf of the mass of the population.

Had I ever carried a Vietcong flag at a demonstration? Carrying the flag of the "enemy" is what separated the men from the boys within the anti-war movement. The great majority of those opposed to the war could not, and did not, slide out from the clutches of the patriotic mystique. On the contrary, they insisted that they were the ones who were the real patriots. This was a self-image I never adopted. My thinking had arrived at the point where I looked upon patriotism as simply loyalty to the chance occurrence of where one was born—tribal loyalty—inculcated in the individual by such heavy doses of a propaganda sing-along that he's convinced he came to his conviction through independent examination and thought. But you might as well toss a pair of dice, and declare your undying loyalty to whichever number comes up. I was a citizen of the world, I decided, no more loyal to the United States than I was to IBM. Principles concerning human rights earned my loyalty. I was concerned with human rights and government wrongs.

Oddly enough, the Pledge of Allegiance was written by a socialist, Francis Bellamy, a founding member, in 1889, of the Society of Christian Socialists, a group of Protestant ministers who asserted that "the teachings of Jesus Christ lead directly to some form or forms of socialism."

"While he denied carrying a Viet Cong flag during these demonstrations, he would not state, either affirmatively or negatively, what he would do if given such a flag."

I had, in fact, carried a Viet Cong flag. There was also the time when a group of demonstrators were walking through the street on their way to the Washington Monument and a police officer came over and angrily grabbed the Viet Cong flag out of the hands of a young guy. The officer walked away and just stood there looking at us, flag in hand, exuding the raw power of the state. With a sweeping motion of both arms, I urged the other demonstrators to walk with me toward the cop. And as we did so, I yelled at him: "OK, if you don't want a riot on your hands, you better return that flag." We kept moving toward him and, much to my amazement, he walked over to us and returned the flag to the guy. I don't know what surprised me the most—the cop returning the flag, my spontaneously taking on the role of militant street leader, or the fact that the others actually followed my leadership so readily.

What did I think about those Americans who aided North Vietnam, they asked—like the guy in Los Angeles making propaganda tapes for North Vietnamese radio. I actually admired the guy's balls, but I responded with some more diplomatic weasel words. . . It was okay "if the individual felt in good conscience that this was a morally justified action." I added that this appeared to be the position of Senator Robert F. Kennedy. Kennedy had defended the right of a Rutgers University professor to declare that he hoped the Viet Cong would win. Even more surprising, the Senator had supported the idea of Americans donating blood to the North Vietnamese.[6] To this day I don't understand what possessed the man to say such things, but to the (unknown) extent that he was sincere, I admired him for it.

In concluding their report, my interrogators commented that "The subject's reluctance to admit to his participations and picketing activities demonstrates he is under strong leftist and pacifist influences more radical than those of just a 'Socialist' which he claims to be." An odd phrasing. Perhaps the word "socialist"—stripped of the kind of radical definition I had put forth to them—brought to their minds some harmless old icon who slept with the establishment like Norman Thomas, while to me it was the *sine qua non* of being a serious advocate for social change, of being a revolutionary. Not without reason has the word been banned from polite conversation in America except between consenting adults.

My reluctance to readily admit to certain actions stemmed from no radical instinct of underground secrecy. On the contrary, it arose, as with the wedding thing, from much more universal sentiments—called, disparagingly, "bourgeois hangups" in the '60s. I did, after all, still work at the State Department. I had joined this institution with the best of intentions, but had decidedly betrayed the trust placed in me. I was a little embarrassed, for I had lived a lie.

But it must be considered that they, with their policies, had betrayed *my* trust, not to mention my ambition. They were lying to the whole world. And I was not leaving a trail of death and destruction in my wake. During my time at the State Department—December 1964 to March 1967—my employer, the government of the United States of America, had seen fit to subvert elections in Italy, Chile and Greece; suppress movements for social and political change in Peru and Bolivia; save the day for military dictatorship in the Dominican Republic and Guatemala; support armed attacks against Cuba; overthrow the government of Ghana; drench itself in the blood of half a million hapless human beings in Indonesia; and bomb the people of Laos back to The Paleolithic Age. Not to mention a place called Vietnam. This is not to say that I knew about all these interventions at the time, but I knew more than enough.

I could not, however, bring myself to yell "McCarthyism" when it was suggested to me that I would perhaps be happier employed in the private sector, probably even earn a higher salary, they were kind enough to point out. My employer and my interrogators had related to me in a decent manner. Under the same circumstances, in any of the dictatorships which enjoyed the active support of my employer, I would have been cast into a cell and subjected to torture, likely carried out with the instructions, tools, and encouragement of the CIA, who would have first furnished my whereabouts if necessary.

The name of Jerry Rubin came up in the interrogation. Yes, I had met the celebrated Berkeley activist more than once when he came to Washington to attend demonstrations and deliver talks. He and his girlfriend had even stayed with me the first time we met, despite some initial reluctance on his part after I told him where I worked. But the Security men apparently knew nothing about this. It was comforting to know that the O'Toole Intelligence Service (OIS) was not infallible.

Rubin's name bleeped across media radar as he became one of the leading symbols of the anti-war movement and the general weakening of respect for authority amongst the young. Called to testify before the House Un-American Activities Committee, he appeared in the costume of a Revolutionary War solder. He understood about using the media before most others in the movement picked up on the full implication, and was extremely articulate, producing one-liners (today we'd call them sound bites) like: "Yesterday America needed pioneers and industrialists; today she needs cops, soldiers, bureaucrats and a mass apathetic public." And, "No kid in America wants to grow up to be like Lyndon Johnson. . ."

In 1969, while we were chatting in the office of the *Quicksilver Times*, Rubin said to me—in a context I now forget—"I'm a Marxist." He said it very simply and matter-of-factly, but I did not take him seriously for a moment. In that time period, in the particular surroundings in which he found himself, talking to a person like myself with members of the newspaper present, it was not surprising—it was almost *de rigueur*—that he would feel moved to say such a thing. In the following years, in a different period, he became a venture banker—this from a man who had scattered money onto the floor of the stock exchange to show his contempt—ran a dating service, immersed himself deeply in New Age spirituality endeavors and jargon, and marketed a wonder nutritional drink. At Jerry's funeral in Los Angeles in 1994, his former wife, Mimi Fleischman, said of him: "He realized that America was the greatest country on earth. He realized that capitalism is the greatest system on earth."[7]

When Rubin told me that he was a Marxist, he may well have convinced himself that it was so, just as in later years he insisted, in response to criticism, that he had been listening to the same muse all along, that in his new roles he was carrying out the same inspired work as in the '60s. An attempt, sort of, to explain this, in a book he wrote in the mid-'70s called *Growing Up At Thirty-Seven,* is such cover-to-cover psychobabble, growthobabble, and spiritobabble that I put the book down no wiser than when I picked it up, though I sincerely was hoping to discover the real person.

Then who was Jerry Rubin? God knows. All I know is the obvious—he was not in it for the long haul. He was not a man at war with society, he only had some technical problems to be ironed out. Once he had seen how easy it was to acquire fame, and had dined heartily and fully on it for several years, he turned his attention to fortune.

Ditto for his pal Rennie Davis, almost as prominent an organizer and orator in the '60s, and one of Rubin's co-defendants amongst "The Chicago Seven." Next thing we knew, Rennie had transmutated into a devotee of Maharaj-Ji, the fat little divine teenage guru, who, like others of his profession, wore the smile of a salesman who knows secrets that are good for you. Davis was convinced that this particular fat little teenager was God. Literally. Here to lead us all to salvation.

In April 1973, Rennie bravely stood before an audience in Berkeley and informed them that "Richard Nixon is truth, knowledge and bliss." In the face of catcalls and tomatoes, Davis predicted that "before this year is up, Guru Maharaj-Ji will have swept America, in 1974 he will enlighten Eastern Europe, and in 1975 he will visit China and have the greatest single following of people the world has ever known. I know this with every fiber of my being."[8]

It was not too long before "perfect master" Maharaj-Ji was replaced by Swami Something-or-other as God of the Month. And not too long after that that Rennie Davis became a partner in a financial-consulting firm. "Rennie's goal is still nothing less than saving the world," commented one of his clients, "but he found that working outside the system was like attacking a mountain with an ice pick."[9] Ergo, he became part of the mountain?

What lures a seemingly well-grounded activist like Rennie Davis, whom I met several times, to the likes of a Maharaj-Ji? Davis perhaps provided one clue when he spoke of the extremely moving and influential first step in his "receiving knowledge"—"I first was shown a technique called 'light', and I saw light in my head that was a hundred times lighter than the sun."

The Maharaj-Ji people closely guarded information about what actually took place in their Divine Light Mission sessions with followers and initiates, but early in 1974 I happened to come upon a young man who had left the organization. We might refer to him as a "disgruntled former devotee" (DFD). This young man told me about the "light" phenomenon, and showed me how it's achieved—by pressing a finger hard against each eyeball; just keep pressing until you see the light. I tried it several times, and each time, sure enough, I saw a very bright light, not a hundred times lighter than the sun of course, but very bright. It was indeed extraordinary, but I was not inspired to become a financial consultant. I later learned from an optometrist that pressing the eyeball hard enough will stimulate the retina, which in turn will excite the optic nerves and cause them to "fire." It's an example of a "phosphene"—defined as "an objective visual sensation that occurs with the eyes closed, and in the absence of retinal stimulation by visible light."

CHAPTER SIX
IBM AND LSD

I left the State Department early in the afternoon of my last day as an employee, and wandered aimlessly in a northerly direction, winding up on a bench in a little park at Washington Circle. I didn't know where I was headed, neither at that moment, nor for the rest of my life, but as I took my tie off, folded it up neatly, and stuck it in my suit pocket, I knew that I'd not be needing these trappings again anytime soon. I was a few days short of my 34th birthday, in excellent health, with $15,000 in the bank—a decent nest egg in 1967 for a single person, considering that my rent was only $95 a month, I had a brand new VW Bug fully paid for, and I was not terribly addicted to upscale living.

But people didn't do things like this, not where I came from, not how I was raised. My foreign service career—tossed into the trash can! And was I also now abandoning an even better-paying career, a career with an unlimited future—much greater, it turned out, than hardly anyone back then ever imagined for computers. And I was really good at the stuff. With a great head for business and an accounting background, if I had stuck with it I could have wound up as King of Silicon Valley, or another Ross Perot, who was at IBM the same time I was there, although I don't think we met. Perot was in sales and thus knew less than I did about the proper and optimum use of computers --the devil is in the details. But I was walking away from it all, as casually as hanging up a new picture on the wall because I was tired of looking at the old one.

My periodic evaluations at IBM back in New York had all been the same, one form or another of: "Good technically, but lacking marketing awareness. . .

should be in an area where his customer contact would be at a minimum level." Customers had to be spared the sight of me because I had not performed well in classes during the simulated sales presentations. I was not a nerd, but the enjoyment of persuading someone to buy something which they might not otherwise do, or even need, seems to be a characteristic that was left out of my DNA. It was not that I was lacking marketing *awareness*—I knew perfectly well how the game was supposed to be played. I just didn't care to play it. I much preferred to lose myself in the marvelous intricacies of designing, programming and testing a computer system than playing my expected role as a member in good standing of the sales "team." Not, it should be understood, that I ever pissed on a customer's Persian carpet.

IBM—like other giant corporations—knows no heresy save maladjustment. They're not really into suppressing individuality as an end unto itself. Their only end is the maximization of profit. If you could convince IBM that hiring 500 bearded, barefoot, hatless, shirtless, pot-smoking freaks would increase their profit significantly, IBM would immediately go out and look for 500 bearded, barefoot, hatless, shirtless, pot-smoking freaks, the best and the brightest they could find. The problem is that the freaks wouldn't take the IBM game seriously enough, an essential requirement for the game's proper functioning. Consider, if you will, the following scenario drawn from real life, circa 1963; only the names have been changed. . .

The chatter of small talk subsides as a gavel strikes a podium three times. The 40-or-so people in the room turn to face the front. Amongst them can be discerned one black, an Asian, three or four women, and, less apparent, two Jews. The others, as a group, can pass for "Princeton 5 to 10 years later." Brant Durrell, sales manager of the midtown office, waits until the last few murmurs have trickled away. He is the only person in the room over 35; tall and trim, ruddy-complexioned, you know that he's always been active athletically.

"I'm glad to see you all survived the weekend," he says with a large, charming grin. The grin is returned by his audience, with a few moved to laughter, the knowing kind.

"A few notes before we get down to business. First, a reminder that Wednesday is the last day you can submit an entry into the Name the Paper contest. So get to it fellahs, I'd sure like for one of us to pick the name of the new company newspaper. We ain't gonna let those guys from downtown beat us, are we?"

He is rewarded with a cluster of "No!"s.

"That's the spirit," Durrell continues. He is in his element and supremely in control. "Also, I'd like to announce that our own Frank Kearney, as of the first of the month, will be working out of corporate headquarters. His new moniker will be Assistant to the Director of Marketing for the Steel Industry—stand up

Frankie boy!"

Frankie boy rises to his feet and is joined in the act en masse by the other salesmen, while I remain cemented to my seat, a seat I occupy due to my poor sales-class performance. Some of the salesmen are applauding vigorously, others are thrusting a clenched fist into the air along with some indistinguishable cry—Princeton has just crossed the goal line.

"I know that I speak for all of us Frank," says Durrell, "when I say that our loss is corporate's gain. I'm sure you'll do the same bang-up job there that you've done here. Best of luck boy, and keep in touch with us, y'heah?"

"Thanks a lot Brant," Kearney replies, still standing. "It's been a real pleasure working here with a swell bunch of guys." His eyes drift out over the swell bunch of guys. "And I sure will keep in touch with you peasants from my exalted position," he says sheepishly as he takes his seat.

A chorus of hisses and boos greet this last remark. Kearney revels in it all. I have a vivid image of a younger Frank Kearney being hazed by his fraternity.

"We'll remember that, Frank," says Durrell in mock seriousness, changing immediately to a chuckle. The chuckle in turn gives way to serious seriousness. "Okay, I think we'll let the movie roll. This film you're about to see is damn good. I've seen it already and I think if you pay close attention you'll all get a hell of a lot out of it. Okay Jim, whenever you're ready."

The lights dim, the blinds are drawn, and a film splashes onto a screen that has been set up in front of the room. The film is entitled: "Getting The Customer To Have Confidence In You." Two actors and one narrator are sufficient to impart the secrets of this most treasured and arcane ability. One actor plays the salesman, the other, the customer executive. They are both handsome devils, in this best of all possible worlds, and equally adept at concealing the fact that they are human.

The first scene concerns itself with the delicate business of not talking down to a customer: "He must be made to feel that even though he doesn't know as much about your product as you do, you don't think him totally ignorant of what's involved. This, after all, is a valid assumption, since to have risen to the position he's in, he must know something." The right and wrong way of approaching the matter are movingly dramatized. The audience learns that one sure-fire technique is to preface certain remarks with: "As you know..."

There follows, the right and wrong way of: shaking hands, looking at a customer when he's speaking (with a closeup of the salesman's eyes radiating the message: "I am vitally interested in what you are saying."), admitting shortcomings in your product, talking about your competition, and transmitting an air of reliability—it is apparently possible to recite the words "You will receive your order on time" with all the same passion and conviction that Patrick Henry bared when speaking of liberty and death.

The lights flick on. The absolute silence that attended the film is broken by the sales manager saying that he knew they would like it. "Hear, hear!" cries the congregation. I am thinking that a few miles away in Greenwich Village the same film might be shown as pop art, and I and the rest of the audience would feel free to break up laughing. As it is, I find myself soaking in a pool of embarrassment.

It was not long after this—the week following the assassination of John F. Kennedy (which brought tears to my eyes a number of times)—that I walked into my manager's office to give notice. His office was neither plush nor pretentious. IBM was like that. Its computers were like that. And I needed no appointment. The company prided itself on its open-door policy, as it did its many employee benefits. The robber baron had been succeeded by "enlightened management." Just don't mention the word "union" within a one-mile radius.

I toyed with the idea of confronting my manager's mind with the ways in which I was not at home in the institution he was so devoted to.

Fred Carpenter was not much older than I, clear bass voice, wholesome, boyish good looks (there were no homely executives at IBM). He was surprised to hear of my plans. "Well, we're always sorry to lose one of the IBM family, but if anyone feels he can do better for himself elsewhere. . . well, that's what makes our country what it is; each person doing what's best for himself and in the end everyone benefits."

I nodded. That sounded about right. Years later, I was to reflect that the system described by my manager was nothing short of anarchy, the polar opposite of what IBM practiced. The company, with its meticulous selection, direction and grooming of employees, certainly wasn't leaving things to the vagaries of the individual; neither was its technology: a computer system would self-destruct if each of the programmers did not interface precisely with each other.

"May I ask who your new position is with?" Carpenter asked.

"Well, I don't actually have one as of now."

"Oh?"

"No, I thought I'd just sort of take it easy for awhile, pursue some interests of mine. . ."

It was his turn to nod, while he adjusted to a redefined set of circumstances, while I wondered why I wasn't saying any of the things I had thought of saying.

"Well, I wish *I* could retire," he laughed. It was not a good laugh. "It takes a lot of guts to leave a job without having a new one all lined up."

I was about to say that I hardly thought it was a gutsy thing I was doing, that I had done it several times before, when he told me that he admired my courage, that most men wouldn't be doing what I was doing, and I realized why

I wasn't speaking out. There was no need to, he knew it all, in a dusty corner of his mind that he rarely visited, no need to scrape my nails over it. He said that when he himself was younger he sort of had a thought to do the same, but y'know how you get caught up in things, and before you know it. . . and then he seemed to catch himself, and he switched over to how good he had it; he had lots of people under him he had, and his office was first in sales it was, and his own potential in the company was never better, and there was a nice wife and kids, and let's not forget the big house in Jersey (commuting was sort of a bother, heh-heh, but it's one of the prices you have to pay, heh-heh), and, well, it was a pretty good life it was. . .

Another of Jerry Rubin's one-liners. . . "The American standard of living is a baby blanket for executives who wake up screaming."

In striking contrast to my repeated job and career changing, my father, a semi-skilled machine-operator, took the IRT train from Brooklyn to the Fulton Street station in Manhattan to the same factory to the same job for 45 (sic) years, two weeks off in the summer, three weeks after 30 years, never earned more than $100 a week, never had a promotion. Then they retired the man with a burlap parachute. He was at most semi-literate in English although he was only a boy of 10 when he arrived from Poland. Never once did I see him open a book except a Jewish prayer book, nor did I ever hear him carry on a sustained conversation or express an idea save a simplistic condemnation of something, be it the price of meat, the weather, or the way the Dodgers were performing. His only interests, and my only legacy, were baseball and poker. But perhaps I was left another legacy: the drive—though wholly unconscious—to not live life like he did, which may account for my risk taking, my acute need for new experiences. My mother—in a rare instance of talking to me as a person, and not as a son or a Jew—lamented to me one day that she had led "a boring life" with my father. "I fell for a handsome face," she said.

Years after his death, I was surprised and pleased to learn from the younger of my two older sisters, Elaine, that our father would sometimes sneak off to porno films in Manhattan. I took it as a sign of life I hadn't known was there. Undoubtedly, though, if I had known of this when I was in my teens I would have been embarrassed down to my toes; parents are not supposed to be real people with real sexual urges.

Part of me sitting in Washington Circle that springlike day in early March didn't really believe that I had "dropped out." Four years high school, four years college, twelve years working with only scattered short breaks between jobs—I had performed like a veritable paragon of normalcy, whatever unorthodox notions I nurtured in a secluded little alcove of my brain. I wondered how long it would be before I was scanning the employment ads in the Sunday paper under "computer." But how many were my options now, given that I wouldn't and/or couldn't work in governmentland again, and was an alien in corporateland?

That was Friday. On Saturday morning I dropped some acid with my friend John James, now the publisher of "AIDS Treatment News" in Philadelphia. I had taken LSD once before and had had an entertaining—albeit weird—experience. On that occasion, when I felt I could handle being outside, I had sat on a bench at Dupont Circle during the evening rush hour, eyeing the people going home after work. It gave me the feeling of seeing truths normally hidden from LSD-free man. The people scurrying by, shoulder bags dangling, attaché cases in hand, each bore the face of an animal: tiger, lion, monkey, sheep, ostrich. . . most of them walked like the animal they were. This was, I was sure, their true nature, or at least their true nature in the working world, although I couldn't figure out what an ostrich symbolized; while on the grass nearby sat a woman, a child a few feet from her, and I was able to see rays of love emanating from the mother's eyes and going out to her child. I am not speaking metaphorically, I actually saw the rays.

Weird, of course, was what LSD was all about, but this morning, my first day of "freedom"—as in "Freedom's just another word for nothin' left to lose"—I violated a cardinal rule of taking acid. To borrow from the streets of New York: There are three things you don't do in this world—You don't piss against the wind, you don't pull the mask off the Lone Ranger,, and you don't get involved in anything personally heavy while you're out there flying on acid.

Suzanne and I had stopped living together a short while ago, but there was still something going on between us. Or so I felt. When the LSD took me over, I was suddenly hit with this overwhelming feeling of love and romance directed at her. I had to speak to her. I picked up the phone, as John asked me what the heck was going on, and called her. She didn't want me to come over, at least not at that moment, but her words meant nothing to a man possessed. I left a confused and concerned John alone in my apartment and raced to my car.

It's called auto-pilot. I had made the trip to her mother's home in Silver Spring so many times, thinking was no longer a requirement. . . left here, right there. . . red light-brake pedal-stop. . . green light-gas pedal-go. If drunk driving is a crime, my condition was a capital offense. My body draped forward over the wheel as if to put me that much closer to my destination. I stared ahead with the focused eyes of a madman, unaware of any other dimension, knowing instinctively that if I relaxed my focus, the acid would dance in my head and put on its famous psychedelic show. I had to keep the jolly monster caged; my mind in struggle with itself.

When Suzanne opened the door, she was clearly not ecstatic about seeing me, but that didn't deter me for a moment from walking past her into the living room. There was a guy standing there. And then I noticed that Suzanne was wearing a bathrobe.

With my head in its normal place, I would have kept my cool—ego, self-respect, all that jazz. But now it was all operatic wails and forehead smiting. "Who is this man?" I loudly demanded to know. "What does he mean to you?" I repeated this refrain several times with only minor variations, if any. If I were to see a video of my performance that morning, I'd crumble to the floor in a heap and pray to my atheist god for life to leave my body as quickly and pain-lessly as possible.

After a nod from Suzanne, the guy excused himself and left. That made me feel even worse—the contrast between his behavior and mine. I did not stay much longer, and I don't remember any of the words that passed between she and I. It didn't matter. I didn't have the right script for this scene. If it hadn't been over between us before this farce, it sure was by the time I left. I managed to find my way home without any vehicular homicide, and threw myself in bed.

The acid trip—the picture show part of it—had been aborted, the projec-tor and screen wrenched from inside my head. But for the rest of that day, and the next day, and every day for the next few weeks, I was in a daze. I took care of all the basics, but it was like I was stoned, permanently, without the laughs. I had had a lot of experience with myself, but nothing to prepare me for the daily bouts of depression, the sudden crying for no apparent reason, the out-of-body element whereby I often watched my own behavior as if it belonged to some-one else, hoping, in fact, that it did.

I couldn't stand to be alone, and spent a lot of time at friends' houses and hanging around with people at Dupont Circle, the charming little oasis which was Washington's center for much of what became known as The Sixties. I kept reaching out—stopping short of being pitiable, I hoped—but no one seemed to understood what I was going through, or even that I was going through any-thing. All these people in their twenties—this "love generation"—had they not yet outgrown teenage unconsciousness of other people's needs?

Late at night, sitting alone with my condition, I took to reading Eastern mysticism literature. The idea that nothing had to be the way it appeared, and probably wasn't, was very comforting. . . pain, pleasure, anger, guilt—they're only mind moments, and there's always a new moment. . . one should abstain from dualistic thinking. . . a compelling play of words upon the mind to evoke emotions, more potent than music for a word person like myself. I could see why people leaned upon such language, especially at troubled times, which was likely how the whole theory and practice arose in the first place; the same with what the West calls religion. This was not to be the only time I turned to such books, but I never considered embarking on a pilgrimage to India, nor becom-ing some guy's devotee; and I find, ironically, that the distinction made between the spiritual consciousness as "real" and the mundane consciousness as "illusion" is the ultimate example of duality.

Many times have I met someone who went on about "unity" and "oneness," and I've always asked them the same question: If you're standing at the edge of a cliff, do you take a step forward off the cliff because the rock and the air are "one"? Their multifarious non-answers have reinforced my belief that such people don't live the way they preach; and they can't, because what they preach is not livable.

After the passage of a few weeks, my usual daily state settled into an intermittent, lower-level psychic ache. I was able to function okay, not happily, but okay. It was not until nine months later that I awoke one morning and knew, I simply knew, that it was all gone. Why then? Why that moment? It would have been fascinating to be able to peer into the process my unconscious, in its infinite wisdom, had gone through to decide that I had been punished enough.

I took LSD just once more, perhaps to prove to myself that it wasn't the acid per se that had fucked up my head so, but the acid combined with an intolerable personal situation. My partners were a young man, Tom Torosian, and his girlfriend. Tom worked at the Pentagon on some sort of military newsletter, into which he'd sneak coded messages, like "Make Love Not War" backwards (that's rawtonevolekam). The trip was pretty much like the first one: strange, but the LSD didn't burn any holes in my genes.

There were those amongst the eminent hippie political scientists who believed that LSD dropped into the water supply would change the world. Right.

CHAPTER SEVEN
THE *WASHINGTON FREE PRESS*

"Do you think you'd be allowed to print this if you lived in North Vietnam?"

Was there anyone putting out an underground newspaper in the United States in the 1960s or early 1970s who did not have that question thrown in their face? The implication being of course that this was proof of how free and noble was our land compared to the enemy's land, and that we should thus seriously reconsider our opposition to the government that ruled over this free and noble land. The further implication was that we should be so grateful for the right to publish such newspapers that we should demonstrate our gratitude by not publishing such newspapers. If the question didn't mean these things, it didn't mean anything.

I began working full time at the *Washington Free Press* a mere two days after the onset of my bad trip, simultaneously a major challenge to and a welcome distraction from my acid-soaked brain. I was one of eight people who had begun meeting a few months earlier to plan the first issue. None of us had a journalistic background worth mentioning. We all came out of the anti-war movement and, for a brief romantic interlude, we thought that that was enough to bind us all together as courageous newspapermen and women crusading for peace and justice.

An old rundown townhouse at 1737 Q St., NW served as the paper's office and the home of almost the entire staff. All room and board was paid for by the newspaper, with spending money provided by being allowed to sell as many copies of the paper each week on the streets as one wished. I kept my own apartment, but I sold papers once in a while and took some meals at the house when I wasn't tired of pasta and chili.

Our planning meetings had not included discussions of anything so banal as journalistic style or standards, but people's leanings in this direction soon became clear enough when there appeared on the office blackboard the dictum: "Grammar is bourgeois." It was meant in only minor part as a joke. It turned out that I was the only one who was truly concerned about the quality of the writing and who seriously and consistently edited the articles, almost all of which needed industrial-strength polishing. I was, moreover, the one most conscious of catering to the hangups and answering the questions of the great American Liberal-Center, a group with which I had had a long affiliation.

The prevailing attitude amongst some of my colleagues, however, was that editing could sometimes border on dishonesty, if not out-and-out censorship. Although rarely put into practice in the publishing world, this was not a new literary thesis. Jack Kerouac had once stigmatized rewriting as a "form of cheating," referring to his *own* rewriting, not simply that of an editor.

Thus, it was reasoned, if an article came in that was not entirely literate or coherent, it should be left the way it was written, not only in fairness to the author, but to capture the true spirit of the times: if semi-literate, semi-coherent, semi-articulate, slogan-waving kids were part of the revolution, then the articles should reflect that—"the medium is the message," in the words, repeated *ad nauseam*, of Marshall McLuhan, all the rage at the time. Here was a perfectly suitable hero for the grammar-is-bourgeois crowd, using revolutionary lingo to disparage the ability of reason, analysis, and clarity of argument to provide enlightenment, consistently refusing to offer concrete examples of what he was getting at, tossing out an occasional truism re the media dressed up as "futuristic insight," all sandwiched between layers of impenetrable neological-babble. By undervaluing substance, and elevating means and process, McLuhan appealed to countless young people who didn't understand the substance of this idea or that issue and were overjoyed to be relieved of the responsibility of actually having to understand the stuff. "Oh great! I've been trying to figure out what the fuck the message was, and now I know! It's—duh—the medium!"

At one point I enrolled for a class in Spanish at the so-called Free University of Washington, and at the first meeting I was flabbergasted to hear the "teacher" announce that he probably didn't know much more Spanish than the students. And that's the way it should be, he informed us—no authoritarian hierarchy. He wanted to learn from us as much as we wanted to learn from him.

Dumb was in! And it was to stay in—New Age and Metaphysical Gobbledygook were standing in the wings. They would call themselves "spiritual" because "religion" had gotten such a bad name, and sneer at the Bible Belt while believing in mumbo jumbo that would shame Oral Roberts.

Anti-intellectualism was doubtless an odd perspective for individuals putting out a newspaper. But we, myself included, did not think of ourselves as newspaper publishers. The paper was merely a vehicle for the anti-war movement, the civil rights movement, and all the other burgeoning anti-authoritarian and social-change tendencies that convinced the good burghers of America that society's fabric was rapidly unraveling.

I did not even think of myself as a writer, except as one of the legion of writer wannabes who never even submit anything for publication. It was only when the first issue was nearing completion that the question struck me—why don't I write something myself? The quality of the writing that I saw going into the paper left me with no doubts that I could match the competition, although the short piece I wrote, called "Life at the State Department," was a relatively amateurish literary debut. Posterity has been kind, nonetheless—a copy of it has resided in my FBI file ever since.

In common with the rest of the mushrooming underground press across the country, our columns were filled with stuff about drugs—the use and enjoyment of, the right to the use and enjoyment of, the determination of the police to prevent the use and enjoyment of; the Black Panthers, Students for a Democratic Society (SDS), the anti-war movement, and police oppression of them all—black activists, white radicals, and peaceniks; Vietnam and other U.S. foreign policy adventures-cum-imperialism; draft advice for conscientious objectors, local campus issues, even a discussion of homophobia and homophilia, still a rare subject for a newspaper.

Where did a bunch of young people—all in their twenties except myself, all of white skin, all bereft of working experience even remotely like mine—get off telling Mr. Jones what was happenin' and the White House where to get off? It was not that we were necessarily "smarter" than those who wrote for the *Washington Post,* for example. Yet, consider: The anti-Vietnam War movement had burst out of the starting gate back in August 1964, with hundreds of people demonstrating in New York. Many of these early dissenters took apart and critically examined the administration's statements about the war's origin, its current situation, and its rosy picture of the future. They found continuous omission, contradiction and duplicity, became quickly and wholly cynical, and called for immediate and unconditional withdrawal. This was a state of intellect and principle it took the professional journalists and analysts of the *Post* until the 1970s to reach. And even then—even today—they viewed Vietnam only as a "mistake;" i.e., it was "the wrong way" to fight communism, not that the United States should not be traveling all over the globe to spew violence against anything labeled "communism" in the first place. Essentially, the only thing that the daily press has learned from Vietnam is that we should not have fought in

Vietnam. Remaining a mystery is the idea that "communism" was simply the name given to any government or movement that posed an obstacle to the extension of The American Empire.

Yet it's part of the American media's ideology to pretend that it doesn't have any ideology.

To this day as well, neither the *Post* nor hardly any other daily newspaper in the United States would ever think of making reference to "the American invasion of Vietnam," although that's precisely what it was, as surely as the Soviet invasion of Czechoslovakia. On a day in August 1968, I joined a group of marchers near the USSR embassy on 16th Street, protesting the Soviet invasion of the day before. I carried a homemade sign declaring: "Soviet Union Out of Czechoslovakia. U.S. Out of Vietnam." A man marching alongside me was so upset by my sentiment his anger could be measured with a Geiger counter. He could scarcely manage to get out of his mouth the words to express his monumental incredulity at the bizarre comparison I was putting forth. This was one of the most singular features of the Cold War: the seeming inability of the militant anti-communists—indeed, the average American—to ever equate American and Soviet actions; even more unthinkable, of course, the idea—the fact!—that U.S. foreign policy was actually much more brutal, repeatedly, than that of "the commies."

David Lawrence, the editor of *U.S. News & World Report*, sat down one day in February 1966 and was moved to put the following words to paper: "What the United States is doing in Vietnam is the most significant example of philanthropy extended by one people to another that we have witnessed in our times."[10]

No one should ever wonder how the overwhelming majority of the German people—with the highly educated no exception at all—were able to bring themselves to enthusiastically support the actions of the Nazi government. I sent Mr. Lawrence a copy of a slick, well-done pamphlet entitled *American Atrocities in Vietnam*, which gave graphic detail of its subject. To this I attached a note which first repeated the above quotation with Lawrence's name below it, then added: "*One* of us is crazy," followed by my name. Lawrence responded with a full page letter, at the heart of which was:

> I think a careful reading of it [the pamphlet] will prove the point I was trying to make—namely that primitive peoples with savagery in their hearts have to be helped to understand the true basis of a civilized existence.

These remarks, I would venture, could have been punctuated with a pinch of snuff.

It took the daily press even longer—decades—to (tentatively) admit that there was a grave police problem in America—routine brutality, planting of evidence, etc. The underground press in the '60s regularly carried first-hand accounts of dissenters experiencing such indignities, for which the newspapers were rewarded by being labeled "paranoid."

When reporter Allen Young's political convictions compelled him to quit the *Washington Post* and join the *Free Press* and Liberation News Service, with which we shared an office building on Thomas Circle, we printed Young's story under the modest little headline: "*Post* Reporter Defects to *Free Press*."

"With its scraggly crew of reporters and editors," wrote Young, the *Free Press* can hardly amass the facts contained in the big dailies. But they can tell it as it is. That's why I like it better here."

One day early in 1968, I accompanied Allen to the apartment of a Foreign Service Officer. There were five other FSOs present, one of whom Allen had known at Columbia University. They had invited us to discuss the war with them because five of the six were scheduled to go to Vietnam in the near future, and whatever this might do for their careers, it was a troubling prospect—not simply because of the looming danger to life and limb, but, it seemed, politically as well.

They all had reservations about the war. One stated flatly that he opposed it—whatever that meant in the context of the Vietnam black-hole dialectic—but defended his upcoming job in pacification work there on the ground that if he resigned, someone worse would take his place. All of them were clearly, and understandably, very eager to somehow feel better about being dropped into the swamp of their employer's latest exercise in killing foreigners with kindness.

How did they expect to achieve this state of mind from a dialogue with two anti-war activists? Perhaps they felt that if they heard the "worst," the most telling arguments against the war, and this didn't faze them unduly, or if they decided that the arguments were a bunch of crap, their pressing concerns would be diminished.

For a long while they eschewed the standard mantras of raw-meat anti-communism proclaimed by supporters of the war: "Communism is an evil system and we have a moral obligation to combat it.". . . "The communists are stirring up revolution all over the world just so they can take over.". . . "We have to draw the line against communism somewhere—if we don't fight them in Vietnam, we'll have to fight them in San Francisco. . ."

Instead they put forth what to them seemed more sophisticated or intellectual arguments, speaking of such things as "national interest," "maintaining the balance of power," "self-determination," and other catchwords of State-Departmentese.

However, when Allen and I subjected their arguments—which we had dealt with repeatedly for some three years—to critical scrutiny, and displayed a knowledge of the history of the conflict far more informed than they possessed, after a couple of hours and a few drinks the young Foreign Service Officers began sounding more like Joe Sixpack, and the discussion became heated for the first time.

I'm unable to say to what extent, if any, they derived what they were looking for. As for me, I could not help thinking the obvious: There but for fortune go I.

Though we eagerly awaited the paper each week when it came back from the printer, after the first gush of excitement our offspring was not a joy to look at. Slanting lines of text, mixtures of type in the same sentence, some words handwritten, columns that wandered creatively around the page, lots of typos, egregious ones, entire sentences missing, graphically retarded, we had it all. Par for the course for the underground press in America, circa 1967. It was facile for our natural enemies to dismiss us out of hand. Desktop publishing and spell checking could have done wonders.

The paper got better in time of course, but it never quite lost the appearance that it had been laid out on drugs, probably for the obvious reason. And laid out by people up all night, working with the first typesetting machine ever built, and a shortage of proper layout equipment and supplies; dragging our tired and hungry bodies home at seven in the morning. I blackened my lungs with a whole pack of cigarettes during a layout session, slashing my cell walls with enough stress to give Mahatma Gandhi an ulcer, and likely beginning the process that some years later developed into duodenitis. Thank god for Tagamet.

Jerry Rubin's Yippies insisted that if a revolution was not fun and games, it was not worth doing. Like many of the things the Yippies said, this sounded great, with a marvelous ring of truth to it, but if taken literally through the ages might have left humankind still in the dark ages politically and socially.

October 21, 1967, the March on the Pentagon, surely one of the most extraordinary and imposing acts of protest and civil disobedience in history—the government hunkered down in its trenches in the face of an audacious assault upon its seat of power by its own citizens; a demonstration much bigger than the Bonus Marchers of 1932, those depression-stricken World War One veterans demanding payment on their government bonus certificates NOW, not in some pie-in-the-sky future—the people peaceably assembled to petition the government for a redress of grievances, violently and humiliatingly squashed by federal troops under the command of a general named MacArthur, and his aide named Eisenhower, and their officer named Patton.

Why did the soldiers of 1932 forcibly crush the hopes of the soldiers of

1918? Why have soldiers acted in like manner virtually at all times and in all places in history? The MacArthurs, the Eisenhowers, the Pattons, the Pinochets, the Duvaliers, the Stalins, the Greek Colonels, the Napoleons, after all their speeches and decrees, after all their pomp and circumstance, have no power to enforce their objectives—absolutely none—without the active cooperation and obedience of *the man with the gun*. . . Praetorian, *légionnaire*, riot police, *gendarme*, redcoat, knight, Special Forces, lancer, doughboy, archer, bowman, musketeer, carabineer, Green Beret, grenadier, fusileer, infantryman, foot soldier, security forces, artilleryman, cavalryman, dragoon, hussar, soldier, sailor, marine, policeman. . . We're all born knowing that the divine right of kings is a little less divine in the absence of troops to carry out the divine will. The inexorable tendency of the human being turned soldier to obey orders, even those he doesn't believe in, to not be inhibited by the consequences of his actions, is one of the greatest barriers to progress the world over.

We would soon be coming face to face with such creatures, thousands of them.

A week before the march I had written the following in the *Free Press*:

> This will not be 'just another march'. The continued escalation of the war has changed the mood of many in the anti-war movement from dissent to active resistance. Everyone is expected to do his 'thing', including, of course, those whose thing is simply to march and make their numbers felt. The Diggers' thing is to expunge the bad vibrations from the warhawks' five-sided, concrete aviary. According to American Indian lore, the pentagon is the symbol of evil. In order to drive out the evil, the Indians would draw a circle around the pentagon. So the Diggers plan to make a circle around the Pentagon with people opposed to the war. Some of them were at the Pentagon last week and blew a few minds there as they measured how many people, holding hands, it would take to form a ring around the Pentagon. They concluded that 1200 would do it. Skeptics about the efficacy of Indian magic will be free to use more conventional methods, such as blocking the Pentagon's doors.

This section of my article was reprinted on page one of the *Wall Street Journal* a few days later, and although I knew it would never have landed on such an august spot if it had contained radical ideas or a militant tone, it pleased me considerably—partly because of the extra publicity given to the upcoming event (though the number of *Wall Street Journal* readers my words would induce to attend might not exceed high single digits), but mainly because it massaged my ego. Though I could denounce the *Journal* with the best of them, and was perfectly capable of referring to it as "the running dog of capitalism," with tongue only partially in cheek, I had by this time developed a healthy writer's vanity, and was only sorry that I hadn't attached my byline to the article because I had another one right next to it which did carry my name.

I was thus deprived of the further pleasure of imagining old friends of mine back in New York—who had not been inspired enough by my example to follow in my footsteps, and instead wound up on the very same Wall Street—staring in disbelief at the *Journal*'s front page while sipping their morning coffee.

It was strange how guys from the same neighborhood, same schools, same socio-economic class, same religion, same everything as me, strange how their social intuitions steered by such a highly selective compass—they could reach for their moral shotgun when the-way-things-are trespassed upon the immediate vicinity of their family, wallet, or comforts, but were otherwise spared the harassment of a community or international conscience.

Eventually, inevitably, my friendship with the more conservative of these old friends became a casualty of the horizontal generation gap so peculiar to the times. The one thing we most shared, the thing which made Brooklynites, particularly of the Jewish persuasion, a fraternity—that special brand of irreverent, sarcastic, sick, racist, sexist, anti-gentile humor—even that didn't help. To be sure, we all still had our sense of humor. It's just that we didn't laugh at the same things anymore. By this time, they were undoubtedly making jokes about people like me.

On a visit to Manhattan to attend a political meeting, I phoned Phil B., a friend of almost 20 years, who was pursuing a career in the world of finance. We were both acutely aware of our "differences," but so far had succeeded in not permitting that little fact of life to slash through the heart of our friendship. I asked Phil if I could stay with him for a couple of days, as I had done on a previous visit. His answer was of one word, said without emphasis: "No."

"What do you mean?" I asked chuckling, certain he was kidding.

"I don't want you to stay with me," he replied, again in a tone suitable for telling me what the weather was like. This was probably painful enough for him without adding an emotional factor.

There was a long pause at both ends of the line, while my mind scrambled to make sense of what was happening. When I came to, I said: "Okay, Phil, so long." We both of course knew it was not "so long," but "goodbye." That was 1968 and he and I have had no contact since.

The previous year, another youthful friend, Frank Brasco, from the same block as me in Crown Heights, had become a Congressman of all things. We had not seen each other since about age 20, and when I read about him being in office, my first thought was to try and remember any flashes of intellect or idealism radiating from him. My second thought was to wonder about myself for instantly associating such qualities with a Congressman. My third thought was that, as a political activist and journalist, it might come in very handy knowing a Congressman. I couldn't afford to own one, or even rent one, but I could still cultivate a relationship with one of the species. (I hasten to explain such cynicism by pointing out that Frank and I had not been long-time, very close friends as was the case with Phil and I.)

So it was that we had lunch together one day at the Members' Dining Room in the Capitol, courtesy of the Congressman of course. I had actually partaken of a little self-flagellation by covering my body with a cuff-linked white shirt, a tie, and a suit on a sweltering spring day. It was either that or a black beret, a Che Guevara T-shirt, and a bandolier. I had considered bringing a copy of the *Free Press* to show him, but, only a couple of issues old, the paper was not terribly impressive, and would certainly not convey to the likes of a Congressman that its editor had "made it." It was a bit painful to me to realize why I wasn't taking the paper with me.

After a few minutes of "What ever happened to so-and-so?", I mentioned my recent resignation from the State Department, which naturally led into a discussion of Vietnam. Frank, while apparently not a hawk, held the view that dissent was okay, but once it had been expressed and the nation's leaders were aware of the substance of the opposing arguments, it was the dissenters' obligation to give the government their full support. I doubt that Frank knew it, but his concept was one practiced by Communist and Trotskyist parties in many countries; they called it "democratic centralism," substituting the party for the government of course.

I had resolved beforehand, and kept reminding myself as I sat there, that I was not going to lose my cool. But the idea that if the government ignored the protestors and continued the war, the protestors had the civic duty to cease their protest, was one that, even as part of a fancy lunch, was indigestible. When Frank told me to lower my voice, it was the first I knew that I had lost my cool. He was stealing glances toward nearby tables.

Here, as well, a "so long" was clearly a "goodbye." Well, it was time to stop deceiving myself and remove the one foot I fancied I could still keep in that other world. As for the Congressman, before long he had to remove both feet from his own world, for he was indicted, and lost his seat, for conspiring to win a Post Office mail-hauling contract for a Mafia-controlled trucking company in return for a bribe.

We return now to the famous March on the Pentagon. After a stirring concert at the Reflecting Pool by Phil Ochs surrounded by 150,000 of his closest friends, most of the protestors marched over the Memorial Bridge to the war factory. Never to be forgotten: the roof of the Pentagon when the colossus first came into view and we marched closer and closer—soldiers standing guard, spaced across the roof from one side to the other, weapons at the ready, motionless, looking down upon us from on high with all the majesty of stone warriors or gods atop a classical Greek temple. For the first time that day I wondered—

not without excitement—what I was letting myself in for.

This was wholly unlike my first protest at the Pentagon. This was not a group of Quaker pacifists sworn to non-violence, who could bring out the least macho side of even professional military men, and who would be received cordially in the Pentagon cafeteria. Today, we were as welcome and as safe as narcs at a biker rally. Our numbers included many the boys at the Pentagon must have been itching to get their hands on, like those in the Committee to Aid the National Liberation Front, with their Vietcong flags, and SDS and other "anti-imperialist" groups, who became involved in some of the earliest confrontations that day.

In sharp contrast to the likes of these were the illuminati like Norman Mailer, Marcus Raskin, Noam Chomsky, Robert Lowell, Dwight McDonald—men in dark suits, white shirts and ties as if to ward off evil spirits with the cross of respectability.

In the vast parking lot to which we were confined, open hostility was kept in check at first, but it was clear that the peace was only an inch deep. Repeated draft-card burnings took place—a veritable performance, with flaming cards held high and flaunted square in the irises of the soldiers, whose faces were masked in studied indifference. Although this augured conflict of unpredictable dimensions, I found it exhilarating to see all those young people acting so principled and fearless. I was sorry that I was too old to have a card to burn.

Scattered pockets of mild confrontation broke out, soon unfolding into more widespread and serious clashes. At one spot a Vietnam teach-in for the troops was broken up by MPs with clubs. Later, 82nd Airborne Division paratroopers, veterans of Vietnam, entered the scene, bayonets fixed, face to face at last with these people they had been hearing about so much, the privileged little sons of bitches whose incessant crying about international law and morality and god-knows-what-else gave aid and comfort to the enemy, the cowardly little snotnose draft-dodgers who wallowed in sex and dope while the GIs wallowed in mud and death.

The paratroopers proceeded to kick ass—after 'Nam this was a church picnic—and many bruised and battered demonstrators were carried away to waiting prison busses, helping to swell the day's total arrestees to near 700. The protestors, whose only defense was to lock arms, appealed to the soldiers to back off, to join them, to just act human, shouting through a bull horn: "The soldiers are not our enemy, the decision makers are." Though this was a sincere declaration, its failure to sway their attackers gave way to angry, impotent curses of "bastards" and "motherfuckers."

I had no big argument with the idea that the soldiers' bosses were the real enemy, but I had real difficulty with the expressions of "love" for the GIs that some silly hippie types allowed to pass their lips. The soldiers, after all, had made decisions, just as others of their generation had opted for draft evasion or Canada. These soldiers, in particular, were fresh from the killing fields. The idea of "individual responsibility" is not just a conservative buzzword.

Several eyewitnesses told the *Washington Free Press* that in other areas of the "battlefield" they saw as many as three soldiers drop their weapons and helmets and join the crowd, and that at least one of them was seized and dragged into the Pentagon by MPs soon afterward. Later attempts to obtain information about these soldiers from the Pentagon were met with denials.

As we were chased about in turmoil by military men swinging gun butts and clubs, I had the feeling I've often had in the midst of street confrontations with police officers—when I almost wish the cops would start shooting and we would shoot back; it would take away the damn *pretense* of a civil game and reveal the struggle for control it really is; stop making the cops look so fucking moderate and more the extremist bastards they really are.

Whence cometh such a belligerent mentality in me? One would think I had been raised in the Warsaw ghetto under siege, or something. I think it's the ritual of it all, the ceremony that demonstrators and police go through, which is, like most ceremony, based essentially on sham—the band plays, the dancers know their steps, the music stops, and everyone returns to their exact same position in the exact same society as before.

Hard to believe, but the following evening there were still dozens of demonstrators congregated on the Pentagon steps and talking freely to soldiers, the smell of tear gas still wafting in the air, along with marijuana and hashish, smells not entirely unfamiliar to those GIs who had been in Vietnam.

It happened that I fell into conversation with a Congressman, William J. Scherle (R-Iowa), who had come there to talk to the demonstrators about the war, admitting that he didn't know as much about it as he should. This was made rather clear when, after I mentioned a few very basic and well known facts about the war and the Geneva Accords of 1954, he said to me: "I'm very impressed with your knowledge of the war, young man, and I want to talk to you further." The impressive knowledge I had enlightened the good Congressman with was stuff we had read and discussed in the study group more than two years earlier, and which had appeared in countless flyers and anti-war publications all over the country.

Though Scherle was to be complimented for his honesty and his willingness to go directly into the enemy's camp to learn first hand what was on their minds, the lack of knowledge on the part of one who had been voting on matters concerning the war was certainly sad and appalling. By all evidence, Scherle was unique amongst congressmen re Vietnam only by virtue of his honesty.

Although my lungs and eyes howled in protest against my very first taste of tear gas, I was neither arrested nor beaten up. I don't remember making a particular effort to avoid conflict, but neither did I stick my neck out as much as some of the "crazies," or purposely put myself in a position to get peacefully arrested as did Norman Mailer, who used the experience as the basis for a book. This is not to imply that he got himself arrested *because* of the book.

The book, *Armies of the Night*, begins with a gathering held at a home in Adams-Morgan the night before the march, which I attended. Mailer goes out of his way to poke snobbish (his word) fun at the hosts, Ted and Suzanne Fields, although he doesn't name them. He puts down the paintings on the wall, the furniture, the carpet, whatever his oh-so-discriminating New York eye falls upon. Mainly he agitates himself about "liberals," and, even more so, "liberal academics," which he associates with the Fields and some of their guests. This was rather ironic inasmuch as neither of the hosts were academics. Ted happened to be my dentist, and Suzanne, although she held a master's degree, did not hold a university teaching position. Amongst other things, she wrote cultural reviews for the *Free Press*, not for a living of course.

Norman Mailer, in-your-face macho individualist that he is, appears to find it demeaning, or at least uncomfortable, to be lumped together with any kind of group thinking or group action, particularly once it's reached a critical mass of popularity or enthusiasm. To make sure that no one would associate him with liberals, liberal academics, leftists, or any other variety opposing the war which could conceivably be labeled, he referred to himself in the book as a "Left Conservative." He informed the reader that "There was no one in America who had a position even remotely" like his, and then proceeded with an analysis of the Vietnam question that suffered from the two most common failings of U.S. cold war foreign policy analysis: placing no explicit weight at all on the economic factor, and using the word "communism" as if it had a precise, universal meaning and "communists" as if the world over they were all clones of each other. Years later, after achieving a measure of prominence in JFK-assassination circles, and in danger of being labeled a "conspiracy theorist," or, much worse, a "conspiracy nut," he suddenly did a 180-degree turn and announced his belief—accompanied, of course, by a new book—that Oswald had killed Kennedy and had acted alone. He then declared that he was "75 percent sure" of this.

At another party at the Fields' home, I found myself standing next to Allen Ginsberg, who was engaged in a discussion-cum-debate of Vietnam with a Foreign Service Officer. After a few minutes of the usual recitation of the two "lines," with the usual lack of making any dent in the other's armor, the poet opted for metaphor—he opened his fly and took his penis out. And there he stood, and there *it* stood (hung actually), as if to say: "If by this time you haven't seen through all the bullshit, I can't waste my time intellectualizing with you. Here's what I think of your rationalizations."

The FSO and his wife at his side were now faced with the exquisitely delicate task of pretending that nothing at all unusual was happening. They kept their eyes focused hard on Ginsberg's face, as if their life depended on it, while the husband continued to calmly and thoughtfully present his government's view of the world.

I would sooner have walked into the White House waving the Vietcong flag in one hand and a hammer and sickle in the other than do what Ginsberg did. Whatever else one might say about such behavior, it takes a very special kind of "freedom"—albeit the same freedom schizophrenics claim; just as on the previous evening when Ginsberg had spoken at conservative Georgetown University and, in the midst of discussing President Johnson's war policies, suddenly asked: "How big is the President's prick?" That actually embarrassed me, perhaps because the words seemed so totally out of context, dirty for dirty's sake, although not entirely inappropriate as applied to the vulgarian who occupied the Oval Office. Perhaps Ginsberg harbored a perverse affinity for the man. But I was also concerned that he would turn off some of the Georgetown students from the anti-war cause. However, from the audience's reaction, at that moment as well as during the whole evening, I think not. The students may have been more conservative than at some of the other local universities, but they were still young, and could revel in things that shocked their teachers, if only *because* they shocked their teachers.

Suzanne Fields is a case in point for what I find to be one of the most intriguing and puzzling facets of the whole sixties phenomenon. For half a dozen years I marched, worked and socialized close up, to one degree or another, with many hundreds of people—comrades, I thought of them as, West-bloc dissidents, all of us part of a movement committed to struggling against U.S. imperialism abroad and economic and police injustice at home. And whatever the different tendencies and branches within that movement, at times antagonistic to each other, we were unified in our common struggle against the forces of darkness.

How unknowing I was. So much was taken for granted that it remained unspoken. Rarely did people illuminate their ideological leanings in explicit sound bites. It turned out that many of the people I marched and worked with, even some of those I slept with, for all their radical posturing, had their own agendas. Many were "simply" against the war—for pacifist reasons, for being of draft age, for having a husband or son of draft age, or to pull the plug on the god-awful napalm pictures on TV. Or because it was fashionable. It pissed me off when the media opined the latter, because I knew it was just wishful thinking—they couldn't accept the fact that so many people could have good reason for being so passionately against what the media supported. But they were right, even if for the wrong reason. Like blue jeans and long hair and Dylan's music, marching in a crowd against the government was fun, challenging authority was exhilarating. To kids AWOL from suburbia it was all a first-class experience, they felt part of something bigger than themselves. And it promised—to those of all ages—more easy sex than they had ever had before.

Sure, they could spout off about "capitalist pigs" as well as anyone, and the treasonous-sounding "Ho-Ho/Ho Chi Minh/The NLF is gonna win!" But they were not serious students of the institutional capitalist structure, of the underlying arrangement of power in the world, even of Why Vietnam?, and they cast a skeptical eye upon anyone who claimed to have a lot of "answers"—such people were labeled "dogmatic." The closest they brushed up against a political or social philosophy was the belief that to change the world you must first change yourself. "The personal is political" was the prevailing mantra. "Free your mind," sang the Beatles, don't blame the institution. This philosophy was not a sixties creation of course; many creeds have long insisted that we must embody in our lives the changes we'd like to see socially. But was this any way to run a revolution?

"I remember very well the first time I heard the slogan 'the personal is political,'" writer Christopher Hitchens has remarked. "I felt a deep, immediate sense of impending doom." He saw it as meaning: "I'll have a revolution inside my own psyche." Calling this "escapist and narcissistic," he added that "With 'the personal is political', nothing is required of you except to be able to talk about yourself, the specificity of your own oppression." [11]

When Vietnam became history, and the protest signs and the bullhorns were put away, so was the serious side of many protestors' alienation and hostility. They returned, with minimal resistance, to the restless pursuit of success, and the belief that the choice facing the world was either "capitalist democracy" or "brutal communist dictatorship." The war had been an aberration, was the implicit verdict, a blemish on the otherwise humane American record. The fear of the powers-that-be that society's fabric was unraveling and that the Republic was hanging by a thread turned out to be no more than rumor.

Suzanne Fields wound up writing a regular column for the *Washington Times,* the unabashedly conservative Moonie-owned daily newspaper, in which she regularly disparaged feminism and expressed affinity for such conservative staples as George Bush, cold-war anti-communism, Zionism, and David Horowitz, the borderline hysteric who, since his reincarnation, has never met an extreme right-wing cliché he doesn't like. (Horowitz, a former radical scholar, is the only genuine defector from the left to the right that I know of. In the case of other ostensible defectors, I surmise that their leftism was only skin-deep to begin with.)

Another *Washington Free Press* writer, a member of the editorial staff, Ellis Pines, once penned a poem which we put on the cover. It began...

We, the bums, the beggars, the horse thieves of the family tree,
We, the jailed, the beaten, the fled and fleeing,
We, the outs, catacomb Christians, cellar Jews, subterranean Communists,
We, the real, the now, always artist and anarchist. . .

In his next incarnation, Ellis could be found worshiping a right-wing guru, and putting his way with words to use at an advertising agency which specialized in defense contractor clients. But he had not forsaken the sixties altogether. One of the firm's clients was Right Guard underarm deodorant, for whom Ellis wrote a commercial in which students are staging a protracted sit-in in the dean's office; after a while the students—who refer to themselves as the Left Guard—begin to smell a bit. "Left Guard!" they cry at one point. "Right Guard!" yells the deodorant, marching in to save the day and relieve the senses.

One of the co-founders of the *Free Press* was Michael Grossman, the coiner of that eternal verity: "Grammar is bourgeois." A stocky, bellicose Norman Mailer type, who frequently would break out in shadow boxing, oblivious of his surroundings, Michael turned to mysticism before the '60s had run their course. Like the psychotic killers who appear to be model citizens until they go berserk because, having sensed aggressive impulses within themselves, they had tried to live the opposite of what they felt, Michael—I would psychoanalyze— became a model saint to hold at bay his own personal devils. Before his sainthood, he took pleasure in finding a person's soft underbelly to turn the knife in, like the time he proclaimed to two *Washington Post* reporters, on a friendly tour of the *Free Press* office: "You guys have been emasculated." Regardless of my own views of the *Post*, his remark made me wince sharply. When I came upon Michael several months after his metamorphosis, he was dressed in some kind of white flowing robe, and I marveled that I could discern scarcely a trace of ego in the man, nothing was there disposed to express an opinion or pursue an argument, nothing for me to bounce an idea off of or have a dialogue with. To him all that was *maya*, the illusory appearance of the world, of no concern.

The last time I met Michael, around 1980, he was on his way—sans robe *et avec maya*—to the Netherlands one step ahead of some folks in California who were after him because of the way a business deal had turned out. I would not venture even a wild guess as to the nature of his present transmutation.

Another case in point was my good friend Bonnie Packer, former Peace Corps volunteer, a director of the Free University of Washington in the '60s, and active in the anti-war movement. After not seeing her for a number of years, we ran into each other in the late '70s in San Francisco. She had become a lawyer, she informed me, and was acting as such for the telephone company. My expression must have betrayed a bit of surprise because she quickly added: "But y'know, Bill, those people aren't so bad. I've met some very nice people there."

I was flabbergasted. So that's what she thought it was all about? That we were the nice guys and they were the bad guys? And having met a few nice ones of "them," she had changed her errant ways? Having met my share of uptight and obnoxious individuals on the left, I had not suffered from any such illusion, certainly not regarding the likes of telephone company employees. The niceness of the Dr. Strangeloves of the Godzilla War Machine was another matter. "We are all ready to be savage in some cause," observed William James. "The difference between a good man and a bad one is the choice of the cause."

In any event, I couldn't help thinking that there were better uses to put several years of studying law to than protecting the rich and powerful.

Then there was Marc Sommer, of Liberation News Service, the AP and Reuters of the underground press. Marc went a step further than carrying a Vietcong flag. He spent two weeks in Hanoi in 1968, during the height of the war, and came back to write a glowing report about the Vietnamese. Today, his name may still reside in crypto-secret FBI and CIA indexes, amongst those to be rounded up in case of a "national security emergency." But in fact, those agencies could probably remove his name in safety. Last time I saw Marc, also in California in the late '70s, I happened to say something in Sixtiesspeak, and he quickly informed me that he didn't like this "us" vs. "them" philosophy.

I asked him if that meant that we're all on the same side—the Pentagon and the peace movement, employer and employee, landlord and tenant, rich and poor. Can anybody be blamed for any shortcomings of our society, I wondered. Or do these problems just "happen," with neither "us" nor "them" responsible, particularly since everyone expresses interest in solving them? Does everyone possess equal power to influence the way things are, from the Speaker of the House to a homeless drug addict? Everyone with the same stake in the economy, from the CEO to the woman who spends her evenings scrubbing his office floor?

Marc and I entered a philosophical minefield, with the discussion being entirely inconclusive except for the loss of a few toes we didn't need. Whether the roots lay in the intellect or in the emotions, this former fellow at the progressive Institute for Policy Studies in Washington had already taken a crucial bend in the road. There was no looking back. He probably looked down upon me for being stuck in a time warp.

There was also Allen Young, my journalist and anti-war colleague mentioned above, who later became a well-known gay activist and author. When I spoke to him on the phone in 1999 for the first time in some 30 years, he was uncomfortable with the fact that I was still highly critical of American foreign policy. This, while American bombs were falling on Yugoslavia. "All governments do bad things," he said. At one point in our conversation, this former red-diaper baby said that I reminded him of his parents. So it goes. So it went.

A British observer of the '60s offered this slant:

As a general rule of thumb, the rebellions of the '60s gave rise to three distinct bands of renegades and rogues: those who wanted to smash the state, those who wanted to run away from it, and those who wanted to rip it off. For a few confused and inquiring years, they all looked alike, swapped sexual partners and believed they were all marching together towards the same new dawn. But the revolutionaries joined the Labour Party, the dropouts got chastened by Nepalese hepatitis, and the hippie entrepreneurs got fat.

In 1969 I proposed a class for the Free University: "Anatomy of a Radical." The idea was to put a bunch of radicals in a room together to discuss, with sufficient time and depth, various aspects of their lives which might allow us to come to a better understanding of what had brought each of us and all of us to a common point. I was not prepared to state beforehand what political or practical use this insight could be put to, but I thought that—besides all of us finding it a fascinating exercise—the results might well suggest something.

After the class was duly listed and described in the Free University catalog with my phone number, I settled back to receive the calls from Washington's radicals. Not one called. I received two or three calls from strangers who didn't have a clue as to what I had in mind. They had a semi-digested idea that simply being against the war qualified them to be part of the group. The class was never held.

Eventually, I came to appreciate that I had raised a taboo subject. Delving into the roots of one's radicalism was regarded with suspicion in certain quarters—it reduced people, it was felt; took away a certain mystique; it might even give information to the enemy that could be used against us. Others felt that either you were a Marxist determinist and said that class background was the primary factor, or you were with the overt Freudians.

The class background interpretation, although a very useful starting point for discussion, must be approached with caution because of the inexhaustible means of the corporate world—of which the media is of course an integral part—to fold, press and stretch the dough of public perception so as to convince most of the poor that they are to blame for their own plight, thus turning their thoughts away from the determining role of the economic system, the *sine qua non* of a radical political consciousness. Some of the worst reactionaries society has had to suffer have been those men who rose from harsh poverty to wealth, with the concomitant mentality: "If I made it, so can anyone," from which stemmed stern attitudes toward helping the poor. Whereas in the '60s, the preponderance of the leading radical activists derived from relative privilege.

The following passage, which I copied down many years ago, is germane to this discussion, but I have not been able to find it again to identify the source.

Early in his teens he was visited by the radical impulse. The radical impulse is a simple yet ultimately mysterious phenomenon—simple, in that either you have it or you don't; mysterious, in that it tends to hit people indiscriminately. It consists of the recognition that a bad or mediocre life is not pre-ordained, that nothing that now exists cannot be improved upon, ripped down, built anew.

CHAPTER EIGHT
GOVERNMENT SABOTAGE OF
THE UNDERGROUND PRESS

Those who proclaimed that the freedom to publish a newspaper like the *Washington Free Press* in the United States, in and of itself, gave the lie to much of what they called the "anti-Americanism" in the paper simply did not know what "freedom to publish" an underground newspaper meant in the United States of America, circa 1967-8.

There were but a few commercial printers in the Washington area who could produce the large tabloid size that we used, and one after another they refused to do so after printing—or just seeing—a few issues. There was very little of a pornographic nature, either verbally or graphically, in the paper, and only the occasional use of the word "fuck" (that marvelous word that carries more emotive impact than any other word in the English language, has no substitute, and seemingly can never become clichéd.) But printers would cite such infrequent occurrences when they canceled, the first instance being an article satirically headlined, in large letters, "Fuck Communism." They also made offhand allusions to the newspaper's politics, never put too explicitly or strongly, because they didn't have to be constitutional lawyers to know that they were treading on dangerous First Amendment ground. The politics, I felt, was their real reason, for we had learned that the FBI and the police had each visited at least one of our printers in Maryland with a view towards ending their association with us.

Thus it was that eventually we had to send two of our staff—after being up all night doing the layout—all the way to Long Island each Thursday morning to a printer that was able and willing to do it. The extra expense this imposed on a budget already on a life-support system was not negligible.

Meanwhile, the cops were busy arresting our street vendors, obliging us to pay bail costs or fines. The arrests were all illegal, as the ACLU argued in several suits it filed against the police in the District, Maryland and Virginia, for "harassing, intimidating, persecuting and attempting to suppress publication of the *Free Press*." This produced only the mildest of restraints upon the police, who kept on busting the young people, some of whom naturally decided to stop selling the paper to avoid going through all that shit again.

The FBI labored in other ways as well in behalf of the First Amendment. The bureau put pressure—as only the FBI can put pressure—on Columbia Records, and perhaps other large record companies, to cease placing full-page ads in underground newspapers. It worked, and it cost the *Free Press* its only significant source of advertising income. It's known that the FBI also sent anonymous letters of protest to local businesses that advertised in particular underground newspapers,[12] but whether this was done with our advertisers has not been revealed.

There was also a continual refusal of the Post Office to grant us a 2nd Class mailing permit though we had met all the requirements. This was not resolved until one day when one of our editors, Art Grosman, passing the U.S. Postal Service headquarters, was inspired to go in and ask to speak to the Postmaster-General. Art wound up making a personal plea to the Assistant Postmaster-General, who picked up the phone, called the Main Post Office downtown, and ordered them to give us the permit. Perhaps the man was a closet reader of the *Free Press*.

There was, however, no one to appeal to over the refusal of the leading periodicals distributor in Washington to carry the newspaper. Nearly all the newsstands and many of the bookstores (sic) also joined the freeze-out, which is why our street vendors were so vital to us.

The District of Columbia government was frequently on our back as well, about zoning, occupancy, garbage, taxes, and whatever else was on the books, but it couldn't be determined if this had any political element to it or was simply your basic municipal oppression. On the other hand, the several fires that were set in the foyer of our office were certainly not happenstance, albeit by perpetrators unknown.

Perpetrators known, however, were behind a break-in of the *Free Press* office, shortly before Nixon's January 20, 1969 inauguration—FBI and Army intelligence were their names. This despite a 1966 order of the Justice Department to the FBI to stop all breaking and entering operations, on the ground that they were... well, *illegal*. The government operatives-cum-burglars were looking for "any kind of connection to an overseas Communist party... literature or funding."[13] Once again, the unshakable belief of American Authority that America's young could not be acting so "subversive" unless they had fallen under the spell of "communist dupery." America's young might have answered: You had the very clay of our young minds to mold any way you chose for 18 years, and you did your best to mold us, and now you think we've rejected your ways all because some "communist" came along and whispered a few magic words in our ears. If that's so, you may as well give up. You can't fight such powerful magic.

While they were in the *Free Press* office, the FBI and Army also stole several hundred pre-addressed postcards that were to be filled out by Washington area residents who were willing to house demonstrators during the upcoming "counter-inaugural." Back at their hideaway, this G-Man boy's gang filled the cards out with bogus names and addresses and mailed them back to the counter-inaugural office, in hopes of confusing and demoralizing the people there.[14] Of such stuff was the battle for the hearts and minds of Americans made... "Main Street is the climax of civilization," wrote Sinclair Lewis. "That this Ford car might stand in front of the Bon Ton Store, Hannibal invaded Rome and Erasmus wrote in Oxford cloisters." [15]

I do not assume that there was a conspiracy to carry out all of the above. None was needed. The police, the FBI, the Army, the printers, the distributor, the Post Office petty bureaucrat, and the good-ol'-boy pyromaniacs did not need to meet covertly in a CIA safe-house to plan a campaign against us. They were all doing what came naturally to every ganglion of their American nervous systems. Which doesn't mean that there *wasn't* a conspiracy.

As a footnote it might be noted that ouur pages were not open to just any advertiser. At one point Coca Cola had wanted to advertise with us, which would have meant some nice money, but after a vote by the staff, we dispatched someone to inform the local Coke executive that we couldn't accept the ads because "Coke was an international symbol of American imperialism." The executive looked at our representative like she had just jumped off the No. 36 bus from Mars. It appeared that the Man from Coke had never heard this said before about his favorite beverage.

What our natural enemies didn't do to us, we naturally did to ourselves, as did many of the other underground newspapers and movement groups in the '60s: disagreements developed, factions formed, and, eventually, a split that rent the organization hopelessly in two—the left's traditional circular firing squad.

Putting it in the broadest terms, there were two species of activists in these large dysfunctional families who kept bumping heads, here, there, and everywhere. We can call them the "politicos" and the "yippies" (subspecies: hippies, anarchists).

The politicos placed their faith in organization and in the intellect—a mass movement, "vanguard" political parties, hierarchies and leaders, heavy on meetings, ideology, and tracts, at times doctrinaire sounding, using words and ideas to convince the great middle class, if not the great unwashed. There were theories to justify these tactics, theories based on class analysis, presented with historical annotation to certify their viability; theories that Norman Mailer disparagingly referred to as "the sound-as-brickwork-logic-of-the-next-step in some hard new Left program." [16]

The yippies looked upon all this with unconcealed impatience, scorn, and unbelief. Said a yippie to a politico back then: your protest is so narrow, your rhetoric so boring, your ideological power plays so old fashioned...

Let's listen to Jerry Rubin, certainly the yippies' most articulate spokesperson:

> The long-haired beast, smoking pot, evading the draft, and stopping traffic during demonstrations is a hell of a more a threat to the system than the so-called "politicos" with their leaflets of support for the Vietcong and the coming working class revolution. Politics is how you live your life, not whom you vote for or whom you support. [17]

The most important political conflict in the United States for Rubin was not of classes, but "the generational conflict." "The respectable middle-class debates LBJ while we try to pull down his pants." [18]

> Is [American society] interested in reform, or is it just interested in eliminating nuisance? What's needed is a new generation of nuisances. A new generation of people who are freaky, crazy, irrational, sexy, angry, irreligious, childish, and mad... people who burn draft cards, people who burn dollar bills, people who burn MA and doctoral degrees, people who say: "To hell with your goals," people who proudly carry Vietcong flags, people who redefine reality, who re-define the norm, people who see property as theft, people who say "fuck" on television, people who break with the status-role-title-consumer game, people who have nothing material to lose but their bodies... What the socialists like the SWP and the Communist Party, with their conversions of Marxism into a natural science, fail to understand is that language does not radicalize people—what changes people is the emotional involvement of action. [19]

Hardly anyone, of course, fit precisely and solely into either of these classifications, including Jerry Rubin. Much of the yippie "party line" was to be taken metaphorically, unless one's alienation had reached the level of an alien, while most politicos were independent of any political party.

Ray Mungo, one of the founders of Liberation News Service, later wrote of

LNS:

> It is impossible for me to describe our "ideology," for we simply didn't have
> one; we never subscribed to a code of conduct or a clearly conceptualized
> Ideal Society. . . And it was the introduction of formal ideology into the
> group which eventually destroyed it, or more properly split it into bitterly
> warring camps.[20]

When Mungo speaks of "formal ideology," he's referring to the "politicos"
who joined LNS after its inception. These people, whom he refers to as "the
Vulgar Marxists," as opposed to his own "anarchist" camp. . .

> believed fervently in "the revolution," and were working *toward* it—a revo-
> lution based on Marx and Lenin and Cuba and SDS and "the struggle;" and
> people were supported only on the basis of what they were *worth* to the rev-
> olution; and most of the things in life which were purely enjoyable were
> bourgeois comforts irrelevant to the news service, although not absolutely
> barred[21]. . . Their method of running the news service was the Meeting and
> the Vote, ours was Magic. We lived on Magic, and still do, and I have to say
> it beats anything *systematic."* [22]

Mungo would have one believe that ideology is a "thing" introduced from
the "outside," like tuberculosis, that is best to avoid. I would argue, however,
that "ideology" is nothing less than a system of ideas in one's head, whether
consciously organized or not, that attempts to answer the questions: Why is the
world the way it is? Why is society the way it is? Why are people the way they
are? And what can be done to change any of this? To say you have no ideology
comes dangerously close to saying that you have no opinions on—and perhaps
no interest in—such questions. Ray Mungo, I believe, was overreacting to people whom he saw as too systematic and who didn't appreciate his "Magic."

Just as I knew instinctively that I wasn't a Quaker or a pacifist, I knew I
wasn't a yippie, hippie or anarchist, which didn't mean that I couldn't enjoy and
even take part in some of their antics. Jerry Rubin was mistaken in my case, as
in many others—language, spoken and print, had played a major role in my
radicalization; equally indispensable had been the sad state of the world, but it
was language which had illuminated and brought home to me the sad state of
the world and proffered explanations for why it was the way it was.

During the American Revolution, Thomas Paine's *Common Sense,* which
sold hundreds of thousands of copies in the first few months of 1776, used language suffused with both reason and emotion to argue powerfully the case for
independence, to strike convincingly at one of the greatest obstacles to separa-
tion: American veneration of royalty; and to point out that beyond the politics
and legalities of the conflict, the colonies were sources of profit the crown
would never voluntarily relinquish. This message clarified the revolution for

thousands of confused rebels who had been debating points of law with London. Imagine if Paine had been a yippie instead of a politico—his primary message might have been to pull down the king's pants.

It was the movement's politicos who stayed the course, continuing to be activists well past the '60s, while Rubin's long-haired beast and Mungo's Magic people—lacking the convictions of their courage—could more likely be found in the '70s sitting cross-legged at the feet of the newest-flavor guru, probing interpersonal relations instead of international relations, or seeking fulfillment through vegetarianism, "the land," or Rolfing. By the '80s they had evolved into yuppies.

If you longed for the world to make sense and have feelings, you would continue to strive for a more humane and rational society, what might be called the aesthetics of a revolutionary—looking for beauty in the social arrangement as others look for it in art. As Kim Philby, the master Russian spy and British class traitor, said: "I hate the thought of people being unhappy."

There was no one particular idea or issue that split the ranks of the *Free Press* in 1968, no big argument or crisis. Yet, whatever trace there was of such was bicycle-pumped into a split—between "the juicies" as they called themselves and "the grims" as they called us. I was lumped with the "grim" politicos though I was responsible for more humor and satire in the paper than all the "juicies" combined. But my serious, analytic side unquestionably placed me with the politicos. The split escalated to the point where the two factions were alternately putting out their own issues. Within a couple of months or so, all the original and early staff members had left.

Knowing today of the remarkable pervasiveness of FBI and CIA infiltrations back then, I am forced to wonder now about this split, which seemed to come out of nowhere and mushroom without apparent logic. In an FBI report, since declassified, about the *Quicksilver Times*, the FBI special agent in charge assured headquarters that he was "continuing. . . to utilize sources to promote political differences in New Left organizations."[23] The later split at the *QT* was much more dramatic than at the *Free Press*, culminating in the use of physical force.

Thus it was that the time came for me to leave the *Free Press*. I had loved a lot of it, like the way a community had formed around the paper, and the discovery of my nascent writing ability. We may even have induced a mind or two to question what previously had been accepted as the natural way of things, or reminded a few souls that they had a social conscience. But more than full time for over a year and a half as reporter, editor, columnist, chief financial officer, street vendor, and compiler of a detailed, full-page weekly calendar—topped by a vexatious split—had left me, in the language of the day, "burned out." I didn't know what I was going to do, apart from an amorphous notion about writing something or other, but I knew it would be easier on the nerves. My intestines might even stop making fun of me.

At this moment in my life I had the money, the time, and the freedom to take off on a trip around the world. Who would not love to be in my shoes? But the thought never came to me. The travel bug lay peacefully dormant inside some warm, moist cells of my brain.

It was embarrassing. No one saw me, no one ever knew, but it was embarrassing. To wake up in the morning and have nowhere in particular to go, and nothing in particular to do; at least nothing pressing or important or exciting; no major ongoing project, outside of and larger than myself; nothing that distinguished me from the mass of humankind. It was a sign of failure, and failure by my own terms. Here I'd already thrown off the shackles of the bourgeois world, the stated aspiration of every self-respecting radical and bohemian artist and writer since the dawn of the industrial revolution, and I was now tormented by the thought that I no longer had an inspiring replacement; and the embarrassment was acute, like the whole world was watching.

Millions of Americans would have ached with envy—go to bed when you want, get up when you want, go for a jog, play some tennis maybe, do a few pushups and situps, a little stretching and bending, take a shower, read the newspaper while you have a leisurely, healthy breakfast of cereal, milk, and fresh fruit, a piece of chocolate to pacify the ol' addiction, and you're all ready, you're physically and mentally fit, to do whatever turns you on. And all this with no house and mortgage to possess me, no suburbs to deaden the eye and soul, no traffic jams, no mind-numbing meetings, no asshole boss's whims to cater to, no counting the hours till you're unleashed from the galley oars, no counting the days till your pitifully short vacation. I was on permanent vacation.

But I and a life of leisure had never been properly introduced. On many a day I envied those with regular jobs. There's something to be said about having a place to go to five days a week, even if it's a job you're not in love with. There's a purpose of sorts, and a steady paycheck, and you're bound to find at least one kindred soul there.

The next indication that something was amiss in paradise was that I suddenly became impotent. I had never been impotent before, not even when drunk or stoned. In the Middle Ages, women were castigated as witches if their men were impotent, but I was not about to blame my current girlfriend, an engaging slim blond who worked at the Office of Economic Opportunity, in the so-called War on Poverty (poverty won). She was one of several women I had gone out with in New York or Washington who I—in deep hindsight—believe I could have been happily married to, even if not forever, but there was some kind of clock in me that told me on each occasion that I wasn't yet ready to choke off certain unknown life experiences that lay ahead at some unknown time. The marriage bug nestled quietly alongside the travel bug.

I went to see a psychiatrist, also a first in my life. (As well as the only time, which may disqualify me from writing these memoirs.) He tried hypnosis, but I had always been a bad subject, usually unable to keep my mind still long enough to just surrender myself to suggestion; or, even when I could, it still didn't work. Olympic-gold-medal conclusion jumpers will surmise that I must be a "control freak," afraid to let go. But to myself it's always felt like I really wanted to experience "going under." I certainly haven't shied away from experimenting with drugs. Having studied hypnosis at some length at one time, I actually wonder whether there really is such an explicitly singular phenomenon. The human infant matures because it is supremely impressionable, soaking up its environment like a giant hungry sponge. To a baby, everything is suggestible, it exists to be suggested to. Might hypnosis be but a special case of this capacity and craving for suggestion, a moment when the subject's adult defenses are gently pushed to one side, the curtain lifted, and the primeval infant mind exposed?

The doctor—Michael Miller was his name, with an office right on Dupont Circle—then invited me to attend a nude group therapy session that he was forming for people with sexual problems. I was somewhat skeptical that this would help me, but the voyeur in me was excited.

There were about twenty of Miller's patients in the group, almost all in their twenties or thirties, the men slightly outnumbering the women. I was amused to see that the two sexes undressed in separate rooms—we were attacking only one social taboo at a time. Minus even socks and shoes, we all assembled in the large center room and took seats in a circle, gingerly if one had chosen one of the cold metal chairs. An individual would then raise a personal or a more general problem, and the session would begin.

At one meeting, just moments after we sat down nude, a new member, a man of around forty, ejaculated, much to his great embarrassment of course. Our first impulse was to politely ignore the matter, but this was hardly a normal social gathering, and so a discussion sprang up. Dr. Miller was of the opinion, as were others, that such a reaction was "natural" and should not be inhibited. But I and some others felt that this was really carrying the thing a bit too far, that a man should be expected to practice *some* self-control. I did not need to witness his dilemma and his mess.

Most of the women tended to sit with their arms crossed in front of their breasts and their legs crossed, or with their hands dangling loosely and "nonchalantly" between their legs. The men, sensitive and shy little flowers that they are, usually sat with their legs apart.

In each discussion, Miller would break in with a suggestion that we experiment with foreplay, for which he had two chairs set up adjacent to each other in the center of the group. He then chose a man and a woman to sit in the chairs and told them to embrace and to feel as free as they could to act very passionately. Each woman did this with two or three men, a few minutes with each, and might then be asked to comment about how passionate or gentle or whatever her naked *amoureaux* had been. The idea that anyone in the room might be homosexual was an idea whose time had not yet arrived, even, apparently, for Miller, unless he had knowingly excluded them.

Some women, although enjoying the necking, were turned off by watching other couples—one remarked that it made her "miserably uncomfortable." That problem was partially eliminated by having three sets of chairs set up to allow three couples to neck simultaneously, thus reducing the number of people who were obliged to watch at any given time. Now try that on for strange—six naked people in passionate embrace but a few feet away.

Several of the women were voluptuous to the eye, and my voyeurism cup overflowed, though I, fortunately, did not. I probably acted more passionate in the necking than any of the men—although I never had much of an erection—because, unlike the others, I didn't really have a "sexual hangup." I didn't know what my underlying problem was, but it wasn't that, and I sometimes felt like I was there under false pretenses.

Ironically, at one point Miller mentioned something to the effect that recognizing the human body as natural would reduce voyeurism and fetishism. *Well!* I thought, I hardly think that the bodies my eyes are feasting upon are unnatural, and why would I want to rid myself of such a great pleasure?

The 58-year-old doctor, who was himself nude, kept escalating the action at succeeding sessions—semi-lying positions and standing up, the latter being a step closer to intercourse. It was remarkable how his suggestions had the power of law in the group. Miller's approval made behavior which would normally be strictly taboo—even amongst people without sexual hangups—socially acceptable.

Not to put too fine a point on it, but as historian Howard Zinn has observed, "Historically, the most terrible things—war, genocide and slavery—have resulted from obedience, not disobedience," a sentiment echoed by Nobel Laureate Heinrich Böll. When asked after World War II what he thought the most dangerous flaw in the character of the German people was, the novelist answered in a word: "Obedience."

War, after all, gives men license to take part in what would otherwise be described as psychopathic behavior.

Many of the participants in Miller's group claimed that the sessions were helping them in various ways—losing a deeply ingrained belief that sex was "dirty," or recalling long-buried experiences, which months of regular therapy (i.e. dressed) had failed to do. One woman became almost hysterical as she recalled the time when she was a child and discovered her mother in bed with a strange man, and also the time she came upon her father making love to her aunt.

Miller had personally explained to me the rationale behind the group thusly: "Experimentally creating an atmosphere where tyrannical taboos concerning nakedness and sex are outlawed can free the individual of his oppressive super-ego, bring repressions to the surface, and enable the individual to permit himself a greater degree of emotional release and improve his sexual relationships."

This was pretty much standard fare of course for this era before Freud was knocked off his pedestal. My own observations of a lifetime have led me to believe that knowing the cause of one's neurosis or discovering the existence and nature of one's repressions is no guarantee at all of reaching the only goal that counts: behavioral change.

Amongst my comrades at that time could be found those who declared that therapists should stop trying to fix up the people so the system works better, and start fixing up the system so the people work better.

Before too long, I stopped attending the therapy sessions. I didn't relish becoming the object and the subject of the group's discussion when I was feeling sneaky about being there in the first place, and I doubted it would be of any help. But I did wonder if they went on to actual intercourse. I also wondered what hangups or fantasies of ol' Doc Miller were being fulfilled.

At this time, I undertook two new projects: substitute teaching in high schools, and writing a novel (about the '60s of course). Without thinking about it, without any such expectation in mind, I soon discovered that I was no longer impotent. What was going on?

Not working = not really being a man = not being able to perform like a man. That was the equation, I reasoned, that my silly bourgeois unconscious had formulated, as simplistic as this might sound. I had new respect for the power of the unconscious.

The novel, after a year's effort, was, alas, stillborn. Terminally unliterary, it was in need of emergency room editorial resuscitation. The one publisher who was gracious enough to respond pointed out what had completely escaped my attention—there was no plot. Oh! I said to myself.

> How to get people to vote against their interests and to really think against their interests is very clever. It's the cleverest ruling class that I have ever come across in history. It's been 200 years at it. It's superb. —Gore Vidal

Washington, DC, Election Day, 1968. . . I had voted in every election I could since turning 21. Now, just for a change of pace, I decided to publicly burn my ballot. The overriding issue of the day for the American people was, of course, ending U.S. involvement in Vietnam, the war that Dick Gregory described as using the black man to kill the yellow man so the white man could keep the land he took from the red man. So what was the choice "they" gave the citizens, who stood with noses pressed against the window of the government candy store? Why, Hubert H. Humphrey, Richard M. Nixon and George C. Wallace, none even remotely a credible anti-war candidate. Sen. Eugene McCarthy passed himself off as one, and was taken as such by a significant segment of the anti-war movement, particularly the young who were starving for an honest and moral leader to devote themselves to. Another significant segment of the movement warned against him, citing the history of betrayal of progressive causes by leading liberals. Would the Senator have been an exception? Well, we must take into consideration the fact that in 1980, Eugene McCarthy came out in support of Ronald Reagan for the presidency against Jimmy Carter.

In America, elections are the opiate of the people. Every four years they get a quick fix and they call it "democracy." Going cold turkey, I stood in the polling station in Adams Morgan with Frank Speltz, another of the co-founders of the *Free Press*. Tall, slim and bearded, Frank was a former seminarian who had forsaken the pleasure temples of Bement, Illinois to migrate to Washington, but his religious leanings—once a seminarian, always a priest, they say—didn't bother me at all, because he was so unobtrusive about it. Amongst other things, he wrote a column of draft advice for the *Free Press* under the name of General Marsbars, a takeoff on General Lewis Hershey, the head of Selective Service.

We had informed the press of our intentions, for our action would have had little political meaning if not publicized. It was reminiscent of the story told of the two Italian mountain climbers in the thirties—"If we were certain that nobody would ever hear of our having conquered it, should we yet try to scale it? Neither of us dared to reply."—albeit that was pure ego, as opposed to our political motivation.

There were about three election clerks, with Frank and I outnumbering the voters in the station by one, as Frank began making a speech about the immorality of the war and the depressing choice being offered to those opposed to it. The bored clerks perked up immediately at the sight of the bearded Smith Bros. standing there. After a minute or so of Frank's oratory, I lit a match, and just as I applied match to ballots, a *Washington Star* photographer made an appearance and began flashing away. By the time the ballots had mutated to ashes, the police were there, three or four of them, with their leader immediately informing Frank and I that we were under arrest. When I asked the kindly gentleman of the law what we were being charged with, he replied: "Destroying government property."

"Destroying government property?" I asked. "You mean those two small pieces of paper? What did they cost, a penny?"

"You were interfering with people's right to vote," he quickly countered, apparently abandoning his first legal brief.

"There was only one person here voting. Shall we ask her if we interfered with her right to vote?" I looked around for the woman but didn't see her.

"Listen, I want you two to leave here immediately and promise that you won't return. Otherwise I'm going to have to arrest you."

It was becoming painfully clear that Frank and I were not going to be able to do an article for the *Free Press* entitled "Fascist Pig Police Brutalize Courageous *Free Press* Editors at Polling Station."

Nothing appeared in the *Star,* nor anywhere else on earth. On the question of protest, Gandhi once said that "Almost anything you do will be insignificant, but you must do it." And the reason I must do it is captured by yet another adage, cited by various religious leaders: "We do these things not to change the world, but so that the world will not change us."

In addition to being an unpatriotic, irreligious, drug-taking ballot-burner, I was a baby killer. Now it can be told.

Like most depravities it began in pure innocence. In September 1967, Patricia Maginnis, head of the California-based Association for Repeal of Abortion Laws, delivered a talk in the *Free Press* house's living room when she was unable to find any other venue in Washington willing to accept her. The talk was attended by more than 150 people, who overflowed onto the front lawn and stuck their heads in open windows to catch her words. Hardly anyone at that time realized that abortion was such a hot issue. We ran a story about it in the paper.

Even before the story appeared, people began calling the newspaper to find out where they might find a doctor willing to perform an abortion, a medical type as rare as a guilty bystander at a time that abortion on demand was not the law of the land. For some reason unrecorded by history or my memory, the first call or two to the paper were referred to me at my apartment. Before very long, word of mouth had spread throughout the country—For a good abortion, call Bill Blum. I was getting phone calls at home literally from Maine to California. I was half expecting to hear that a caller had gotten my name and number off the wall of a YMCA or YWCA restroom.

In the meantime, I had begun asking around in the lowlife circles I habituated for a lead to an abortion doctor. I quickly hit paydirt—Dr. Milan M. Vuitch, a 52-year-old Yugoslav immigrant, in nearby Silver Spring. I went to see him, and though he was understandably concerned that I might be an undercover cop, gave me permission to refer patients to him. The arrangement was that a woman would call him and, after mentioning my name, was to complain of any female-type ailment. That, a sanitary napkin, and $300 was all she needed.

Over the next year or so, I referred close to a hundred women to Dr. Vuitch, and it wasn't until some time had passed that it occurred to me that I should have been asking him for a cut; $300 was a lot of money at that time. But my priorities had been captured by the stories I was hearing over the phone from women old and young, tales of how giving birth would be disastrous to their life situation, teenagers terrified of their parents, women terrified of their husbands, desperation and pleading and tears washing over the phone line. Although in later press interviews Vuitch described himself as a "crusader," I have no idea if he really had any motivation other than the money. His 1967 income, it was reported, was between $150,000 and $160,000,[24] and I foolishly never asked him for a penny, even as I watched the sum total of my modest worldly wealth diminish with each passing day.

Before all this transpired, I had not given the question of abortion any particular thought, but as time passed, a point of view came into focus: I could not buy into calling it "murder." I thought of the embryo as little more than a clump of cells, with no consciousness, and that to label its destruction "murder" was stretching the bounds of hyperbole. I figured that those using that word probably had their own agenda; perhaps they associated abortion with promiscuous sex, feminism, liberals, or whatever their hangup was; most of the same people didn't call the American bombing of babies in Vietnam "murder." Or religious dogma entered the picture—Would it not be nice, I thought, if church leaders forbade Catholics from partaking in the military's killing fields with the same fervor they tell them that abortion is a sin?

Females seeking to become unpregnant were not the only complete strangers who felt perfectly free to call me at any time of day or night. During the period my name frequently appeared in the underground press, I received literally hundreds of phone calls from individuals who seemed to confuse my number with the Department of Social Services or Revolution Central or several other agencies not yet invented: teenage girls, usually in pairs, giggling over explicit sexual suggestions; other teenagers needing to talk to someone older and "hip" about their parents' oppression (one teenage girl called me every couple of weeks or so for six months); young people in need of money, legal advice, a place to sleep, a friend; distraught parents looking for runaway children; people condemning me to eternal hell for my political views, others blessing me and offering heartfelt crackpot ideas on how to make The Revolution a reality within weeks, if not days—"We have to get the word out, Man!;" those on bad LSD trips in urgent need of help, or wanting to buy drugs, or sell; pathetic would-be agents provocateurs dropping heavy hints about drugs, weapons or bombs and more obscure hints about god-knows-what; others who sounded balanced for a couple of minutes or so, and then it would suddenly hit me that they were rambling this way and that way—veering from a disastrous run-in with the police to the moon landing to what's wrong with "the fucking schools," and "don't forget what the CIA did in Iran in 1953". . . until I had to cut them off, at a loss to understand why they had phoned me. It was a generation of lost souls coming out of heretofore camouflaged urban caves, broadcasting their hurts and quests and revelations—Yes, me too! I, too, have a vision of How Things Ought To Be!—for it seemed that now, amazingly enough, there was a world out there that was listening, or at least a media looking for good copy. Today, such cave dwellers all have their own websites.

If my phone was tapped, the FBI was getting several earfuls. It probably confirmed their worst fears and prejudices.

CHAPTER NINE
SURROUNDED BY INFORMERS

Mae Brussell, the renowned California researcher into the multi-layered world of the covert (or the Queen of the off-the-wall conspiracy nuts, depending on your bias) once declared: "I'm not a movement or an organization, because if I had five people, one would be an agent."

Brussell may have believed that no one well-known ever died a natural death, but as to agents she was right.

There was Irwin Bock, a husky shlub who arrived at my door one day in January 1969, referred by the committee planning the "counter-inaugural" against Nixon, or so he said. I put him up for a couple of days, during which time he informed me that he was working with the Vietnam Veterans Against the War, and had come to town to help prepare for the veterans participation in the upcoming protest. He said was taking time off from his job with American Airlines, and he had all the right things to say about the damn war, his god-forsaken role in it, the government's interminable lying about it, etc., etc.—one could learn to recite the anti-war litany as easily as one could learn to recite the anti-communist litany.

Although I didn't see it, at a pre-demonstration rally, Bock reportedly led cries of "Stop the bullshit and take to the streets!" while a Vietnam veteran was addressing the crowd.[25] Next thing I know, in November, Bock is appearing as a prosecution witness in the riot conspiracy trial of "The Chicago Seven," presented to the world as a police undercover agent, telling of his conversations with Tom Hayden and Lee Weiner, two of the Seven, and leaving a hint that he might have acted as an agent provocateur to encourage bombings.[26]

I once attended a planning meeting for a local protest against the war. There were only about 15 of us in the small room of a church, and we began by going around and giving our names. One guy, in his mid-twenties, gave his name as Philip Friedman and suggested that we pass around a sheet of paper for everyone to sign, along with address and phone number, to facilitate keeping in touch. And any organizational affiliations would be useful too, he added. No one raised any objection. This was 1969, after almost five years of serious anti-war protest, speeches and articles warning *ad nauseam* about "pig infiltrators" of diverse species, "paranoid" being the most commonly used word after "the," and here we were with no one questioning that "There's a man goin' round takin' names," a man who's the new kid on the block no less.

Finally, for me at least, the coin dropped. "Excuse me," I said to him. "Why do you need all this information?"

"I think it's good for creating an effective and efficient group," he replied. "Too many groups are just chaos."

"That may be," I said, "but I've never seen you before. I have no idea who you are."

"Well," said he, as unfazed as can be, "I have no idea who *you* are."

"There are several people here who can vouch for me," I said looking around. Two or three people nodded their agreement. "Does anyone here know this guy?" No one gave any sign. The meeting proceeded without any list being passed around.

A few months later, on August 12, Max Philip Friedman—that was his full name—testified before a Senate committee. It turned out that Friedman had been going to anti-war conferences in various cities, including Cleveland and several in Washington, and in unspecified ways, gathering lists of attendees. He presented a number of these lists to the committee, and the names, hundreds of them (including one Irwin Bock), appeared in the committee's published report on its hearings.[27]

In his testimony, Friedman stated: "to my knowledge, the communists have completely and utterly taken over the peace movements in the United States of America."[28] By "communist," he said, he meant not only The Communist Party USA, but also the Trotskyist organizations: the Socialist Workers Party, the Young Socialist Alliance, and the Spartacists, as well as the Maoist group, Progressive Labor Party.[29] Just as my State Department co-workers disparaged me as a person because I posed a threat to their beloved feelings of patriotism, Friedman—I'm always taken aback to hear of a Jewish right-winger—was trying, like many others of the day, to demonize the entire anti-war movement as nothing more than a tool of the "communists" (by whatever definition of that overused and abused word) and so flush it from the system without having to deal with its ideas intellectually or morally.

In actuality, all the groups he named not only had tiny memberships, but they were at least as hostile to each other as they were to U.S. foreign policy. The Trotskyists were more disciplined and hard working than your average peacenik and thus achieved a prominence in some anti-war committees out of proportion to their small numbers. But their members were sincerely opposed to the war and did not hide their party affiliation, so there was no hidden agenda— they were not part of a conspiracy to. . . to. . . to what? To recruit more members? Yes, but this was neither unprincipled nor very successful. No group had taken over the peace movement, much less "completely and utterly."

I would have made a terrible spy. It's one thing to hide your occupation, as do CIA officers who regularly pass themselves off as employees of other government agencies or businessmen. It's quite another matter to pretend to believe passionately in one side of a highly controversial and emotional issue when in fact your heart and mind belong to the opposing side. The revolutionary in me would scream in silent agony at having to feed people's ignorance, the very same ignorance I was at war with. Kim Philby wore this second skin for 30 years and never became fully snug in it. He later wrote of being closely interrogated by his superior in British intelligence after the shadow of suspicion had finally fallen across him—"It was distasteful to lie in my teeth to the honest Sinclair; I hope he now realizes that in lying to him I was standing as firmly on principle as he ever did."[30]

Friedman had given me reason to be suspicious. Bock had not, nor had Jan Tangen, mentioned earlier. Probably another score or more informants who crossed my path will remain unknown to me forever. We return now to Salvatore Ferrera, my partner in the CIA license-plate caper. His is a case apart.

In early 1969, I received a phone call from Sal. He told me he was a graduate student at Georgetown University in international relations, and that he'd heard that I and some other people were planning to start a new underground newspaper in Washington, in which he expressed an interest to take part.

It was true that I and some others were looking to found a new paper for Washington, for the *Free Press* had been taken over by a whole new crowd, a ragamuffin bunch of hippies and dopesters, putting out a drugs-as-panacea, sabotaging-schools, mystical, bombmaking, lotsadirtywordsandsex sheet, with writing and layout actually worse than our first issue. It was embarrassing to see my adolescent son reverting to infancy.

Sal was a slim, mustached Italian of medium height, with a ready laugh, who had played in a rock band in his native Chicago. Over the next couple of months he and I met with several others discussing the whys and wherefores of the new paper. I finally bowed out when promised seed money of $5,000 from a fat-cat liberal fell through. I just didn't have the stomach (no pun intended) to go through the same daily poverty-aggravation I had had on the *Free Press*, particularly since the life expectancy of underground newspapers had a lot in common with that of infantrymen in the first World War. But Sal and some others went ahead and eventually gave birth to the *Quicksilver Times*.

In the meantime, despite our 12-year age difference, Sal and I became close friends, seeing each other virtually every day, eating meals in and out, traveling to Western High School in Georgetown to substitute teach, going to political events, spending time at the *QT*. (For reasons never clear to me, Sal did not want his name to appear in the paper. He used the name Sal Torey as a byline.) We discussed political and other ideas without clashing, vented anger toward the same inequities, laughed at the same American foibles, and relished the notion that while there may not be justice in the world, at least there's irony.

One day in July, Sal came to me with the idea of identifying CIA personnel by recording their license plate numbers as they entered the Agency compound. He told me that the idea had been suggested to him by Karl Hess, a Washingtonian whom we were both acquainted with. Hess had been a speech writer for Barry Goldwater during the 1964 presidential campaign. Since then, he had come to the realization that his social and political principles made him feel more at home in anarchist and left libertarian circles, and he was now associated with the Institute for Policy Studies. In his journey of conversion, Karl had traveled across a greater distance on the political spectrum than I had, and it seemed to me that he was not yet sure where he had landed.

I never did ask Karl whether he had in fact given Sal the idea for the CIA escapade, because that had carried no weight in my decision to take part in it. (It turned out that, amongst other targets, Sal was reporting on Hess to the FBI.)[31] But in hindsight I realize I should have checked on all kinds of things concerning my friend Sal, just to go through the formality of "verifying his *bona fides*," as they say in the CIA. It was to be several years yet before I acquired the full set of automatic distrustful instincts essential to a political activist.

Like I should have checked with Georgetown University to verify that Sal was really a student there. And I should have asked him about where his money was coming from, particularly since more than one other person in the Washington movement had asked me just that. Our teaching assignments were few and poorly paid, and Sal lived in a semi-fancy high-rise apartment building near Dupont Circle, he had graduate-school costs, he showed up one day with a brand new expensive camera, and another day with a bugging detector he said he'd bought at "The Spy Shop" downtown, an establishment not for the faint of wallet. With me as his entrée—and only because of that—he visited several of the "movement houses" shared by activists, where he proceeded to "sweep" the walls, the phones, the radios, and so on, looking for hidden bugs planted by, presumably, the FBI. He didn't find anything, he said. Sal explained his inclination to search for bugs on having attended a detective school in Chicago. Again I asked no questions. Perhaps I should have gone to a detective school myself.

February 19, 1970, the day after a guilty verdict came down upon the heads of the Chicago Seven. "The Day After" is what the demonstrations were called all over the country. In Washington, it took place outside of the Watergate complex, in honor of Attorney General John Mitchell who lived there. Little could anyone imagine that day what Mitchell and Watergate would come to mean two years down the road. And who wrote the story of the demonstration for the *Washington Post?* A relatively unknown reporter named Carl Bernstein. Only the week before, he had interviewed me for a story about the death of the *Washington Free Press,* the last issue of it finally, and mercifully, having appeared.

For me it was five years, almost to the day, since I first stood in front of the White House that cold morning handing out flyers on the war. And here I was still, showing my support for fellow anti-war protestors, while the war still continued. . . and continued. I had to be there. It could have been said of me that I was addicted.

If only it wasn't such a tame affair; it was like a generic '60s demonstration, all the usual suspects were there, with all the usual signs and shouted slogans, going through the motions, us on one side, the cops on the other. It didn't satisfy the anger that I felt about my comrades in Chicago facing long stretches in prison.

Suddenly I saw Frank Greer, a guy I had a nodding acquaintance with, being forced along by a man behind him. The man was dressed casually in a plaid zipper jacket. None of the demonstrators showed any reaction. In an instant, my mind came to a conclusion and made a decision. I stepped in front of the two men forcing them to stop. Then, I swung my right fist in a round-house blow directly into the face of the man, taking care not to hit Frank. To this day I don't know what the effect was upon the man I hit, for I was immediately clubbed to the ground from behind by a policeman.

The activist in me would like to say that I was inhumanely beaten about the head without mercy by a vicious running-dog-of-capitalism swine. But I can't say that. For reasons I will never know, the swine—I mean the officer and gentleman of the law—completely pulled his punches. He delivered barely more than a tap to my cranium. Then a second tap, and a third. Instinctively—strange how these things work—without even seeing the face of my assailant, I knew from the very first tap that I had to go along with the charade; otherwise I might make him look bad and he'd be forced to really club me. By tap number two I had fallen to my knees. (If Mae Brussell had learned of this, she would likely have concluded that I was an undercover cop. What other explanation could there be, except that the officer—Belcher was his name—had no stomach for rearranging my brain cells? Which makes me wonder how much longer he remained a cop.)

Moments later, as I stood with my hands cuffed behind me, and the officer standing at my back, Sal appeared with his camera and took pictures of my ignominious being, one from the side and one from the back, the latter showing the handcuffs more clearly. I still have copies of the photos. The photos presumably wound up in the files of some government agency.

My instincts about the man I slugged had been correct. I later learned that he was a cop, one E. D. Talbot, whose picture Greer had taken, whereupon the cop had struck Greer, thrown him up against a tree, taken his camera, and handcuffed and arrested him, all of course without benefit of law.

I spent the night in jail along with more than a hundred other social misfits and one jogger. This fellow, still in his white shorts and sneakers, had been jogging past the demonstration, had stopped to look for a moment, and was arrested when chaos suddenly broke out; chaos, I believe, that was sparked or escalated by my action.

With the assistance of a team of civil liberties lawyers who were practiced in such mass arrests—the '60s spawned its own kinds of specialists—most of the arrested were released without charges because the police were unable to testify as to which specific individuals had actually done what. I was released on my own recognizance, but only after being charged with assaulting a police officer, a felony. I was no longer a virgin.

When I stopped by the local office of "The Conspiracy," the national organization set up to support the Chicago Seven, which was monitoring the mass arrests, I didn't know whether to be amused or insulted after being told by more than one person of how surprised they had been to hear that Bill Blum had been arrested for assaulting a police officer. Like I was the mild-mannered reporter trying to act like Superman. In truth, no one was more surprised than myself.

There followed over the next three months a cynical tap dance with the law. My attorney, Richard Sobol, petitioned the Assistant U.S. Attorney to reduce the charge against me to the misdemeanor of simple assault; i.e., assault of a human being, not a pig. His argument was that I had no way of knowing that the man I hit was a police officer, but that I "thought he was a heckler or troublemaker, harassing one of the demonstrators." It was true that I couldn't be absolutely certain that Talbot was a cop, particularly since I didn't see the cuffs on Greer's hands behind his back. Nonetheless, at the time of the incident, there was no doubt in my mind of the man's copness and I acted upon that conviction and that alone. Like many other '60s veterans, I had developed an almost unerring ability to spot a police officer trying to dress and act like one of the boys, ditto an FBI agent, whether in or out of his dark suit. It's a certain way these men have of looking out at the world, and they're the same all over, like they're grown in special hothouses.

My attorney was fully cognizant of all this. We were not into deceiving each other, only the venerable institution of the law. Such was the dynamic of the time—it was indeed "us" vs. "them," and all was fair in law and war. And "they" were doing it as well, officer Talbot for one; and, much more telling, consider the Nuremberg example.

After the Second World War, the International Military Tribunal convened at Nuremberg, Germany. Created by the victorious Allies, the Tribunal sentenced to prison or execution numerous Nazis who pleaded that they had been "only following orders." In an opinion handed down by the Tribunal, it declared that "the very essence of the [Tribunal's] Charter is that individuals have international duties which transcend the national obligations of obedience imposed by the individual state."

During the Vietnam war, a number of young Americans refused military service on the grounds that the United States was committing war crimes in Vietnam and that if they took part in the war they too, under the principles laid down at Nuremberg, would be guilty of war crimes.

One of the most prominent of these cases was that of David Mitchell of Connecticut. At Mitchell's trial in September 1965, Judge William Timbers dismissed his defense as "tommyrot" and "degenerate subversion," and found the Nuremberg principles to be "irrelevant" to the case. Mitchell was sentenced to prison. Conservative columnist William F. Buckley, Jr., not celebrated as a champion of draft resistance, noted shortly afterward:

> I am glad I didn't have Judge Timbers' job. Oh, I could have scolded Mr. Mitchell along with the best of them. But I'd have to cough and wheeze and clear my throat during that passage in my catechism at which I explained to Mr. Mitchell wherein the Nuremberg Doctrine was obviously not at his disposal.[32]

In 1971, Telford Taylor, the chief United States prosecutor at Nuremberg, suggested rather strongly that General William Westmoreland and high officials of the Johnson administration such as Robert McNamara and Dean Rusk could be found guilty of war crimes under criteria established at Nuremberg.[33] Yet every American court and judge during the Vietnam War, when confronted by the Nuremberg defense, dismissed it without according it any serious consideration whatsoever.

Eventually, the charge against me was indeed reduced to simple assault, and I was sentenced to $50 or 5 days. But in the same wave of his hand, Judge Harold Greene suspended that and placed me upon probation for one year. When I told the judge in court that I was about to move to California and asked whether I could serve the probation there, he waved his hand again and told me to forget about the probation. I walked out in the May sunshine of Washington, my long ordeal of court hell and prison torture over. Free at last! Free at last! Thank God Almighty, I was free at last!

To conservatives this would be an egregious example of being soft on crime, violent crime, and against a police officer no less. This is technically correct, but the supposed danger of softness on crime is the encouragement it gives to the accused to repeat his offense, and, although sorely tempted and justified on numerous occasions, I never again assaulted a cop, though more than one assaulted me. No, the legal monopoly on force and violence enjoyed by the police and the military was not endangered by the release of Bill "Mad Dog" Blum.

In any event, for those who push for harsher and still harsher punishment to place on the altar of the god of deterrence, I offer this little reminder: At one point around the middle of the 19th century, the English were having so much trouble with pickpockets, and the fury of the citizenry had reached such a high pitch, that the authorities began to hold public hangings of pickpockets. But they soon had to stop this, because the crowds gathered to watch the hangings were such lucrative fields for pickpockets.

CHAPTER TEN
CALIFORNIA BOMBING

I made the big trek across the continent in June. I felt compelled to do so. To live the full life in America meant at some point experiencing California. In 1970, there was still optimism astir in the land; one could think hopefully in terms of "starting a new life," even if just the same old life in beautiful new surroundings.

Two hours out of Washington, on the Pennsylvania Turnpike, I skidded on rain-slick roadway, smashed into the guard rail, and totaled my VW Bug—gone forever, with only 28,000 miles on it, an infant. . . oh Johannes, I hardly knew ye. In various ways, not worth going into, I crawled the rest of the way to Oakland, barely escaping from the cannibals at Donner Pass, arriving for my new life without a car and less than a thousand dollars in the world. The bulk of my worldly possessions resided in a dozen boxes left in Sal's care (sic!!), to be shipped to me when I sent him word.

My first home in California, albeit only for crashing until I found a permanent place, was a magnificent house in North Oakland of some six bedrooms, lush gardens in front and back, and a kitchen twice as big as my entire Washington apartment, located on a street lined with palm trees. I instantly fell in love with palm trees for life. My entrée was courtesy of one of the tenants, Bill MacGilvray, a former school teacher from Portland, Maine, who had been a fellow "grim" at the *Washington Free Press*.

Living on his savings and help from his brother in Portland, Bill seldom ventured outside into sunny California except to buy food or books. A visitor to his small room would remember nothing but the books—books wall to wall, books floor to ceiling, books, books, books. And there ol' Bill would sit, day after day in the ol' arm chair, readin' away. He might spend a month digesting 19th century British colonialism, then a period of prose literature of the Ch'ing dynasty; then, perhaps, it might be the right time for a little philosophy of science or existential phenomenology. Although I was hardly a Philistine, I couldn't understand what all this book larnin' was a-leadin' to. Being the best-read person in the universe? Winning big on Jeopardy? Was he planning on writing something learned, or rousing the rabble with his erudition transformed into flaming oratory? But MacGilvray did not deem my questions even worthy of his intellect, much less an answer. He just kept on reading. I would have told him to "Get a life!," but that marvelous expression had not yet been invented.

One day, a few weeks after my arrival, I walked into the office of the *Berkeley Barb*, the grandaddy of the underground press, and met its well-known founder, Max Scherr, a full-bearded man in his mid-fifties, tending a bit to portly, unpretentious in the extreme. I was soon the paper's most prolific reporter and for the first time in my life was being directly paid for my writing, precisely by the column inch. The pay of course was very modest, but it made a big difference, for not since I was a teenager at home was I having to count every penny so—I was walking long stretches to save a bus fare, or trying to hitch, buying everything I could second hand or not at all, never passing by a trash area without scanning it for usable or saleable stuff, selling my blood as often as the law and my body allowed. It was not a lifestyle that I readily admitted to, to family or to people I met, particularly women, but neither did I find it humiliating. It was simply the price one paid for living outside the system, and I found it challenging to make do on a paltry income. Moreover, I was not alone—the San Francisco Bay Area was full of people traveling down the same road. To be sure, in my case at least, it was what has been called "voluntary poverty." I had the option of taking a job in the business world, or at least venturing onto that fearful ground to find out if I was still hireable. The "non-profit" world with decent paying jobs had not yet come into its own.

What I did find humiliating occurred a few months later when I found out that I needed a hernia operation. I had to plead and plead and exaggerate and lie in my dealings with the hospital in San Francisco to talk them into performing the operation with just a token down payment. In the end, the people I dealt with probably knew that I was never going to pay the full bill, and they may have found the whole process almost as distasteful as I. National health insurance, such as practiced in civilized countries, would have spared us all.

For the *Barb*, amongst other beats, I regularly covered the meetings of the Berkeley City Council, a microcosm of political America 1970, where openly-leftist council members openly sparred with openly-rightist council members—with the audience irrepressibly shouting their two cents as well, and council members throwing back jibes—on local, national and often foreign-policy issues of the day. Not for nothing was the city known, by both friends and enemies, as The People's Republic of Berkeley. There was precious little craven Clintonesque searching for the safe middle ground. I always took pains to be accurate, but my readers were never in doubt as to which side I support-ed, and I had great delight poking satirical fun at "the bad guys." One of "the good guys" was Ron Dellums, who went on to be a very long-serving Congressman.

Max could sometimes get caught up in putting out a "newspaper," instead of an *underground* newspaper, which is to say a newspaper as a money-making machine more than as a tool of a movement. One evening when the staff was working late on a new issue, I went out to pick up a takeaway. While outside on University Boulevard, a couple of blocks from the office, I came upon a police scene—a police officer had just been shot and killed by an unknown gunman while the officer was writing a traffic ticket. It was much later in the evening that I happened to mention this to Max, and he exploded—Why the hell had-n't I gotten all the information and called the office to send a photographer? "We coulda scooped the *Chronicle!*" he yelled. I was shocked. It hadn't occurred to me for a nanosecond that this was a story for the *Barb*. It had nothing to do with why I was there working for poverty wages. Max was angry at me for some time afterward.

And the *Barb* did indeed make money. At its height, the previous year, "The Off-Broadway of History" had an international circulation of 93,000, and the classified and display ads—for which the paper was famous and infamous—brought in even more revenue. When the FBI succeeded in killing the *Barb's* record-company advertisements, the paper turned increasingly to sex ads. Many people were turned off by what they saw as the porno, sexism, and just plain "filth" that filled the columns, like the guy who offered to "be your toilet." I had to ask a co-worker what this meant, and learned that the advertiser liked to lie on the floor while someone stood above him and had a bowel movement. (I forget if his ad said "discreet" or not.) I worked in the office at times, and one day I chanced to meet this particular chap when he came in to renew his ad. Peering deeply into his eyes, reaching verily into his soul, I sought to discover the childhood trauma that had produced a human toilet. But the bathroom door was closed. He was not the kind of guy I would choose as a friend, nor even to lie on the floor below me, but I was not troubled by his ad or any of the others, equally charming. I think being older and thoroughly habituated to ultra-crass New York City humor made me more tolerant than many younger radicals who were turned off by the grosser parts of the *Barb*.

Today, however, I don't feel quite the same about this. What I call being "tolerant" then was really in large measure being "desensitized." It all seemed so natural back in the streets of New York. And so funny.

In a 1981 obituary for Max, David Armstrong wrote that "Max Scherr stood radical journalism on its head, declaring that mind expansion, avant-garde art, and combat in the erogenous zone were as important as seizing state power." This was of course another spin of the old yippie vs. politico record. Personally, though I liked the *Barb*, I would still choose seizing state power any day.

In August, a notice on a bulletin board led to my moving into a shared house in North Oakland, just off Shattuck Avenue and a few hundred feet from the national headquarters of the Black Panther Party. It was a small room, short on furniture and charm, in a rundown house, in a shabby neighborhood, no palm trees, nothing like my introduction to California. But the rent was only $70 a month. It would have been even less if the guy who ran the house, Willie Brandt (not to be confused with Willy Brandt, the West German Chancellor, although I didn't think you would), paid his share. But, as Willie explained at our first meeting, he was the most revolutionary person in the house and the others were therefore obliged to support him so he could devote full time to the revolution. Uh-huh. Very interesting, I thought. But since he had been the first one there, had set the rules to last for all eternity, and the rent was so low anyhow, no one challenged him.

Willie was a 23-year-old college dropout, tall and solidly built, who had never worked a day since he was 17 and a grocery clerk back in Chambersburg, Pennsylvania. That's when he came to the firm conclusion that his home town, his job, his parents, school, church, and society all "sucked," and set out for California. He now lived by his wits, which were not inconsiderable, and his command of the English language had grown somewhat since then, he being able now to explain "sucked" in proper socio-economic terms.

Before allowing me to move in, Willie asked me for something to verify my radical bona fides, so I gave him a copy of a short story I had written earlier in the year in Washington about some young people who, as a protest against the war in Vietnam, plant a bomb in a men's room at the Pentagon, which explodes and causes a lot of damage. It was the kind of fantasy that visits people who have been reduced to snapping harmlessly at the ankles of those on the board of directors of the planet.

I had actually cased out the Pentagon—it was still an open building then—before writing the story, and had gotten some worthwhile praise for it from a couple of magazines, but they immediately began to look for a ten-foot pole to not touch it with. Perhaps they were wise. In March 1971, about a year after they read my story, it became surprisingly real. Some young anti-war activists planted a bomb in a men's restroom of the Capitol in Washington, which exploded and caused extensive damage. I had nothing to do with it—YOU MUST BELIEVE ME!—but I was very glad that I didn't have to defend myself under the hot lights of a third degree from an FBI under great pressure to indict someone, and suggesting that my use of the Pentagon was merely a diversionary tactic to cloak the real target.

One year later, a bomb went off in a women's room at the Pentagon itself, bringing ruin and flood to a considerable area. Credit for the blast was taken in the name of the Weathermen, but this may not have been entirely legitimate. In any event, the chance of selling my story plummeted to zero.

Willie was very impressed with the story, telling me later that "No FBI agent could have written that." Little did I know the main reason he was so taken with my modest literary effort. For I was now living with the principal bomber of California, if not the United States. Mr. X himself.

It was very surprising that the same Willie who wanted me to prove myself before moving in, and who had every reason to be careful about who shared the house with him, apparently couldn't care less about the others; or perhaps his security consciousness was of recent vintage.

There was Frank, a postal worker (variety: undisgruntled), seemingly oblivious of the era he was living in. I once asked him why he thought the United States was in Vietnam. He thought for a few moments. . . "Well, I guess you'd have to ask each of the soldiers there why they're there," he said rather matter-of-factly. Somewhere there was a village that was being deprived of its idiot.

And there was Tom S., a graduate student at UC Berkeley in mathematics, not particularly political, hopelessly into intellectualizing everything and unable to express his feelings. His predominant manner of relating to other people was telling them what he thought they wanted to hear, a trait that can be viewed as a form of interpersonal paralysis, one not at all uncommon amongst the inhabitants of this planet.

There was also Alicia (not her real name), a tanned, blond and pretty undergraduate at UC, the Miss California/Miss America shiksa that every good heterosexual New York Jewish boy grows up having wet dreams about and never completely expels from his psyche or loins. And to think that she lived like ten feet away from me! She had the innocence of a native Californian, who refers to Chicago as "the East," and assumes that everybody has spent their youth camping and hiking amongst mountains and deserts, under rainless blue skies. She was surprised at my fear of snakes.

Both Tom and I slept with her occasionally, although never at the same time. She was also in the habit of picking up guys on campus and bringing them home for an afternoon fuck. After I got to know her somewhat, I tried to give her some fatherly/older brotherly advice that the sexual path she was walking down might be fraught with emotional tripwires. I was not moralizing. I had walked the same path without any scars that I was aware of. I could simply see that it was not making her happy, that she really didn't even enjoy sex all that much. At the same time, I was conscious of the irony of maybe killing my own golden goose. In any event, neither she nor I had the illusion or the desire for a single moment that a "relationship" would blossom between us. From my point of view, for age, intellectual and every other reason save sexual turn-on, that was a non-starter. Even the sex. . . fantasies, wet or dry, never quite live up to their hype; in the end, fantasies are always just that.

Finally, there was Willie's girlfriend, Wendy Yoshimura, later of Patty Hearst-kidnapping fame. She and Willie had met on a Venceremos work brigade to Cuba to harvest sugar cane. Wendy had been born in a Japanese internment camp in the United States during the Second World War, and had been raised in Hiroshima until about 12, then California. She spoke English with a slight accent. I liked her; she laughed easily, and was gentle without being fragile, although I sensed that she was not native to radical soil, and would not be leading anything like the political life she was if not for Willie's powerful influence. Years later, when she was out of prison, and no longer involved with Willie, this former art student undertook the painting career that had long been her first love. She did a lot of vases and flowers and other still lifes, to me the artistic equivalent of composing a poem beginning "Roses are red, violets are blue," not the usual stuff of a hard-core urban guerrilla.

Willie survived not only by paying the lowest rent on earth, but by innumerable scams he devised to obtain merchandise from stores and corporations. To this end he created several identities for himself, some obtained by looking through old newspapers in the library for death notices or news stories of children who had died young, who would be close to Willie's age at the present time. With the basic information of name, date of birth, and place of birth, he might be able to obtain a birth certificate; that in turn would lead to a driver's license and a Social Security card, and, *voila*, his new persona was alive and well, born knowing how to fill in applications for credit cards. This method—for whatever end—became so common in the '60s and '70s, that federal, state and city governments finally began to clean up their act and make it more difficult to obtain these documents. They even began to match birth and death certificates.

Willie also used variations on his own name for one scam or another: William Henry Brandt became William Henry Barrows, William Henry Brown, etc. At some point, when law enforcement agencies began to take a keen interest in the varied doings of William Henry Brandt, they very well may have been confused about a William Henry Blum receiving mail at the same address. Yes, my middle name is Henry, too. I enjoyed thinking that the FBI was convinced that William Henry Blum was just another of Willie's pseudonyms.

The oil companies, the airlines, the department stores, all jumping on The Great American Bandwagon, screaming "Buy now! You don't need money! All you need is a little plastic card that fits into your wallet." "It's a deal," said Willie. "I do indeed have no money, and I'd like two of those GE Cassette Recorders, a few of those Transatlantic Radios, some of that smart Samsonite matching luggage, and, oh yes, around three or four of those cute Minolta miniature cameras. Charge it please."

I would sell these items at the Alameda Flea Market on Saturdays—announcing that my prices were a "steal"—to people ecstatic over the bargains, along with other goods I was acquiring; it's amazing the stuff people throw out if you look for it; and lots of records, cassette tapes, and books from book and music clubs, who seemed oblivious to the fact that about a dozen people, each with a different last name, lived at the same address. I was surprised to discover how much I enjoyed spending a day outdoors, kidding with people who came to my spot, and making some money. I could see why so many people long to have their own little business, being their own boss.

At one point, Willie and one of his "gang" members used credit cards to rent two cars. After using them for a week or so, they gave me one of them to sell because I knew a mechanic whose class on auto repair I had just taken. He bought the almost new VW bug for parts and gave me $250, about a sixth of its market value, but that's the way it went with all of our schemes. We were not doing these things to get rich, to indulge of the grand lifestyle. We were petty criminals, just making enough to escape the clutches of the 9-to-5 warden; more examples of "us" vs "them," and "them" could easily afford it.

On Saturday night, about four or five of us piled into the other car, a fancier sedan, and drove to the North Beach area of San Francisco. The lights of Columbus Avenue were aglow with cabarets, dining spots and theaters, the street crowded with strollers out for a good time, as we parked the car right on the Avenue. After we piled out of it, a small jar of gasoline suddenly appeared and was poured over the seats, a lit match was tossed through the open window, and we all walked away, quickly but nonchalantly. From a safe distance we watched the flames and the crowd's gawking reaction.

Why did we—or rather they, since I took no active part and had not even known of the plans—do this? To show their disdain for private property, the trappings of wealth, "the system". . . choose your favorite revolutionary cliché. But if you had given each of the persons on Columbus Avenue who witnessed the fire ten guesses as to the reason for the strange sight their eyes beheld, there wouldn't have been one answer even close. If my *compañeros'* purpose was to somehow "enlighten" the public, to move them a step closer to "a higher political consciousness," I'd have to give them a grade of zero. But 100 percent for radical masturbation. Yet I must admit that it was a fun adventure, although I'd still rather have had the car or the money for it.

While the getting was still easy, I acquired two Social Security cards myself under fictitious names without even a birth certificate. Prevailing revolutionary wisdom had it that we all had to be prepared for some depth of underground life, where multiple IDs were bound to come in handy.

Another thing that was bound to come in handy was proficiency with firearms. Accordingly, Willie and his gang and I—or was I now part of the gang?—went to a shooting range in Alameda on Sunday mornings, where we learned the rudiments of firing shotguns and handguns, and, at home, the disassembly, cleaning and reassembly of same. In my life to that point, I don't think I had ever seen a single person so much as hold a real gun in his hand, except for the police and military. (Surprising as it may seem, my parents were not deeply into the hunting culture.)

On several occasions at the shooting range, our neighbors using the next target over were a group of right-wingers. We always exchanged a little smile or nod, a few words of small talk, each side fully aware that the other was there preparing for the very same Armageddon. And I would invariably tell myself that the use of these dreadful weapons was perfectly suited to such people as they, it may even have been in their genes. Indeed, I was surprised to see that they still needed any practice. More than once an image flashed before me, of one of them confusing one of us with the target.

My side, on the other hand, was of course being forced to acquire such a distasteful skill purely out of political necessity. One way our superior virtue was clearly demonstrated was that we always had at least one woman in our number, usually Wendy, while they were uniformly a bunch of macho bastards.

Arms, disguises, bomb-making, multiple IDs, jujitsu, knot-tying, survival in hostile environments, surveillance, locks and keys. . . Willie acquired manuals on all of these and related subjects, many prepared and sold by the Defense Department, others by private companies. He eventually put together and distributed his own little manual, a sort of "What you need to know and do before, during, and after The Revolution," dedicated to John Brown. I'm pretty certain it never made the *New York Times* best-seller list. It was more like one of those limited-issue monographs sold in rare-book shops that the *cognoscenti* are thrilled to stumble upon. Willie could have done wonders with the Internet.

Did I think The Revolution was coming next week? No. Did I think it would come within my lifetime? No. Did I think it should? Depended on whether someone like myself was in charge or not. Did I think we'd all wind up underground? Not myself, but I figured that Willie and his gang should be out looking for shovel sales.

How would it be if Willie were in charge? Well, there was the time I went to

the fridge, looking forward to a nice hamburger with fried onions, only to discover that my ground beef was missing. Willie, it turned out, had fed it to Alicia's dog. Now why would he do a thing like that? Because I had bought it at Safeway, which was being boycotted in California for purchasing non-union lettuce. Willie thought it was hilarious what he had done. He actually had a very exuberant and infectious laugh, and a great sense of irony and of the absurd—
"Bizarre!" was one of his favorite expressions, spit out with theatrical flourish—
not what you'd expect from someone so often uncompromising. It's what made him sufferable. He liked to stand outside places like shopping centers, crying out to the multitude coming in: "Consume, America, Consume!"

But in the case of my hamburger, I was not amused at all. Willie and I had a shouting match, and I later deducted the cost of the dog's meal from my rent.

He also frowned upon smoking, although he never gave my cigarettes to the dog. I would just repeatedly be treated to another Quotation From Chairman Willie: "The tobacco companies have colonized your libido." Ironically, Willie had to smoke to practice his vocation; he used a lit cigarette sticking out from the inside of a match cover as a fuse; when the cigarette burned down far enough, it ignited the matches, which in turn ignited the explosive material.

Not smoking was a matter of health, keeping in shape for. . . would you believe—the revolution? And for that same noble end, he regularly led a bunch of us foot soldiers in a jog around a high-school running track. I must admit that as I huffed and puffed through two or three laps maximum, I had no consciousness of running for the oppressed masses. I was running for my health. But I was usually the first one to call it quits, not so much due to lack of stamina, as to boredom. Although I've always exercised on a regular basis, I invariably wish I were doing something else. Indeed, I have an extremely low threshold for boredom, another by-product, it would seem, of my 20 years trapped inside a synagogue, not intellectually engaged, just aching to get out and resume being myself.

CHAPTER ELEVEN
KILL YOUR PARENTS

Bill MacGilvray left his books long enough to drop by one day. I was shocked to hear that he had cancer of the colon. He was younger than me. Bill was unable to hold back the tears as he told me his tale of woe. But a few minutes later, the readings on both my shockmeter and sympathymeter fell sharply when I realized that what I was hearing was a self-diagnosis. No doctor had told him that he had cancer. He frowned with impatience when I tried to bring him down to earth.

A few months later, a beaming Bill was to inform me that the vile cancer cells had departed his body. From what fount had this miracle sprung, I wondered, tensing up to hear the inspiring story of yet another Radical for Jesus.

Coffee enemas. He had cured his colon cancer with coffee enemas. Radicals for Coffee Enemas? His voluminous studies into the matter, including much material not usually found in the University of California Medical School curriculum, had led him to the promised land and a sparkling clean bowel. I never did ask him if it would work with decaf. Cappuccino? That seemed more appropriate to the San Francisco Bay Area, where the first stirrings of New Age alternative this and alternative that were being felt, like a low-level earthquake that presages a Big One. Coffee, after all, was "natural," and, as Isabel Allende has written, "Those not searching for Buddha are searching for the perfect cappuccino."

This medical vaudeville was my first exposure to a side of MacGilvray I had never seen before. Whatever it was, this may have been its initial venture into daylight, but it eventually was to take the poor man over and lead to a very trag-ic end.

I was also in touch with Sal. He and I exchanged phone calls every few weeks or so, courtesy of phone credit card numbers belonging to one unde-serving corporation or another. In the face of this growing practice nationwide, the phone company introduced a secret code to go along with the credit card number, without which the operator would not accept the call. The code con-sisted of a series of 10 individual letters, one for each digit, corresponding to a particular position of the phone number. They changed the letters and position each year. And each year, the entire new code information was published in the underground press. All it took was one phone company employee with higher loyalties.

I kept Sal posted about such mundane things as what classes I was taking here and there, mundane things that I was later to come across in my CIA file. Sometime during 1971 he told me that he was moving to Paris, a move that was to precipitate the climax to his double life and our friendship.

Willie's father came to visit one afternoon in between planes. If I didn't have much in common with *my* father, imagine that Willie's father worked for the Department of Defense, something to do with logistics. He was returning to the east coast after a trip to Vietnam; yes, the same Vietnam I've mentioned before. This tall, thin man, who looked more like a weather-beaten farmer than a Pentagon functionary, sat in the living room, trying not to notice the TV set that had been smashed to bits when Willie fired a shotgun into it because of one commercial too much or one inanity too many. This was before my time and I was grieved to have missed this acting out of a fantasy harbored by millions round the world.

So there the man sat, ignoring not only the TV but the sign directly above his head that said, in foot-high red letters: "Kill Your Parents." This was one of Jerry Rubin's show stoppers. Rubin later wrote that the inspiration for it derived from hearing someone say: "Anyone who is not willing to kill his parents for the revolution is not a revolutionary." Jerry subsequently came to realize that it meant kill the *parents-in-you*. But that isn't what the sign said.

Who knows what aching confusion filled Mr. Brandt's heart and head about how his son had turned out? His first born and only son, who had left home so young. What could he as a parent have possibly done to spawn such a mutation? And his ache derived from only the sketchiest of information about the later Willie. If the man knew but a quarter of the story about how his first born and only son had turned out, he might have volunteered for front-line duty while over in 'Nam.

"The people there don't always like what we have to do to their villages, but they know that we're there to help them and they're mighty grateful," he told us, continually nodding his head up and down, with a vacant look in the eye that never seemed to focus on Willie or me for more than a second at a time. "And our boys are real proud to be doing their job, yes sir, real glad to be there."

Willie just laughed out loud. "Dad, you're totally insane!" he shrieked, with his usual reserve. "Who'd you speak to? Only the officers?" and laughed even louder.

I could think only to jump up screaming some horrible karate cry, grab this man by the neck, and throw him to a monstrous electric-shock machine that would wipe clean from his mind the 50 years of his life, leave him as unprogrammed as a newborn babe, and dump him into a Vietnamese rice paddy under falling napalm.

I did not have to wonder why a callow Willie had taken flight from the nest of such a bird.

Does a son have the right to wonder about the way his only father has turned out? After Brandt Senior had departed, it was an evening filled with "Bizarre! Bizarre!"

Willie's poor mother fared no better at the hands of her first born mutation. One day a five-inch reel of tape arrived from her, containing a sermon delivered by the local minister, with an attached note asking Willie to record his reaction on the other side of the tape. The sermon was your basic appeal for the lost sheep to return to the fold, the kind of appeal I'd heard too many times in synagogue, which assumes that the sheep have wandered simply due to lack of understanding of the joys offered by the fold, and not because the sheep understand them only too well.

As Willie ran the tape to the end and turned it over, I sat there and thought about a kindly-looking, plump, middle-aged woman in small-town Pennsylvania, borrowing a tape recorder from a neighbor and taking it to church one pleasant Sunday morning, after getting the minister's permission of course. I saw her at home listening to the playback, proud of her technological achievement, packaging the tape carefully in the special envelope she had purchased at the local stationery shop, smiling hopefully as she read for the third time the letter she was enclosing, and proudly presenting her finished product to the friendly Post Office clerk whom she'd known for years.

"Let's blow her mind," I said.

Taking microphone in hand, calling forth my deepest voice, I said in crisp authoritarian tones: "Hello there, Mrs. Brandt, I'm Dr. Stimson at Napa State Hospital. Willie was kind enough to play your tape for me and I must say I was rather moved. Your son has been very cooperative since he's been our guest here. The fits are happening less and less often. He still talks of violence a bit too much, but we think that we can help him on that. And we hope that the fellow sharing Willie's room, Charles Manson, will have a steadying influence over him. The main thing we're concerned about is the loaded machine gun young William insists on taking to bed with him. But on the other hand, some of our other guests refuse to sleep without their teddy bear. And now Willie has asked me to record some of his favorite music for you. He hopes you enjoy it and wants you to know that as he lies in his bed with his loaded machine gun he is always thinking of you."

Following my professional diagnosis were obscenities from The Fugs, treason from Country Joe and the Fish, threats to all that is decent and holy from Dylan, drugs from the Beatles, incomprehensible, deafening noise from various rock nonentities, and closing with a few weirdos from the Mothers of Invention and Tiny Tim, all designed for a long-suffering woman in a world grown increasingly incomprehensible, designed to drive her. . . well, to Napa State Hospital?

The reader may notice a similarity between this Mother Pushing Religion and another MPR previously referred to, and conclude that the latter explains my hostility towards the former. Well, I must say that to believe such is to cast doubt upon my powers of objectivity and pigeonhole me as one of those unfortunates who can never heal the scars of their abusive childhood, which is not to say that there's nothing to the idea.

Willie and I had a pretty good laugh over that one of course. A week later, the phone rang and when I answered it I found I was talking to Mrs. Brandt. She had called Napa State Hospital and was told that no one by her son's name was a patient there. Nor was there a Dr. Stimson. She didn't understand. Where was her son? What's happened to him?

Oh my gosh. Willie wasn't home, I told her, and it was all a silly joke, but that didn't register in her troubled mind. I spent several minutes on the phone reassuring her that the story wasn't true, until she finally closed the conversation, maybe two-thirds convinced.

She should have seen her son in my room one day. Sitting on the floor, making a bomb. I saw it, and at first I was fascinated. My room was at street level, just off the alleyway that separated our house from the next one. At one point in the process a lot of smoke would be suddenly produced and Willie would need immediate access to the outside. My door was left open a few inches, and as soon as it began to smoke he put the container (I forget now what it looked like) out in the alley until the smoke dissipated. This happened a couple of times. What our neighbors might have thought if they saw this smoking thing, only God or the FBI knows. This was not exactly your high-security need-to-know eyes-only crypto-secret CIA covert operation.

But neither did it make security sense for the likes of Willie, Wendy and myself to be living with the likes of Tom, Alicia and Frank. I don't know if Frank knew about anything under heaven or on earth, but from time to time, from a word or a grin here, a wink or a nod there, Tom and Alicia made it plain that they knew that Willie was into bombings. It was a measure of the times that they didn't inform any authorities. I think they got a kick out of being so close to something that made headlines, and probably couldn't resist dropping joking hints about it on campus. But I don't know how many of Willie's specific targets they were aware of. Patty Hearst, in her account of her kidnapping, has written that Wendy told her that Willie was involved in at least 40 bombings over a two-year period, including banks, nuclear laboratories, and police cars, under the banner of the Revolutionary Army,[34] of which Wendy was one of the grunts, and Willie Chairman of the Joint Chiefs of Staff. From things mentioned by Willie to me or in my presence, the only targets I knew of for sure were a Republican Party office in Oakland, a police station parking lot in Oakland, the Iranian Consulate in San Francisco, more than one Bank of America, a Foster and Kleiser billboard company office (they maintained commercial billboards in Saigon), an Army Recruiting office in Oakland, and one other I'll get to presently.

The bombing of the Iranian Consulate, in October 1971, caused significant damage and was in retaliation for the obscenely lavish party the Shah of Iran was putting on at the same moment to celebrate the 2,500th anniversary of the Persian Empire—a five-hour formal dinner for 500 presidents, prime-ministers, majesties, highnesses, eminences, excellencies, grand dukes, sheiks, sultans, and other underprivileged; several thousand horses, hundreds of camels and water buffalos, floats, boats, and chariots; several million dollars for the affair, while the multitudinous poor of Iran survived in the manner normal to the multitudinous poor. Anti-monarchists in the Bay Area were blamed for the bombing, but they, rightfully, denied it.

How many people in this sad world, I wondered, were offended by the Shah's extravagance, not to mention the systematic and routine torture he was renowned for, to the extent that they wished they could find some way to express their moral outrage?

As usual, Willie didn't send a message to the mass media, but only to Radio Station KSAN in San Francisco, which sympathized with the left. Willie regarded the "official press" as part of the enemy and didn't want to have anything to do with them, just as the "official press" tended to ignore KSAN. Willie's policy bothered me. Although there was a bit of public speculation that the bombing may have been, somehow, related to the Shah's festivities, the absence of an explicit statement considerably blunted the political impact of the deed. Willie also didn't know that the Consul and his family lived in the building and would still be there late at night. Neither did he consider that what "may have been the most powerful bombing in the city's history," as the police labeled it,[35] would do serious damage to many nearby houses. As far as I'm aware, no one was ever hurt in any of Willie's bombings, but it was just pure luck that no one was injured or killed in this one.

Back to my room. So I'm standing there watching this young guy use his college chemistry and some instruction he's picked up in a mail-order manual to fashion a powerful bomb, at least powerful enough so that a single mistake would mean the instantaneous, inglorious, and eternal end to William Henry Brandt and William Henry Blum as players on the stage of life. Their one and only role. Not long before, in March 1970, a Greenwich Village town house had Ka-BOOOM! disappeared, killing three young people of SDS, busy concocting a bomb. The house belonged to the family of Cathy Wilkerson, formerly of the *Washington Free Press*. She survived.

I'm thinking of this and another time Willie had posed a danger to my health: driving around downtown Oakland one night, Willie, I and a third guy who's driving. Willie's in the front passenger seat and I'm sitting behind him. We stop in front of an office building of the State of California, the nearest symbol of authority at that moment. The street's deserted and quiet as Willie sticks his rifle out the window, aiming to annihilate the large glass front door. He fires, and hits the marble steps instead. The bullet ricochets instantly, smashing the window I'm looking through, passing an inch or two in front of my face, and exiting out the other window. My lap is filled with broken glass as the driver makes a tire-screeching getaway. Needless to say, Willie found it hilarious. I didn't.

I've thought enough. I leave the house and visit a friend. A couple of hours later I'm driving home, and as I turn into Fairview Avenue, I'm at least half expecting to see fire engines, police cars, spotlights, a crowd of people, the whole circus. But the ugly adobe house is still standing.

I left the *Barb* in late 1970. I left because I no longer wished to deal with the critical remarks I frequently encountered, particularly from women. Yes, the last few pages of the paper were full of ads for strip shows, topless bars, massage parlors, sex devices, porno films, sex shops, S & M, you name it, with lots of drawings. I still wasn't bothered by it, but I was very bothered, repeatedly, by the look I'd get, and the mini-lecture I'd receive: "How can you lend your name to such trash?" It was reminiscent of the flak I had received for working at the State Department, and it did no good to point out that there was nothing, explicitly or implicitly, of violence toward women in the newspaper, and that my name was lent only to progressive political articles. To my critics any connection to exploitation of women was simply non-negotiable, just as a defense of the war in Vietnam was with me. Eventually, I stopped defending myself. Then I began to not readily reveal where I worked. On occasion I covered it up. Finally I quit.

I soon could be found at *The Berkeley Tribe*, which had been founded about a year earlier largely by people who had been at the *Barb*. Max Scherr shook his head. "I can't keep anyone who's radical," he told me. But we remained friends. The *Tribe* was the more radical newspaper, receiving and publishing communiqués from the Weatherman Underground, with a consciousness about security which was absent at the *Barb*. There were no sex ads of any kind. But it paid no money to writers, and didn't even satisfy the ego with a byline, for this was a clear manifestation of "bourgeois individualism," as well as a sure way to provide the FBI and their infiltrators a bit more information with which to shred the First Amendment. I never learned the real names of some of the staff who used pseudonyms, or should I say *nommes de guerre*.

In the Spring, I also left Willie's house, moving to a furnished studio apartment in the prettier Lake Merritt area of Oakland—Athol Avenue, a name I could never say without thinking of someone with a lisp. Oddly enough, I don't remember now exactly why I moved out. I don't think it was fear of arrest or danger to life and limb—nothing so sensible. I think I just longed to live alone again.

Shortly afterward, one of Willie's lieutenants, Don Church, was arrested for two Berkeley bank bombings. Don and his girlfriend, Kathleen Brooks, lived around the corner from Willie, and I had met them often. Kathleen was also indicted for the bombings, but the 20-year old managed to flee, while pregnant. Willie, understandably not wishing to be associated with the likes of an accused bomber, asked me to visit Don at the Alameda County Jail. And I, off on Bill's Excellent Adventure, blithely did so on several occasions, although I had always had a difficult time with Don. He was like the Yippies' worst nightmare—a humorless, intransigent, doctrinaire politico. One time he had frowned on my reading a novel instead of one of The 100 Great Revolutionary Books of the Western World. On another occasion, when I mentioned in passing that I liked to play tennis, he reacted as if I had just confessed to being a multinational garment manufacturer running a child-labor sweat shop in Thailand.

Incarceration did not appear to mellow Lenin, Jr. very much. He expressed no gratitude for my visits and the tidbits of news and gossip I brought him. That, after all, was no more than my revolutionary duty. It was like he was Jimmy Cagney and I was Pat O'Brien, the long-suffering priest with the big heart. When I brought him a book from Willie one day, the jail wouldn't allow him to receive it, for it seems that someone had given a prisoner a book with one or more pages soaked in LSD, and since that time police mentality—no less dogmatic than Don's—dictated NO BOOKS except for new books sent by a publisher, which presumably would be LSD-free. I had a jiffy bag from a publisher returning one of my many rejections, which I fashioned into a mailer for the book to Don. And it worked, even with the same postage-machine stamp, whose date I updated with a red pencil. I got as much satisfaction out of saving the postage as I did from fooling the jail.

Don was in jail for nine months before being released on $10,000 bail, put up by his mother with her house as collateral. He then promptly fled into hiding. Cagney would have broken out into one of his devilish grins. Whether Don's mother actually lost her home I don't know, but these were not good times for mothers. For all my own mother knew of my actual life, despite my occasional postcard, I could have been a Buddhist monk in Outer Mongolia using a California mailing service.

Don eluded the authorities until 1983, when he was arrested near Bentonville, Arkansas with $6 million of cocaine. The governor of Arkansas at the time was one William J. Clinton; no connection between he and the drugs is inferred here (I think), although the governor's alleged approval of a CIA cocaine smuggling operation going on at the very same time in Mena, Arkansas, 120 miles away, has been widely discussed.

Kathleen Brooks, who was as tough a cookie as her boyfriend, had been with him in Arkansas, but she again managed to escape the clutches of the law. Finally, after living the life of a fugitive for 17 years—hunted by the FBI in Canada, England, Spain, France, and Luxembourg—she surfaced in 1988 in Oakland and, for the sake of her three children, she said, turned herself in; one of a number of wanted radicals who gave themselves up in the late '70s and the '80s, writing *finis* to what was probably the most bomb-filled period in American domestic history.

Meanwhile, I was suffering a financial crisis, again, still, serious enough to drive me into seeing how much of a marked-down commodity I was in the computer field. I knew that in four years a lot had changed technically, which I had no usable knowledge of, but the lure was strong because the work paid so well—I could save enough in less than a year to live for at least the next two.

"Please list all places of residence during the preceding 10 years. Account for all periods of time."

I look at the five blank spaces. I've had five residences in the past year and a half alone.

"Please describe the kind of person you are in a biographical sketch. If more space is required, attach a separate sheet. . . Have you ever been refused credit?. . . Have you ever been fired from a position? If so, please explain. . . Have you ever been arrested?"

"I don't care what kind of trouble you've been in," says the hiring boss to Humphrey Bogart. "We've all had our troubles. You just give me a day's work for a day's wages and we'll get along fine."

"Why did you leave the computer field?" he asks. . . "What did you do from October to December 1959?" He wants to know about this gap on my application. What did I do from October to December 1959? Why, I was molesting children, mugging blind, crippled women, and overthrowing the government by force and violence. What the fuck do you *think* I was doing, you asshole? I was looking for a job! No, I take that back. I also sat in the park a few afternoons and read a little, frequented shopping malls, pool halls, and fleamarket stalls; threw all decency to the wind by seeing a movie or two; totally unproductive I was, doing nothing to increase the Gross National Product or any of the Leading Economic Indicators, displaying no driving ambition whatsoever, no get-up-and-go, not even a self-starter was I.

Maybe I can tell him I was sick. What's a good three-month illness?—hepatitis? No, not respectable enough. Can't tell him I was sick at all. They want good robust Americans, no one keeling over the desk during business hours, very messy, bad for the insurance. . . Maybe I was with the CIA and I'm not at liberty to divulge the nature of my mission. . . Maybe I should get up and leave right now. Maybe I should piss on his desk first. . .

"You indicate here, Mr. Blum, that you left a position because of job dissatisfaction," says the man, whose station on the planet is Assistant Manager of Personnel, Bank of America, San Francisco; an odd place for me, to be sure— one of the banks Don and Kathleen had bombed—but banks at that time were the foremost users of computers in the private sector. "Could you kindly clarify exactly which of your duties you found dissatisfying, as you put it?"

Oh how he knows how to weed out the misfits, he does. His eyes are so clear, his skin so unblemished, his teeth so straight. What's the last thing that made him cry? What did he last question? Was there some secret he carried he'd die before telling his wife? Can I tell him I quit because I found the undiluted commercialism suffocating? May as well tell him I didn't like getting up early every morning and putting on a suit and tie. You gotta use everything you've ever learned about Americans and act the part. You gotta run their questions through a computer, just like they did, that tests for human content and branches to a translation sub-routine that prints out all they need to know about fitting the right man to the right job. And Christ, you can never say you didn't like the work because it was socially useless. They won't know what the hell you're talking about. They'll have to run back to the ol' database and check under "Religions: esoteric and extinct sects." That's if you're lucky. If they *do* understand your quaint language, you better start rolling your ass out of there before they call the FBI.

"I notice that you've changed careers several times, Mr. Blum, as well as changing jobs often. It all sounds very interesting, but we have to be concerned here more with. . . stability."

"You want to know whether I've settled down," I offer.

"Well, for example, why are you looking for a job right now? Why don't you use your freedom to write, which you seem to enjoy a great deal, or. . . ?"

"I couldn't even if I wanted to. I don't have the money saved to do that."

"And when you do have enough money saved, you'll just take off again?"

"No, no," I protest, cursing my carelessness. "That's not what I. . . no, those days are over. For one thing, I haven't had much success as a writer. I can't make a living at it, to put it mildly."

I shift in my seat, careful not to cross my legs, not because I think it would be too casual looking, but to make sure I don't reveal the bottoms of my shoes with their gaping cleavage. Concealing my sport jacket is not as simple; it's a blue and grey splash thing that was once new and cheap looking, now it's old and cheap looking. If I had another jacket. . . well, that would make two.

"Can you tell me, Mr. Blum, why you would like to work here?"

I've prepared several responses to this inevitable question. But they all sound like bullshit. Primarily because that's what they are. Can I tell this man the truth, that for the first time in my life, the very first time, I don't know where my next month's rent is coming from? Finally. . .

"Well, we all need jobs, obviously."

"Of course, but why do you want this *particular* job?"

"Well, what do you want to hear? That for years and years I've dreamed of helping to automate Bank of America's check processing system?"

"No, I'd just like to hear the truth."

"Okay. I need a job. I need a job to pay the rent, to buy food and gasoline, and to go out with women. . . and I'm a conscientious worker."

"Okay, fair enough."

But the Bill Blums of the world know that the Bank of Americas of the world do not hire on the basis of fairness. No more than people marry for such reasons. The thought actually crosses my mind that I could offer to guarantee that the bank would not be bombed again.

We both know the dance is over but the man from personnel needs to complete the standard turn and curtsy. "Tell me, Mr. Blum, what do you expect to be doing five years from now?"

This question—this quintessential corporate tenet of how people should look upon life—had depressed me the very first time I was asked it in my twenties. It did not improve with age. "I suppose," I say at last, "you also want a *team player*, right?. . . And someone who can *fit happily into our little family*, right?"

Oh well, I wouldn't have passed their security check anyhow.

A few such interviews and a dozen such application forms propelled me into the arms of the temporary employment agencies, which were more like Humphrey Bogart's hiring boss. But at four or five dollars an hour, I still had to count pennies at every turn and any stupid waste of money was enough to drive me up the wall. . .

"Didn't you see that the light was red when you crossed?"

"Yes, but I also saw that there were no cars coming."

The officer's eyes flash at this unexpected lack of humility. "May I see your identification, please?"

I sigh deeply as I hand over my driver's license. "Don't you think," I ask, "that the spirit of the law is aimed at people crossing the street recklessly and endangering themselves and motorists? That's not what I did at all."

"I'm not paid to think," he replies flatly, already writing out the ticket.

At least he didn't say he was just doing his job.

The officer is now on his radio talking with police headquarters, giving them my vitals. I'm pretty sure I'm not wanted for anything, yet my mind races anxiously in search of something I may have forgotten about or been unaware of. When you live on the edge, particularly with the likes of Willie and his gang, there are lines you cross that can trip silent alarms and feed you into police databases.

I'm tempted to pursue the dialogue-cum-monologue with the officer out of pure hatred, but that very same hatred means that I can no longer bring myself to face the man. Essentially, I'm very uncomfortable feeling the hatred, but I've convinced myself that the officer deserves it, and I don't even want to look him in the eye lest I see something too human to hate. And if I saw it, it would only make it more of a tragedy, the human being turned policeman. Comes the revolution, no one who wants to be a police officer will be allowed to be one.

The report comes back negative and I'm given a ticket along with a lecture and warning. "Is that clear?" the officer asks, as he's asked a thousand times before.

I hesitate. How far gone is this guy's power trip, I wonder. Do I have to kiss his ring? "If I say that it's not clear, will you arrest me?"

He looks at me now as if for the first time, stares at me with eyes wide—the words are enunciated slowly—"Don't let me catch you again."

As the officer returns to his motorcycle, I breathe a real sigh of relief that the guy didn't call my bluff. That would have meant handcuffing, squad car, police station, photos, fingerprinting, prison cell, hours of hassle and humiliation; above all, humiliation; at their mercy within a closed system; yes Your Honor, no Your Honor, I promise Your Honor, thank you Your Honor, *fuck you Your Honor*. They can always find a charge, and they don't necessarily care if it's dismissed later as long as they've extracted their pound of flesh. I think that cops are not much bothered by crime per se; it's part of the game of cops and robbers, and the criminal is a necessary player in the game, which cops enjoy because the rules favor them so. They can act decently toward the criminal as long as he knows his place, but if he acts uppity—i.e, stands up for his rights—

there's no limit to the cops' rage. And of all the causes for which I might nobly suffer the slings and arrows of outrageous police fortune, jaywalking must be last on the list.

I look at the ticket. It's gonna cost me about two hours of temp work. And I won't pay it when it's due, out of principle, out of anger, and someday they'll catch up with me and I'll have to pay more than double; that's more than half of what I earn in a full day. I know this, it's perfectly clear, but I can't pay it now.

CHAPTER TWELVE
RADICAL PSYCHIATRY

Berkeley, 1971, everything is up for grabs; no institution or tradition is immune from penetrating analysis or fundamental reorganization; anything, including yourself, can be reinvented. Let's see, today I think I'll become a psychiatrist; no, even better, a *radical* psychiatrist.

Claude Steiner was the founder and head of the radical psychiatry movement. . .

> All persons competent in soul healing should be known as psychiatrists. . . Extended individual psychotherapy silently colludes with the notion that people's difficulties have their sources within them while implying that everything is well with the world. . . Adjustment to prevailing conditions is the avowed goal of most psychiatric treatment. Persons who deviate from the world's madness are given fraudulent diagnostic tests which generate diagnostic labels which lead to 'treatment'. . . Psychological tests and the diagnostic labels they generate, especially schizophrenia, must be disavowed as meaningless mystifications. . . Psychiatric disturbance is equivalent with alienation, which is the result of mystified oppression. Paranoia is a state of heightened awareness. Most people are persecuted beyond their wildest delusions. Those who are at ease are insensitive. . . Psychiatry is a political activity."[36]

This was a philosophy that was custom made for the time and place. Steiner was not saying that people who sought out psychiatrists were not hurting, and in need of relief, or that radical psychiatry would not try to offer relief. It was the approach and the premises:

> A radical psychiatrist will take sides. He will advocate the side of those whom he is helping. The radical psychiatrist will not look for the wrongness within the person seeking psychiatric attention; rather, he will look for the way in which this person is being oppressed and how the person is going along with the oppression. The only problem that radical psychiatry looks for inside someone's head is how he empowers and enforces the lies of the oppressor and thereby enforces his own oppression.[37]

Steiner hedged his bet a little by stating that every psychiatric diagnosis "except for those that are clearly organic in origin" is a form of alienation. Today, of course, the trend is to ascribe biologic causality instead of environmental factors to more and more aspects of behavior—from intelligence, shyness, and anxiety to happy marriages, violence, and children's personality and interests. But a radical psychiatrist, or even a non-therapeutic radical, might reply that this is primarily a defense mechanism—we're losing control over an increasingly crazy and scary society and we have to convince ourselves that it's not our fault, that nothing much can be done about it, that it's in the genes; at the same time lending scientific credence to a conservative agenda of preserving existing social inequalities by making them appear natural and inevitable.

My introduction to radical psychiatry came in a public lecture by Steiner to a large audience sitting on the floor of a Berkeley high-school gymnasium. I was receptive to his words, for in one way or another I often reflected about how much of our private pain is rooted in the way we collectively organize our social, political and economic lives, in areas like health care, education, employment, and consumption. As a socialist, by definition, I saw problems in a social/systemic context. Otherwise, I would just go around telling people to be nicer to each other, like the people who gave me a migraine at interviews, but who were just doing the job they're paid to do: eliminate the American expatriates still living in America, who are not prepared to kill, die or lie for the bottom line.

At one point—in the touchy-feely climate that was California of the day—Steiner suggested we choose a nearby person to hug and kiss. Without further ado or ceremony, the woman next to me and I began to. . . well, hug and kiss. It quickly became pretty passionate. (I should mention that she and I were both there alone.) The one moment I came up for air and opened my eyes I saw the damnedest thing—a roomful of people hugging and kissing. Finally, at Steiner's command, we all parted from each other and listened to the rest of the lecture. It would have been uncool of me to make anything of what had happened, to take it as any kind of invitation from the woman; so we left separately, like train passengers getting off at different stops. In the small town that was Berkeley, I

ran into her occasionally, and learned that she was the wife of a fairly prominent Marxist professor of philosophy at the university.

It was of course another example of unquestioning obedience to authority,
like with Dr. Miller. And the people in the room, with perhaps a few exceptions,
were not even under Steiner's care, not beholden to him for therapy. "People
like being given orders," Colin Wilson has observed. "It helps them to throw off
the feeling of responsibility—civilization neurosis. The aim is to make them feel
like innocent children again."

I also liked to hug and kiss.

From this distance of many years, it's hard to say if I was really serious
about carving out a new career for myself—I'd never had a thought of becoming any kind of therapist—or whether I was just letting the tide of the time
wash me up on whatever beach was close at hand and sounded interesting. But
I did attend a few sessions of a training group, in which I heard a lot of talk
about learning how to give and receive criticism, and on making the group
"safe" so that people would feel free to ask for what they need; members were
encouraged to brag about good things they did—women in particular for acting "potent"—and the others were to give them "strokes" for doing these things.
. . It all seemed so transparent and patronizing, unspontaneous, even childish.
The group leader would tell someone "I support you," seemingly without any
real caring, merely following a script.

At one session, a fellow from India happened to lament the United States
killing of so many Asians and he decried the American public for not protesting enough. Given the countless actions of the anti-war movement, his com-
plaint seemed to me odd in the extreme. I questioned his conclusion and began
to give a mini-history of the past six years, when I was cut off by the group
leader, Hoagy Wyckoff, who was the number-two person after Steiner in the
radical psychiatry movement. She accused me of being a "bourgeois liberal." In
Berkeley, California, circa 1971, this was roughly equivalent to being identified
as a "Jew" in Nuremberg, circa 1935. Before I could say a word in my defense,
Wyckoff called upon the group as a whole to "give Bill some critical feedback,"
whereupon three or four people proceeded to say negative things about me.
One went so far as to accuse me of defending American policy in Vietnam. As
absurd as that was, I was more upset by the other remarks because these had to
do with my character—some rad-psy clichés, from people possessing virtually
zero knowledge of me. Is ignorance a point of view? I was stunned into atypi-
cal silence.

Outside, after the session, one of my critics told me that he didn't really
mean what he had said about me, and another person, who hadn't spoken, said
that she didn't agree with the sentiments expressed.

The bloom was off the rose for me. I returned to the group one more time to avoid the appearance of quitting under fire, and I was told by two or three others in private that they didn't go along with what had taken place the previous week. But none of the people who spoke to me in private either week said a word about the matter in the group, nor did any of the other ambassadors from The People's Republic of Berkeley raise a diplomatic eyebrow. Did they have rad-psy ambitions? Hoagy was not only Number Two, she was Steiner's mate. Or was playing Get-Bill yet another example of obedience to authority? Without even a sexual reward.

So, again the question: How shall I spend the rest of my life? While waiting for my next radical epiphany, I kept body and soul together by toiling away at the occasional eye-glazing temp job—boredom is to the mind as torture is to the body—and penned reportage and commentary for Alternative Features Service, a Berkeley news agency that regularly sent out packets of such to many underground newspapers as well as a few above ground. AFS of course made little money, for itself or its writers, but felt compelled to transmit some alternative views out into the ether. Then, as now, one could studiously read and memorize forever every word printed in the *New York Times*—All The News That Fits Our Ideology—every day of the year, yet wind up seriously ignorant and/or thoroughly misguided about a multitude of controversial happenings and issues in the world. The American public has an inordinately difficult time believing a statement like this.

In the Third World, guerrillas have had to kidnap someone prominent in order to get a full-page in the daily press explaining their political views. In the United States, radicals have turned to alternative newspapers and news agencies. The guerrillas have been more effective. Today, if one scrutinizes the remarkable international journalistic and other resources of the Internet, one is more aware than ever of the critical pieces of the puzzle omitted by the establishment media (often material which was made available to them from the likes of Reuters and AP) as they decide: a) which issues to cover in the first place, and b) how many sides there are to each issue, thus setting the narrow limits of respectable debate.

Every once in a while, I ventured an article for the likes of *Esquire* or *New Republic,* and told myself with smug satisfaction that the reason for my unblemished record of rejection was that I hadn't learned to censor myself sufficiently. But the truth was that I also hadn't learned to write in the proper "slick" style, to which I was resistant for I tended to associate it with "slick" people, writers as much taken with *le bon mot* and the clever turn of phrase as with substance, and keeping a professional distance when the material cried out for some measure of involvement. Yet their bias was still plainly evident, right there between the li(n)es.

I was now living in Berkeley, sharing the upper floor of a duplex on Parker Street with Jeff Cohlberg, a post-doc student in biochemistry. Like your basic Berkeleyite, I was spending time on Telegraph Avenue, the epicenter of '60s protest, still in its golden age. After a browse through the marvelous used and new bookstores, like Moe's and Cody's, I would take up table space in the Cafe Mediterraneum, chatting with Max Scherr, Art Goldberg, Bob Dylan (okay, I made that last one up), and other veterans of the '60s, some of them still in their twenties. One day I ran into Frank Teruggi, a fellow I had gotten to know when he lived at "Hearst Castle," a communal house on Hearst Street, and I had written several articles for the *Barb* about the commune's battles with its landlord, the University of California. Frank told me he was about to leave for Chile, where Salvador Allende, a socialist—a genuine one, not a social democrat—had been elected president. I knew immediately that I had to go there too, surprised that I hadn't thought of it myself. I was not cut out to be any kind of therapist, working on one individual at a time, even if employing social concepts. History was happening in Chile, a social revolution, a peaceful revolution, the CIA permitting. I would observe Allende's "socialist experiment," and be its John Reed.

The only problem was money. Chile was half a world away. Later, at home, I took stock of my financial situation. I had just paid my rent. I had a few days worth of food in the frig, about 20 dollars in food stamps, and about 30 dollars in cash. After 38 years on earth. I was both surprised and amused that my balance sheet didn't alarm me. Was there serious denial at work here, or what? I was only sorry because the needle on the dial said I was not going to Chile.

I would have had more in food stamps, but I had recently chosen to drop it. Although I was eligible based on income and assets, I could no longer deal with the shit the welfare office dumped on me, the new ways they came up with every month to hassle me—a new document had to be turned in, or a letter from someone, some new long, complex forms to fill out, interviews, an inspector coming to my apartment. . . and the American public likes to believe that welfare is a racket, that anyone can walk in and get it just for the asking. And this was only for food stamps, the easiest thing to get. However, it must be added that being a white male college graduate made me a marked man. The black clerks I dealt with had a difficult time accepting me as someone really in need.

I had also applied for unemployment insurance, believing that I was eligible for a small benefit based on several temp and other little jobs along the way. The unemployment office had rejected my claim and I had an appeal pending. Thus it was that I found myself faced with the same revolting prospect facing the rest of humankind—I had to find an (ugh) job, an (ugh) steady job for an (ugh) few months, to build up a nest egg for Chile.

It was early 1972. Tax season was at hand. Hey, I used to be a tax accountant, about a hundred years ago in New York. I got me a current tax manual and studied it intently. This wasn't easy. Chloroform in print, as Mark Twain put it. But in fairness to my former pencil-pushing colleagues, I must say that I resent the familiar stereotype of an accountant as an uninspired, uninspiring, "unpoetic" technician, nose close to the desk, adding up his endless little columns of numbers, with or without a green eyeshade. It ain't necessarily so. Some of the funniest and wildest guys I knew back then were those who spent their daylight hours performing calculations and moving figures around on pieces of paper.

Lo and behold, I answered an ad to do taxes for an accountant in the port area of San Francisco, who specialized in seamen, and the guy hired me.

The day before I was to begin at the job, I received a notice in the mail that my claim for unemployment insurance had been approved. My first thought was—oh, what a shame, if only I could receive both, the unemployment and the wages. My second thought was—why not? I would work at the job and collect the unemployment benefits as well. I would be caught of course. Sometime in May, the State of California tax department would send a report to the State Unemployment Office listing the earnings for the first quarter of all workers. The Unemployment Office would compare the names on that list with the names of individuals who had received unemployment benefits during the quarter, and if they found a match, would check to see if the individual had reported the earnings to them. In my case, they would find that no earnings had been reported. But when the shit hit the fan, I would be somewhere deep in the heart of Latin America, maybe going jungle in the Amazon, and wouldn't care. It was truly living for present gratification and willing to pay the price later.

I wanted to travel feeling as financially secure as I could, so I put up signs around Berkeley offering my tax services, and after my day job, went to people's homes and did their taxes for them. I found it remarkable that some people would hire a tax accountant based on a note sticking to a tree or a supermarket bulletin board, although amongst our species there are undoubtedly those who would consult a doctor the same way, or even find a spouse if the price were right.

I was still in touch with Willie. He and Wendy, spurred by Don Church's arrest and heightened FBI questioning of neighbors, had decided to move to a less hot locality and wound up in a flat on Athol Avenue, just a couple of blocks from where I had been living. Willie and I came up with a scheme, also to do with taxes. I filed two phony tax returns, using the names and Social Security numbers on cards Willie and I had acquired. To each return I attached a W-2, with a real employer's name and federal ID number from cruise ship lines I had copied down at work. Each return called for a refund of about $300, hopefully sent out by the IRS before they verified the information, a practice they foolishly still followed at least until the late 1990s. The returns gave Willie's new address, where he once again was receiving mail under a small army of names. In his inimitable way, he'd find a way to cash the checks and we'd share the money.

No, I didn't think this was a revolutionary act, except to finance my trip to Chile to report on a real revolution. Willie probably told himself that it meant less money for the Defense Department and his father, or something even more grandiose. But I felt no guilt. Deceiving the IRS was as American as apple pie, and no individual would feel the pain of a direct loss of money.

My plans were coming along fine, saving lots of money, studying Spanish, planning my route very carefully. One day in mid-March, Willie proposed that I accompany him and another guy, Paul R., on one of their adventures. Paul was visiting from St. Louis and had crashed on my living room sofa for a few days at one point. It bothered Willie that I had never taken part before, and I guess it must have bothered me a little too, because I agreed. But all I did was drive the two of them, at five in the morning, to a spot a block or so from Telegraph Avenue. I left them there in the cold and darkness and drove back to my warm bed and my "normal" life. I didn't know what their target was.

As the *San Francisco Chronicle* reported it: "A powerful pipe bomb exploded at 5:55 a.m. in front of the British Motor Car agency in Berkeley yesterday, shattering two showroom windows, severing the trunk of a pine tree, and showering several expensive autos with glass and debris."

The police were at a loss to explain the reason for the bombing. But a look at the calendar would have told them that it was St. Patrick's Day. The Irish and the British. Get it? Willie and Paul did. I was underwhelmed. Once again, Willie didn't send any communication to the press. He may have thought that the politics of his action were obvious enough, but in this case, whatever one thought about the British role in Northern Ireland, a store selling cars in Berkeley, California was too many layers of responsibility and logic removed.

Did this now make me a "bomber"? I didn't feel like one. And when I strolled over to the scene of the crime and saw the damage and the harried personnel of the showroom, I felt sorry for them. This was not the Pentagon or Dow Chemical.

The penultimate day of March. I've left the profession of tax accountant, for life. Jeff and I are both packing up to vacate the apartment. He, like a true career academic, is soon off to Madison for post-post doc-doc work. The next day I'll store my life's little belongings in my friend Nancy's garage, she being the only person I know that owns her own house and can reasonably be expected to be in the same place at least a year from now. At about five the following morning, the phone rings. I stumble out of bed to answer it and hear the voice of Willie. He's calling from the Berkeley Jail.

Two hours earlier, Willie, Paul, and Michael Bortin (also of Patty Hearst-fame-to-be) had gone to a garage in North Berkeley, which Willie rented to store various of his goodies. Unbeknownst to them, a strong odor of gasoline or something, emanating from the garage that afternoon, had resulted in the police being called, discovering the dubious goodies, and staking out the place. This being Berkeley, one of the neighbors had called KSAN to post an announcement that there was a police stakeout of 2575 LeConte Avenue, to warn an unknown comrade of a known danger. But Willie never got the word.

When the three young men arrived at the garage at three a.m. and entered it, they were suddenly bathed in bright lights—"We're armed!" cried the officers from outside. "Come out with your hands up!"

In addition to a quantity of printed material—bearing such folksy titles as "On Organizing Urban Guerrilla Units" and "Instructional Manual on Recoilless Rifles and Rocket Launchers"—the garage had contained rifles, shotguns, a machine gun, gas masks, blasting caps, sundry chemicals, fuses, pipes, ammunition, and explosives, including one device "ready to go," which the police detonated at a remote location, resulting in a reported "considerable hole in the earth."

Also discovered were layouts and photos of the Aspen, Colorado home of former Defense Secretary Robert McNamara. Willie had once showed these things to me and casually apprised me of a plan to kidnap the man whose hands were caked with the blood of the Vietnamese carnage. It seems that one of Willie's cohorts had smoked dope with McNamara's son at the Aspen house on one or more occasions, and had used the opportunity to case the joint. I didn't know how far, if at all, the plan had progressed since then, but certainly it was now all kaput.

When Willie told me of the plan, I think he was hoping I'd offer to take part. While I had no more regard for Robert S. McNamara than he had for the people of Vietnam, I told Willie that whatever the political ransom demand—like exchanging McNamara for Angela Davis and/or other political prisoners behind bars—the choice of kidnapee was ill-fated, if not out-and-out dumb. McNamara was no longer in office, his resale value had plummeted—Richard Nixon would sooner admit to a cross-dressing affair with J. Edgar Hoover than capitulate supinely to "terrorists" on behalf of a John F. Kennedy appointee. I suspected that McNamara was being targeted simply because the necessary information had fallen into Willie's hands, and it was too juicily opportune to waste. To pull the caper off would be BIZARRE! In any event, although I could—at least on one occasion—punch a plainclothes cop in the face, I was not cut out for this kind of stuff. Where and how would they keep McNamara? If their demands were not met, were they prepared to live with the man in his prison for weeks or months on end, and then perhaps "dispose" of him? Were they prepared to kill anyone else in his house who resisted? Their plan, I felt, had all the chance of success as a ground war against Russia in the wintertime.

Willie and his gang were not the Tupamaros. This was not Uruguay. And I was not crazy.

The trio—with Willie giving his name as William Harvey Barrows—were held on the usual shopping list of charges: possession of destructive devices, possession of components for destructive devices, possession of explosives, possession of a machine gun. . .

I despaired to think of the consequences had I been their chauffeur on that night instead of two weeks earlier. Papers found in the garage and in their car indicated that their target for the evening was probably the Naval ROTC office at the university. A much more appropriate target than British Motors, to be sure, although I wouldn't have liked to see the beautiful Berkeley campus disfigured. It was very ironic. For once Willie had prepared a "communique" to be sent to the media, and he was caught with it.

I clearly had ambivalent feelings about this revolutionary custom of planting things that go boom in the night. Many people in the movement were unambiguously against it, insisting that it distracted drastically from any other message, while tarring us all with the "crazies" or "terrorists" brush. This was not, they argued, the way to win the hearts and minds of Americans.

But there was a simplicity to such an equation that drove every other consideration into the ground. I was concerned also about my *own* heart and mind. The infinite ability of the *powers-that-be* to be casually cruel and proudly stupid routinely left me with the feeling that the world had gone on perhaps a year or two too long. These leaders of the "democracy" in which I lived had a structure of power many dictators might envy. "In America," writer Paul Goodman observed, "you can say anything you want, as long as it doesn't have any effect."

Vietnam was now in its second decade. I and the rest of the army of the powerless needed a few points up there on the scoreboard against the lords of the national-security corporate state. A bombing—with suitably diabolic target and enlightening publicity—told the bastards that we were still out there, that their immunity was not total. Armed propaganda. It told the public that there was something more serious going on than a town-hall difference of opinion that could be reasonably resolved by reasonable people discussing things in a reasonable manner. Like an unhappy child having a temper tantrum, we needed some instant gratification.

On the phone, Willie told me simply that he had been arrested and that I should call his "girlfriend." I quickly threw some clothing on and went out into the cold night. I knew that even if the police knew what number Willie had just called, they couldn't instantly set up a tap on my phone to learn what number I was about to call. But I was taking no chances, a precaution that in the long run may have saved me a lot of grief.

A couple of blocks away, at a pay phone, I called Wendy, and changed her life forever.

Willie had given a false address as well as false name, and the police didn't actually know where he and Wendy were currently living. But it couldn't be too long before they found their way to the Athol Avenue apartment to arrest Wendy—at least two of the weapons found were in her name, the car was in either her name or her father's, and the police could have little doubt that she was the "young Oriental woman named 'Anne Wong'" who had rented the garage. Within hours of Willie's arrest, police converged on several residences in North Oakland where Wendy or her friends had lived, or were still living. One young woman was taken into custody.

That morning, groggy with sleeplessness, I and some other friends of Willie and Michael Bortin met with an attorney to try and line up a defense for them, a task—given the contents of the garage and car—that might well have given pause to O. J. Simpson's legal team aided by Clarence Darrow in his prime. Afterwards, I drove to Wendy's apartment to help her get rid of everything not suitable for the eyes of children or police officers. As we listened with ear and nerve for the arrival of the police, she filled a couple of suitcases with the life she was taking leave of, giving me a gun to hold onto.

I drove her to the home of Sam Goldberg, his wife and child. Sam, an Olympic-level track star, had achieved his greatest fame when, at halftime of a UC football game, he had run out onto the field waving aloft a large Vietcong flag. Chased by members of the UC Marching Band and others, he circled most of the field before being captured. Sam would be a way station on Wendy's underground railway.

I could not stay. I was to leave for Chile in a couple of days, and had to be all moved out of my apartment in a few hours. Wendy and I embraced good-bye. Her brave side was doing its best, but what could be more unnerving than to be suddenly ripped from a life you've carefully sculptured, your comfortable daily routine, and flung into a tornado of unknowns? Could she as much as call in to her commercial art job and tell them she would not be coming in to work that day, or any other day? They'd have to read about it in the newspaper. So would her parents in Fresno. Where and when would we meet again? Before that was to happen, her name was to bleep non-stop across media radar because of her being arrested together with Patty Hearst, and she would achieve modern civilization's highest cultural achievement—celebrity.

I think I felt more sorry for Wendy at this moment than I did for Willie, a survivor of the first order. He probably saw his arrest as a medal of honor and was having spirited discussions with his jailers, laughing out loud at their "bizarre" attitudes. It was to be a long time before I was able to visit him.

Was my trip in jeopardy? I had too many ties to this whole scenario and its actors, in addition to Willie calling me from jail. Were there things in the garage with my name on it, perhaps my short story about bombing the Pentagon? I wasn't so much afraid of being arrested, as of being ordered to stay put for months as a material witness, or whatever the correct legal terminology is. I rushed to finish my packing, after wrapping the gun in a plastic bag and burying it in the soil alongside the house. I didn't want to be surprised by a police visit with that little plaything lying around, particularly after taking my first good look at it and realizing that it had a silencer attached, a great big legal no-no.

And what would the police have thought upon finding me packing?

"Were you planning on going somewhere, Mr. Blum?"

"Yes, as a matter of fact, to South America. But it has nothing to do with what's happened. I assure you it was planned months ago."

"Oh? May I inquire as to when you made your plane reservation?"

"Well, I'm not actually flying there. I'm going by land."

"Oh? Well since you're going such a long way anyway, perhaps you wouldn't mind adding one more little stop on the way, down at our station."

What awaited me, I was certain, was being put through a great deal of unpleasant interrogation, minute examination of my belongings and papers, and several other varieties of official shit. I was glad for Jeff's sake that he had already left.

After storing a dozen or so boxes of my things, half of them books, at Nancy's, I settled into her house for my last day before the first leg of my trip, a car ride to San Diego. The next morning I borrowed her car again and drove over to my house on Parker Street. I stole glances at the parked cars I passed, looking for your basic men in dark suits just sitting there in the middle of the day for no apparent reason; or perhaps an FBI agent studiously pretending to read his Agent's Manual on how to look natural reading a book in public. Then I saw a police car parked directly in front of my old house. I kept on going.

It was only to retrieve the gun that I had gone back. I returned again in the evening and had to squeeze slowly by a police car that was double parked. My heart was pounding as I came within a couple of inches of the copmobile, being forced to turn my head away at the same time. If I had hit the car, imagine the expression on the officer's face as he read the name on my driver's license. I didn't know whether they were carrying a photo of me with them.

Tomorrow was departure, so that was it. The gun itself was not important to me, but I had no idea of the story behind it. (I forget now whether I had wiped off my fingerprints.) Well, the gun, hopefully, could wait for my return, along with the unemployment fraud. I was behaving like I had received official immunity from everything as long as I was in South America. I was only sorry that I hadn't given the gun a proper long-term burial. As it was, the first heavy rain might well expose it.

That was it also for the tax refund scam. The checks were due to arrive at Willie's house any day now I figured; they might already be sitting in his mailbox. I could picture some unsung IRS civil servant looking at the returned checks and wondering about all these people just so careless about their money.

CHAPTER THIRTEEN
TEN THOUSAND MILES
OVERLAND THROUGH
LATIN AMERICA

Willie was a jailbird, Wendy was a fugitive bird, and I, free as the proverbial bird, left for Chile early in April, $1600 in cash and traveler's checks stuck deep down in a zipped-up pocket, hopefully secure against the South American badlands of Yankee mythology. I carried one large suitcase and one smaller canvas bag, each filled to uncomfortable heaviness, but I shunned wearing a backpack. An old olive green army-type jacket I had inherited from somewhere, jeans, clodhopper hiking shoes—all okay—but a backpack did not make my self-image happy; it had "youth" or "student" or "hippie" stamped all over it, or maybe "old eccentric birdwatcher;" funny where we draw our lines.

The next day my ride took me to San Diego and put me up for the night. In the morning I took a bus to the Mexican border, which I crossed by foot and then into Tijuana, straight to the first place I could sit down and put down my luggage. Already tired, and more than 7,000 miles to go, more than coast to coast in the U.S. and all the way back again.

Tijuana is often disparaged as being too Americanized, but I instantly felt like I was in a different world. This was going to be good. A few days in Cuba 14 years earlier, and three weeks in Europe a decade ago—that was the logbook of my world travels. I now had all the time in the world. The revolution in Chile would wait for me.

Or would it? During the past year and a half, enough of the real world had leaked through the official Washington mask to make it plain that the United States of America, Superpower, was not happy with what the people of the land of Chile, population ten million, had freely voted for. But even without any leaks, to all those not born yesterday the American threat to the Allende government was a natural fact of imperialist life. A successful socialist society would set an example for the Third World that Washington could not tolerate. I actually was afraid a military coup would occur before I got there, and avidly looked for news about Chile in the press of each country I passed through.

Nonetheless, I was determined to proceed at a nice, leisurely pace, spending more than a week en route to Mexico City, staying for a few days in Guadalajara at the home of an American woman I knew from Berkeley. Marilyn Pursley was a former member of the Communist Party USA, and at an art exhibition of an expatriate American she introduced me to five or six other expatriates, CPers and fellow travelers who had flocked abroad in the 50s after McCarthyism had either ruined their careers or otherwise made life in America intolerable.

These CP types in Mexico, like the many I had met in the States, and like the many more I was to meet in other countries. . . it was richly ironic when one thinks of the indoctrination long drilled into the American mind. . . these CPers typically were, and are, so mild in their political expression: liberals, social democrats, unMarxist socialists, unmilitant, peaceniks; often advocating hardly anything more revolutionary or violent than the idea that if only people were kinder to each other, if only the corporations were more considerate of their employees' needs, if only nations would seek peaceful solutions to conflict, if only we could elect more Democrats, the world would be so much nicer. I had come a long way since being shocked at encountering Arnie the Bolshevik. I wonder if J. Edgar Hoover had ever had a real and relaxed conversation with a current, card-carrying Communist. He would have convinced himself that the fucking commie's moderation was no more than a false front.

While I was in Mexico, J. Edgar finally revealed that he did, after all, have something in common with the rest of humanity. He died. They must have been partying in Berkeley.

Mexico City, one of the world's grand metropolises, can not fail to impress. But to go along with the incomparable Museum of Archaeology and the Boulevard of the [so-called] Revolution, are the Chiclet families; women sitting on the ground in the midst of fashionable commercial neighborhoods selling Chiclets to maintain respiration for another 24 hours, young daughters at their side, their unstimulated minds preparing them for their future occupation. The street is their only school, death their only doctor. All the livelong day, these children of god camping on the pavement, selling their little boxes of Chiclets. What do mother and daughter eat? Where do they go to the bathroom? What awaits them at whatever it is they call home? Place the daughter in a different environment before the cast hardens around and inside the head, as was the good fortune of young Benito Juarez, and what would you get? Maybe another President Benito Juarez.

My entrance to Guatemala was as deceptively tranquil and beautiful as walking through the idyllic woods before coming upon Buchenwald might have been to a wanderer three decades earlier. Lake Atitlan, set in the mountains, is usually the gringo's initial port of call. As I sat by the lake shore contemplating the postcard-perfect picture and my gringo navel, if someone had asked me whether I knew that I was in a brutal police state, after a moment's thought I would have nodded my gringo head. But no one asked me.

On a hike up the mountain the next morning, I encountered a solitary young man, clearly a full-blooded *indígena*. He was carrying a heavy sack over his shoulder, filled with his pathetic little produce, struggling up the long, steep road to the next village. When I offered him one of the rolls I had brought with me for my breakfast, he unburdened himself of his sack and sat down on a large rock, opposite me perched on my own rock. Much to my pleasure, we began a simple conversation, in what was a second language for both of us—Spanish. After a month in Mexico I had passed the stage of preparing entire sentences in my mind before uttering them. I could now begin a sentence reasonably confident that the proper words would reach my tongue when needed.

I gazed upon my breakfast partner with some of the wonder I would have felt upon encountering an alien. Here was a fellow creature who knew no other life, perhaps yearned for no other. His manner and expression made me think that he rarely encountered the likes of me. Or did his deference derive from having encountered too many of my ilk, like the soldiers and police who brutalized and killed his people to keep them from aiding the scrabbly, hopelessly outmanned band of desperate men who passed for guerrilla fighters? He perhaps didn't dare decline my attention. Nor might his empty stomach have the courage to refuse the roll.

Guerrilla recruitment amongst the Indian peasants was in fact painfully slow and difficult. People so preoccupied with a daily struggle to stay alive are compelled to devote almost all their energy to that end, fearing to risk even the virtual nothing they have; people so downtrodden hardly think they even have the right to resist.

Guatemala City, the capital, does not have an abundance of charm, not at all in the same league as Mexico City. No city I would encounter on my trip was. But I still treasured each day there for all the foreignness that surrounded me.

This included the regular appearance of jeeps filled with soldiers rolling through the crowded streets, a soldier no more than 17 with a machine gun lying across his lap, the barrel facing toward the sidewalk pedestrians, his finger within an inch of the trigger. If this teenager were asked: "Who is the enemy, and why?" his answer would be of interest only as part of a study of political indoctrination.

My first stop, after finding a *pension,* was a medical clinic, where I received the third in a series of three inoculations I had begun in Berkeley against typhus and typhoid. The room at the clinic did not look properly hygienic, the nurse wore a filthy apron, and within hours I thought I was at death's door with my finger on the bell. Whatever the medical explanation, I lay in my bed at the *pension* for nearly two full days, writhing in the grip of a spinning head and fevered and aching body, willing to bear the anguish of raising myself from the bed only when nature adamantly insisted. Repeatedly, the scenario played across my inner screen: He died in Guatemala City? Is that in Guatemala? At age 39? What was he doing in Guatemala City? All alone? In some tiny fleabag room? Why wasn't he at work in the United States at corporate headquarters? Or at home with his wife and kids? How did he die? What do you mean, no one knows?

In Mexico I had also had visions of an early departure from this plane of existence, while ruing my disbelief in reincarnation. Several times I was afflicted with major-league diarrhea and vomiting, actually falling to the street almost unconscious at one point, and spending 24 hours in bed. I finally figured out it was the milk. The idea that milk should be kept refrigerated had not yet made its way south of the border. Or, like so much else, refrigeration was a luxury which the places I patronized could not indulge in. During my entire stay in Latin America, I never again had a glass of milk with my breakfast, and learned to drink coffee black, a habit that became permanent.

I sent my first story back to Alternative Features Service after interviewing one Livio Gomez, a law student and former head of *Unificación Democratica,* a socialist student group. In Spanish and in English, he and two of his friends described life in Guatemala for me: You haven't seen a close friend for a couple of days. He's not at his home. His family doesn't know where he is. Because he's done some labor organizing, or been a student activist, or worked with the peasants, you check with the police. If you, and your friend, are lucky, he's been beaten up by the military and is in a cell for a while musing over his "lesson." More likely, the police tell you they have no idea where he is. And that's it. You never see him again.

Gomez and his friends pressed upon me a number of copies of their newsletter, urging me to distribute them in my further travels and amongst friends in the States. This I promised to do, though fully conscious of the futility of their little journal, or my little article, influencing the terrible facts of life in Guatemala. But like them, I could not do nothing.

"My" government—which could start or stop a coup in Latin America with a frown—could easily change the situation, which it had created 18 years earlier by overthrowing a democratically elected and benevolent government. But this it would not do. I wonder if Livio Gomez became one of the *desaparecidos*. I hope his torture was not terribly prolonged.

On a long bus trip to the marvelous jungle and Mayan ruins in Tikal, in the north of Guatemala, my seating partner was another Californian, a school dean from the Palo Alto area. (I don't remember his name, but let's call him Izzie in honor of my father, to whom neither I nor anyone else ever paid any honor of any kind.) At one point the bus was stopped by an army patrol, which came aboard and announced that it was checking papers and passports. "Oh shit!" I exclaimed to Izzie. "I left my passport at my pension. I didn't think I'd need it inside the country." And I had a copy of the very "subversive" newsletter with me. As a soldier approached us, good ol' Izzie got up from his aisle seat, purposely blocking the soldier's view of me, as I sank deep into my seat. As ridiculous a tactic as this may sound, it worked. The soldier looked at Izzie's passport and never glanced behind him. An elite special forces, military intelligence, ranger commando he was not; just another wretched Indian peasant dragged from his people to help repress them; he probably could hardly read a word of the passport. If only he and all the other soldiers like him would join forces, turn to their officers and shout *Basta ya!* (Enough already!). It would be so simple. Without them their superiors were sheltered by a house of cards. But then the United States would send in genuine elite special forces, military intelligence, ranger commandos—as many as needed—and squash the revolt.

Before reaching Tikal—where monkeys swing through the trees above as you stand in awe of ancient giant pyramids—Izzie and I stopped for a couple of days in the town of Flores. Izzie had been there before. Some people know their way around Paris or Buenos Aires. Izzie knew his way around Flores, Guatemala. We wound up visiting a family who lived in a cave. I stood in the cave in the one area that an adult could stand fully erect, looking at the pots and pans hanging from the walls of rock, a small wooden bench or two, the parents with two or three children, and I wondered what century I was in, or what age. Some poet somewhere would be inspired to compose an ode to the indomitable human spirit and its sublime adaptability. Those were not my thoughts.

Similarly in the next country I came upon, El Salvador. In the heart of what passed for downtown in the capital city of San Salvador, I saw a sight that has remained vivid for me all these years. . . early evening, in front of a bank, stretching from one corner to the next, the homeless are preparing their beds for the night, dozens of them; a family, with a naked young child moving his bowels in the street, the father using a page from a newspaper he's picked off the ground to tenderly clean his child's behind. The child, I'm sure, didn't think that it was doing anything unusual or abnormal. But I wondered to what extent the father knew that this was not the way people are supposed to live.

Despite my uncompromising remarks above about Washington's policies in Latin America, the fact is that at this time in 1972 this attitude of mine was not yet set in cement. I still had not arrived at the understanding that the foreign policy of my government literally did not have any moral factor built into its DNA; that it was invariably more at home with a laissez-faire military dictator than with a leader concerned about his people's welfare; that to a CIA officer a specialist in torture was much more one of the good ol' boys to be cultivated than was an idealistic human rights advocate. And—most difficult for me to grasp at this time—that there was nothing one could say to an American policymaker to yank him from this frame of mind. If he actually came around to your thinking, he'd have to quit his job, or be fired, whichever came first.

Many later events and much research were to harden me. As one example: There were indeed many people in El Salvador who did not for a moment think that the father-son story above was the way people were supposed to live. And throughout the 1970s, they tried to effect change by working within the system. They won elections, but were fraudulently denied any real power, and when they took to the public squares to protest, they were shot down *en masse*. When the inevitable happened, and they picked up the gun in 1980, good ol' Uncle Sam was there to provide the Salvadoran government billions (sic) of dollars of firepower, airpower, training for its forces, and American military specialists to make sure that the children shat on the sidewalks, and not on American multinational corporations.

It will not have passed unnoticed to the reader that I was not raised in leisurely splendor. Yet, I was virtually a stranger to "roughing it." My time had now come. There was, to begin with, the buses. The intercity ones in Mexico were modern, the busses in Central America had arrived, I believe, either with Cortez or Columbus. From the Mexican border to Panama City, I was subjected to repeated 10 or 12 hour rides over scarcely paved roller coaster roads. I was faced usually with the choice of keeping my window open and winding up literally covered with sand, or closing it and boiling to death. I partook of both delights, while my stomach and other organs experienced a shaking and rattling that three million years of human evolution had not prepared them for. Unfortunately, this did not fully dampen my appetite, for Howard Johnsons were very few and far between. When I was not queasy from the shaking and the heat, I was faint from hunger and thirst. Eventually, my stomach learned to narrow itself, while my bladder learned to expand.

It was the thirst that was the worst. When I finally reached my destination,

I would gulp down half a dozen bottles of terrible Inca Cola within minutes, with the feverish intensity of a man who had just crawled in from the Sahara.

My next great bodily need was a shower to remove the pile of sand fused to my perspired hair, face and arms. This could be difficult. Though I was eating well enough when not on a bus ride, I was saving my money by staying at minus-five-star *pensiones*, which cost me about a dollar a day on the average. This sometimes turned out to mean no shower or bathtub, sometimes no running water at all. On several occasions, I had to move my bowels on top of an already-formed pile. I learned to carry my own toilet paper.

At times in my bed I had to contend with multi-legged creatures as long as two inches, or sleeping on one side of the bed because rain was dripping in on the other; while in a room in Panama City I was up half the night listening to something that was alive, gnawing its way under the floorboard beneath my bed. To add a flourish to this charming tableau, in Costa Rica I came down with a case of gonorrhea, courtesy of a prostitute. Luckily it was there, the only passably developed country in Central America.

My traveling companions on the bus trips from hell were predominantly that variety of the species that never seems to leave history's stage, more numerous today than during feudalism—your basic impoverished, illiterate peasant; always a large new contingent waiting at the next bus stop, the next town, or the next country, their backs forever arched under the weight of oversized sacks filled to bursting with all manner of goods, dead and alive. More than once my seating companion held a live chicken on his lap, one time a pig, as docile as their human masters, perhaps because they expected as little from life.

I never became accustomed to seeing these beaten little people, with their gaping missing teeth, standing in silence for hours in the sweltering bus, or sitting hour after hour without reading anything and scarcely any conversation. I did not know then, and do not know now, what it feels like to have a mind that does not require continual stimulation. This has to be conditioned exceedingly early, perhaps beginning with the absence of a rattle. The peasant and his lot have not noticeably evolved over the centuries; scarcely less superstitious and religious, able to bear this life only because of the promise of an afterlife of eternal bliss, encouraged by the Catholic Church to believe this as the Vatican's contribution to squelching revolt against the blessed status quo.

There are those—Noblesavageists, et al—who would argue that I'm being racist, that these peasants may well have the proverbial "rich inner life" that fortifies and occupies them. I'd like to think that was true, for their sake and to relieve my own discomfort when observing them, but I don't have the means at hand to investigate either this hypothesis or my own.

As I crossed the Honduran border into Nicaragua, the customs official decided to single me out, as customs officials since the glory days of the Roman Empire have been singling people out, employing a selection process totally occult to the rest of humanity. This particular mystic decided that my luggage needed a thorough examination. It must be kept in mind that this was during the reign of Anastasio Somoza II, heir to the Somoza clan's 36-year dictatorial dynasty, valued clients and servants of Washington's ceaseless war against "communism."

The customs agent exhibited special interest in my books. One by one he picked them up and announced out loud the key word of each title: "Chile!"... "Allende!"..."Socialismo!"..."Cuba!"..."Castro!"... I wondered whether I'd be sent back to Honduras, or even held in custody, and there was no way to continue my journey by land without passing through Nicaragua, sandwiched between the Atlantic and the Pacific. But then, one by one, the same man put all the books back in my luggage, gave me a nod, and waived me on. Even small men in small jobs need to feel the surge that comes with exercising power. Because they can.

Only a few weeks earlier, Nicaragua had been hit by a major earthquake. Managua looked awful, but after a few days there I began to realize that even before the earthquake there wouldn't have been much reason to open your eyes in the morning. It was easily the ugliest capital city I had been in, or, as it turned out, was going to be in. The presidential palace, rather unimpressive as such edifices go, sat on top of a hill in the center of the city, surrounded on all sides by drabness and decay—lower-class drabness and decay, and middle-class drabness and decay. I was ignorant of it at the time, but the Sandinista National Liberation Front was already in existence. In 1979 they would finally overthrow Somoza and his despotic, impoverishing rule. Then they only had to deal with Uncle Sam. And lost.

Before I left on my trip, one of my main concerns had been that I would suffer from loneliness—all those months, all those miles, all those Spanish-speaking people, all by my solitary self. But this fear proved entirely unfounded. In each new town or city, fitted with map and guidebook, I would just walk and walk and walk, glad that I was alone, for I could linger for as long or as short as I wanted at any place. At the Panama Canal, I stopped in front of a wall on which was inscribed a long history of the canal. For more than half an hour I stood there translating it word for word with the help of my dictionary—noting how it made no mention of the United States's infamous role in inducing Panama to secede from Colombia—with no one to crow at me: "Bill, are y'gonna stay there all day? I'm getting hungry!" It's well established, is it not, that long trips can be an acid test for couples or friends.

I also kept bumping into the same travelers again and again, North Americans and Europeans, most of them headed for Chile. We would greet each other like old friends, exchange traveling tips, and discuss the latest news about Chile we had heard or read. We were a privileged group; our workaday worries and legal entanglements had been left unpacked in California or Toronto, Zurich or Amsterdam.

In Mexico I had gone to a bullfight for the first time in my life. Without any preformed opinion, I was sufficiently turned off by the cruelty to the dumb beasts so that it was also the last time. And ditto in Panama City where I went to a cock fight. I've also gone hunting and fishing each exactly one time in my life. The idea of digging a metal hook into the flesh of a fish's mouth and tugging and twisting it was even worse, since I was not just a spectator, but rather the perpetrator. Contradiction that some may see it as, this is no impediment to my love of eating dead animals.

After a month in Central America I was anxious to maintain my plan of reaching Chile by land only, but the Pan American highway ran smack into the Darién Gap, about 90 miles of jungle between Panama and Colombia. I inquired about a boat—at least it would be "surface" travel only—but the only ones I could discover were scarcely more than rowboats, each operated by individual "captains," no crew, only me and my luggage. I took one look at the boats, a second look at the captains, and I dug into my precious little budget for a one-hour airplane ride to Barranquilla, on Colombia's Caribbean coast.

The news reports I read and heard were not encouraging. The United States was imposing an economic blockade on Chile. Credit from American banks and international ones controlled by Washington was being choked off. At the same time, Nixon was requesting more military aid for Chile. What could conceivably be the purpose of that except to woo the military to take action against the government? And Allende was caught between the devil and the deep blue sea, reluctant to refuse this "assistance" for fear of antagonizing the military leaders.

As I write this, more than a quarter of a century down the road, civil wars, drug wars, and the inexorable steamroller of globalized, privatized, unregulated economies have left the period of my sojourn in Latin America looking like a Golden Age. Today, passing through lands of utterly desperate men, walking alone for miles burdened with heavy luggage, walking through city streets late at night, the most conspicuous of bearded sitting-duck gringo tourists, I fear that I would never make it alive to Chile. If I somehow made it as far as Colombia, that would certainly be the place from where my casket would be flown back to the States. Even in 1972, it was the one place travelers were constantly warned about, particularly about the pickpockets.

Sitting on a city bus I suddenly felt a hand in my pocket. I pushed it away, only to find it there again a minute later. I got up and walked to the center of the bus and stood there. I could hardly believe my eyes when the guy who was enamored of my pocket got up, walked over, and stood right next to me. He must be about to get off I told myself. In a moment I stopped telling myself that as I felt his hand in. . . yes, my pocket.

"Que hace?" I shouted at him as I drew away. All heads turned.

I got off at the next stop after making sure the obsessive-compulsive wasn't following me. Could it be that there was a subculture in Colombia which regarded picking the pockets of "rich" foreigners as a normal—even reputable—way to earn a living? As normal and reputable as drug trafficking was to become a decade later? Today, the Colombian pickpocket has a gun, and is part of a guerrilla movement, of the left or the right, looking to kidnap not your wallet but your entire body.

But at last I was in South America! And that meant the Andes. I had discovered in California something that I had never had an inkling of during my years on the East coast—I loved mountains.

On a bus ride from Colombia to Ecuador I feasted upon a scene of marble-like mountains, and only mountains, mountain within mountain within mountain, wall-to-wall mountain, nothing but mountain as far as the eye could see. And then the bus broke down, one of many times this happened on my trip. At least it was on a plateau, and the bus hadn't gone over the side as it went round one of the narrow mountain turns, a happening in Latin America not terribly uncommon.

As the driver worked on the bus, I walked a little ways from the other passengers, turned my back to them, and I was alone; looking around and down from the top of the world; just me and the mountains. I was transfixed. . . one of those moments when the intellect is stilled and the senses are the only things awake. Soon, a feeling of "this is enough" came over me. I needed nothing more in this world to feel happy and fulfilled.

The fact that I didn't feel anything of what I would call a religious dimension did not reduce the experience for me. Later, when I reflected upon it, I surmised that my unconscious had been in awe of the permanence of what my eyes were taking in compared to the transience of everything else: the mountains had been there a billion years before me, they would be there a billion years after me, and the world had been unplugged.

There are many who would call this "spiritual." Fine. Then it's a matter of semantics, and we might even have a dialogue, at least up to the point where they began to babble about "the pure rhythm of the essence of the universal life force energy. . ."

In Ecuador, I wound up in the town of Santo Domingo de Los Colorados, where some kind of civic celebration was taking place. I was thus fortuitously positioned to be able to witness what may have been the most pathetic parade since the 13th century Children's Crusade. Without military or floats, virtually without music or costume, a few poor souls would march by, followed a full minute or two later by a few more, perhaps one tooting on a flute, all grinning and waving to the crowd. Their moment in the sun—*gracias al Dios*—had arrived at last.

"One would have to have a heart of stone to read the death of Little Nell without laughing," observed Oscar Wilde. Not for the first time on my trip did I view so many of the natives as droll little children. But that's what incurable poverty can beget—an utter dependency on, and fear of, *el patrón* that mimics a child and his authoritarian father.

The region's aboriginal Indians, *los colorados,* had come to town with their traditionally painted hair—not dyed hair, mind you, but painted, with a thick mat of red paint. I wondered how they ever got the stuff off when they wanted to do so. Some of their women would pose bare breasted for a fee. God knows how that quaint little custom began, and how the women really felt about it, but there they were, bare from the waist up, sometimes smiling, men (who else?) clicking away with their cameras.

As July broke and I crossed the border into Peru, the news from Chile was another dose of bleakness. Railway and bus employees were on strike, paralyzing public services throughout the country. I was confused. Why should such lowly workers be throwing a monkey wrench into the operation of a socialist government? A few days later, the Chilean Congress, controlled by the opposition, again blocked some of Allende's socialist program and were trying to impeach several members of his cabinet. There was talk of impeaching Allende himself. That would take two-thirds of the Congress, a majority the opposition didn't have.

I was again—still—most anxious to get there, as if somehow the worst could not take place if I were bodily present in the land. But first I had some serious tourism at hand. This, after all, was Peru, the fabled land of the Incas.

I traveled down the coast, spending more than a week stopping at some towns on the way to Lima. My most enduring memory of those places is the relative darkness of the streets after sunset, presumably due to the cost of maintaining a system of bright lighting. I wondered if the people there who had never lived elsewhere imagined that this was the way cities were all over the world, even New York. But to me it was eerie and unreal, even disorienting; dark corners everywhere, harboring who knew what. Yet it seemed like many of the citizens were outside in the evening, strolling about carefree, chatting away noisily, eating ice cream. The ice cream might have been dinner for some of them, and most were probably outside to escape the heat and crowded confines of their dwellings, but after all the unmitigated poverty I had seen it was nice to see the "peasants" enjoying some of life's little pleasures. The Peruvian rich, I imagined, looking upon such a scene, would use it to convince themselves that the so-called poor were coping rather well and didn't really need the succor that bleeding-heart liberals were demanding for them.

In Peru, as elsewhere on my journey, the hills and lakesides were typically inhabited by the poor, most ironic in light of the North American pattern of such picturesque locations being eagerly sought after by the wealthy for their homes and playgrounds. The explanation may have something to do with the Latin American attitude toward private ownership of such public spots of nature.

Lima's old town offered a welcome return to a charming colonial setting. Like in most of the cities and towns I had passed through, there was a large central plaza—as usual, called Plaza de Armas—an open circular park with lots of wrought iron benches under large shady trees, interspersed with monuments and floral pots, and surrounded by impressive colonnaded government buildings and an old stately church. Is there any American city which could not benefit from such? Nearby was the building which had housed the local rendition of the Spanish Inquisition. I was enthralled by the torture racks and other devices designed to elicit confessions from those who, in some way, had not fully embraced conventional wisdom. (I was certain that the CIA was responsible for the whole setup.)

On the way to the tourist meccas, Cuzco and Machu Picchu, I spent a few days in the Andean city of Ayucucho, where I contacted the brother of a Peruvian woman whose taxes I had done in Berkeley. He was a teacher of English at the local Universidad de Huamanga, with a surprisingly poor command of the English language. After dinner with him and his wife, I complied, reluctantly, with his request to record a tape so his students could hear what a "New York accent" sounded like. Mine was nowhere as pronounced as, say, Art Buchwald's, but I was still rather sensitive about it, both for aesthetic and pigeonholing reasons.

I have no idea if my host was aware of what I certainly wasn't, that at his university at this very time the first secret cells of *Sendero Luminoso* (Shining Path) were being organized, guerrilla by guerrilla, to burst upon Peru in 1980. Throughout the '80s and most of the '90s, *Sendero* fought the usual hopeless battle, in behalf of the usual desperate people, against the usual despotic government, which was supported by the usual U.S. military machine. I would presently be in a country where—miracle of miracles—a different historical scenario was being played out.

CHAPTER FOURTEEN
THE CHILEAN SOCIALIST
EXPERIMENT

On the first day of August, 1972 I stepped foot in one of the most polarized places in the world. I was 25 pounds and $900 lighter than when I left California four months earlier. Before the day was over, I was listening to a crowd of people in the Plaza de Armas in the city of Arica arguing heatedly about the Allende government's programs. My Spanish by this time was halfway decent, but there was no way I could break into that give-and-take crackling static of shouts and interruptions. I just listened, and felt like I was present at history.

By the time I reached the capital city of Santiago about a week later, I had come to appreciate that the press was every bit as polarized. In sharp contradiction to what U.S. conservatives at the time would have had the world believe—that Allende, like all "communists" was strangling freedom of the press—the press in Chile was uninhibited to the point of burlesque. Although the conservatives controlled about 80 percent of the media, every stopping point on the political spectrum, from the far right to the far left, had its own national daily newspaper and weekly or monthly magazine, if not its own radio or TV station, a state of affairs the U.S. democratic process has never been introduced to.

The anti-government newspapers, dispensing with any semblance of nuance, featured daily scare headlines and stories which spread rumors about everything from nationalizations to bad meat and undrinkable water, or "The

Marxist Paradise Gives Us Gifts Of New Price Rises"..."Economic Chaos! Chile on the Brink of Doom!" was good for at least once a week..."Bloody Rightist Gangsters Seek To Destroy Chile!" screamed page one of a leftist daily... all in the largest type one could ever expect to see in a newspaper... rightist papers raised the specter of civil war, when not actually *calling* for it, literally... alarmist stories which anywhere else in the world would have been branded seditious... the worst of London's daily tabloids or the *National Enquirer* appear as staid as a journal of dentistry by comparison.

The only story able to push this headline lunacy off the front pages during my time in Chile was the crash of an airplane into the Andes in October, which wasn't found until December, amidst reports that the survivors had been reduced to eating the dead, a story later to be enshrined in several books and films, called *Survive!* and *Alive.*

Polarization and confrontation: Businessmen close their shops to protest government economic policy, the government claims that this further aggravates scarcities and sends the police to cut the locks, a shopowner dies from a heart attack in the process, the store closures expand nationwide in mourning and protest. Crowds form outside closed stores, employees protest their employer's action, other employers shout at these employees, everybody exchanges insults, the police wrap it all up indiscriminately with tear gas and water trucks.

High-school students shut down their school because the newly-appointed principal is a leftist, the leftist students forcibly evict them, the rightists claim that the leftists beheaded the school mascot dog in the process, a rightist newspaper headlines "Barbarous Marxists," the leftist papers have a field day showing photos of the dog with head in place alongside a collage of rightist headlines.

Daily marches, giant painted graffiti, unending political posters, leaving no rest for the eye; the left on one side of the street, the right on the other, both jumping up and down like cheer leaders, ridicule and slogans and songs fired back and forth, the left locks arms and charges the right, the right disperses, the left returns only to repeat their act, nary a blow is landed. More tear gas.

The police released tear gas so often in the central area of Santiago that even when none had been used for a few days it still hung distinctly in the air.

I did a double take one day when I came upon a rock-throwing clash between long-haired young people and construction workers. The longhairs— I figured out after a couple of minutes—were right wingers, the workers supporters of the government. I felt so angry at what I saw as privileged, snobbish brats ridiculing decent hard-working men, that I found myself wishing that the police would crack down hard on the young people, as well as all the other anti-government protestors, and not make any concessions to them. I realized, with some embarrassment, that this mimmicked how many Americans felt about me and other anti-Vietnam protestors, although we fought against police, not laborers. More importantly, each circumstance involved a vital issue, and the bottom line was which side were you on.

Not all was pose and rock throwing. There was a murder a week—former landholders shooting at campesinos working the land which had been idle before, rightists gunning down socialists in covert corners, or on parade.

Anywhere, in any situation—which side are you on?... stated or wondered, subtle or blunt, how far left? how far right?

I go to look at a room in a house advertised by a woman. Because I'm American she assumes that I'm anti-Allende, the same assumption she'd make if I were European, for she wants to believe that only "Indians," only poor dumb *indígenas* and their ilk, support the government. She is pleased by the prospect of an American living in her home and is concerned that he might be getting the wrong impression about her country. "All this chaos," she assures me, "it's not normal, it's not Chile." When I relieve her of her misconception about me she is visibly confused and hurt, and I'm a little uncomfortable as well, like I've betrayed her trust. I make my departure quickly.

I was soon a member in good standing of the international community. Much like a previous generation of leftists had gone to Spain in support of the Republic, we had come to Chile in response to the Socialist government, albeit without risking our lives in a war, or so we thought. I wondered if any of the foreigners were the children of Brigadistas.

An easy bond formed among us all, in many cases one that lasted for years after we had left Chile. Amongst our number were Marc Cooper of Los Angeles, Walden Bello of the Philippines, Hannes Frischknecht of Switzerland, Gary Crystal of Canada, Vince Santilli of northern California, Ignacio Sosa of Mexico City, Charles and Joyce Horman of New York, and the one person I knew beforehand: Frank Teruggi of Chicago and Berkeley, who had given me the idea to go to Chile. The many South American expatriates tended to hang out in their own communities. Most of them were political exiles from extremely repressive regimes in Brazil, Argentina, Uruguay, and elsewhere. For them, a socialist government in Chile was a godsend and lifesaver, literally.

The government was in the hands of the Unidad Popular (UP), a coalition composed of Allende's Socialist Party, the Communist Party, and three other parties. The Communist Party of Chile was the least revolutionary segment of the coalition, differing in this respect from other Communist Parties through-out the world only by virtue of the words "of Chile."

Those on the left, foreigners and Chileans alike, were not of one mind in their support of the UP. Sentiment and analysis ranged from uncritical support or the belief that we had to act and be as unified as possible in the face of the powerful conservative threat, to the conviction that the road Allende was pursuing did not represent steps along a straight-line path to socialism, but rather were merely changes within the capitalist system; that without complete nationalization of production and distribution, overall economic planning leading to the revolutionary transformation of Chilean society was impossible, and doomed to culminate in yet another "social democracy," content with peaceful coexistence with the bourgeoisie and putting a human face on capitalism. They felt that when Allende had taken power two years earlier, the right was most disarrayed, and that was the time to smash them and take full socialist power. Now the job was much tougher, they felt, especially since the government, in the intervening period, had discouraged independent mobilization and arming of the masses, while miseducating them with open appeals to put their trust in the institutions of the still-capitalist state and in the army and the police. In short, they felt that the government had failed to prepare its supporters politically and organizationally for the inevitable confrontation.

The inevitable confrontation. Everyone on the left and the right said it was—well, inevitable. Not the street clashes, rocks and curses, and the occasional murder, but military power, aiming for the extinction of the whole socialist experiment by armed force. Wiped out. *Finis.*

I would nod my agreement with the conventional wisdom that it was inevitable, at the same time thinking that surely the conservatives here and in the United States won't be that stupid and obvious, or cruel. They won't risk international condemnation of such a blatant usurpation of the democratic process. Apparently, yet one more nail was needed in the coffin of that young man who once yearned to be a Foreign Service Officer

It was because Allende was determined to act within the Chilean constitution that he could not leap frog to socialism. The Congress and the courts were in the hands of hidebound reactionaries, not to mention the police and army, all waiting for one false move by the UP to yell "Aha! You see? Communists have no respect for the law!" All the while plotting their bloody coup d'état.

The UP's accomplishments in two years in the face of such powerful obstacles were not inconsiderable: several nationalizations managed within existing law; significant increases in production by enterprises already under state control, ascribed to employee ownership under a socialist government; a landreform program that greatly trimmed the large estates of the landed gentry, turning the land over to peasant and state cooperatives, in the process releasing tens of thousands of agricultural workers from a semi-feudal state; reductions in unemployment and infant mortality to their lowest levels in Chile's history; a 50 percent increase in the minimum wage plus a general wage hike; and free milk distributed to infants, school children and pregnant women. Allende, who was a medical doctor, explained his free milk program by pointing out that

"Today in Chile there are over 600,000 children mentally retarded because they were not adequately nourished during the first eight months of their lives, because they did not receive the necessary proteins."[38]

There was, moreover, an ambitious program of housing construction which provided visitors like myself a moving experience upon entering some of the many slums that fringed Santiago. I walked along muddy lakes of "streets," past rows of depressing hovels that were home to families—boards thrown together, cardboard here and there, some sheets of tin on the better ones, whatever was lying around; running water, electricity, and proper sanitation were of course only a dream—the archetypal Latin American shantytown, which I had come upon in every country on my trip down. But suddenly I was confronted by dozens of small, modern apartment houses and two-family homes, newly built by the same slum dwellers for their own use, on land adjacent to their former shantytown, the builders learning valuable skills in the process. Each family had to pay ten percent of its annual income up to the point where it achieved full ownership.

The conservatives tried to sabotage these and other programs, and dampen public enthusiasm for the UP, in ways too numerous to detail here. Perhaps most telling of all were the scarcities—symbolized by the words "*No hay,*" "There isn't any"—the little daily annoyances when one can't get his favorite food, or cooking oil, or toilet paper, or the one part needed to make his TV or car run; or, worst of all, when a nicotine addict can't get a cigarette. The ways to create scarcities were without number, the money available for the purpose unlimited, even without the CIA chipping in.

In short, anything to wear down the patience of the people, to convince them that "socialism can't work in Chile," to instill in them a deep longing for a return to order, to "normalcy;" without demonstrations, police and soldiers patrolling the streets, curfews, tear gas and water hoses; without scarcities and interminable waiting lines; without fear and loathing. And all aimed at the congressional elections in March 1973 or the presidential election in 1976, or reaching a state of chaos where the military would feel "obliged" to step in and take over the reins of government.

I bought cigarettes on the black market. It was either that or (horror of horrors) stop smoking. Unlike most Chileans, I could afford to pay the inflated price because I also changed dollars for Chilean *escudos* on the black market, getting around ten times the official exchange rate. It bothered me to deprive the government of badly-needed foreign exchange, but it was either that or leave the country, for I had to put the bulk of my remaining dollars aside for my trip home.

The dollars were reportedly being bought up by rich Chileans who were planning their escape abroad when the communist menace arrived on their doorstep to eat their children; some of them could already hear the beast smacking its lips. So I could rationalize that I was helping to rid the country of some of the worst element—those who were opposed to the social changes no matter what benevolent effect they might have for most people.

The Americans lived rather well in Chile because of the black market. Marc Cooper and Gary Crystal resided in a three-bedroom apartment in the center of town for all of $25 a month. We could go to some of the finest restaurants in Santiago and enjoy a five-course meal, complete with lobster and very fine Chilean wine, for about 50 cents a person. In no time, the 25 pounds which had said goodbye to my body, came back home.

Marc, who wrote for the *Village Voice* and other publications, certainly made more than the $20 or $25 a story I was getting from Alternative Features Service, but I was thrilled at being paid for almost everything I sent them. I was in the right place at the right time. I also sold a couple of articles to Dispatch News Service of Washington, DC, the agency which, in 1969, broke the story on the My Lai massacre in Vietnam.

My ace-investigative-reporter news gathering system consisted of perusing several daily papers of various persuasions (my Spanish reading ability was by now almost "advanced"), visiting relevant government bureaus, touring agricultural cooperatives and copper mines, attending Allende's press conferences, being on the spot at as many demonstrations and street incidents as I could, walking around a lot and listening, and talking to the Chilean man and woman in the street, mostly on park benches.

I particularly sought out those opposed to the government, and was puzzled for awhile as to why they would so often assure me that they, too, were socialists. I finally came to understand that, unlike in the United States, the masses of Chileans had not been raised to instinctively equate "socialism" with the devil incarnate. They in fact associated it with having a social conscience, with being concerned about the underprivileged, and they didn't want to concede this aura of benevolence to the UP, although they might not—and usually didn't—have a clue as to the profound economic and social implications of socialist change. Having thus established their humanitarian credentials, they would then proceed to express all manner of illogical and irrelevant anti-UP arguments, or just wail "*No hay! No hay!,*" or simply insist that "Allende is going too fast." To which I would respond: "You mean, if he made the same changes, but only slower, you would support him?" To which they would invariably reply: "No," or freeze in silence.

One afternoon I called upon Marc and Gary and was surprised to find the door opened by a stranger, who told me to come in. I did so and came upon two other men I didn't know sitting with Gary around the living room table. I was told to sit down on the sofa. It was not a polite request, but a command. The three men were Argentineans and they were berating Gary, claiming that Marc had sold them counterfeit traveler's checks. Marc was away, leaving Gary in the position of denying the accusation and trying his best, in his less-than-fluent Spanish, to placate the men, one of whom had a gun he made it a point not to conceal.

This went on for some time, long enough for me to have some unhappy visions of the outcome. Finally, the Argentineans contented themselves with taking some goodies—a camera, tape recorder and such—in return for the money they said was owed them.

Perhaps because of this incident, as well as for "the inevitable confrontation," Marc somehow found a source for guns and convinced his friends that it was their revolutionary duty to be prepared. I thus became a gun owner for the first time in my life—a .22 caliber pistol as I recall, costing me about $15. Not long afterwards, I was at Marc's apartment when his American girlfriend Heather came in complaining about having been grossly insulted by a lewd Chilean outside the building. Marc and Gary immediately grabbed their guns and ran down the stairs, with me and Heather, gunless, in pursuit. I could scarcely believe that I was part of a gang of revolutionaries hell-bent on saving a lady's honor with bullets. Marc—short and a bit chubby, pugnacious and witty; a radical, Jewish Danny de Vito—spoke excellent Spanish and proceeded to give the Chilean guy a verbal tongue lashing. In the face of this armed and crazed mob, the guy's *machismo* quickly crumbled.

A closer call for me occurred one evening during one of the periodic curfews, instituted to cool down passions. Based on my press credentials I had obtained a pass which allowed me to be out after hours. Walking home around midnight from the apartment of Vince Santilli—a biology professor, formerly of the University of Buffalo, now the University of Chile, and one-time member of the Communist Party USA—I came upon a group of soldiers at a street corner. One of them said something to me as I approached, which I didn't make out, but I reached into my pocket to get my pass. With my hand still in my pocket and his rifle pointing directly at me, I realized what he had said in Spanish: "Raise your hands!" These words are of course being written here only because that young soldier had not yet been reduced to automaton.

Although fascinating because of the political dynamics, Santiago was not particularly charming. A hill stuck incongruously in the center of the city, with a marvelous ornate marble staircase leading up to the first plateau, was one of the few beauty spots and escapes from the noise, bus fumes, and congestion, as well as the countless street vendors hustling desperately to earn their family's meal that evening.

There was also an old monastery, set back from one of the main boulevards, which I would sometimes duck into to walk through the cool, quiet cloister and be immediately transported back to the 18th century, with Santiago completely shut out.

After a couple of months or so, I took a train trip south to the beautiful lake region with Walden Bello. Walden was working on his PHD at Princeton, and was later to become a well-known author and activist in the area of third-world development and globalization.

On trains, one meets people one seldom encounters on buses. Thus it was that in the dining car I found myself sitting opposite a Chilean woman who spoke perfect English, a gift from her Irish mother. We began talking about the lakes, the weather, her son studying journalism at the University of Wisconsin—polite talk we both knew was but a brief preliminary to the inevitable turn to politics, the subject that could not be avoided in Chile 1972.

Her appearance was wholly Caucasian, European, not a hint of Indian blood. Her salon coiffure and fashionable outfit completed the portrait and left me with little doubt as to which side she was on. But her cultivated manner and the absence of any language barrier promised an intelligent discussion, a rare phenomenon for me up to that point with conservatives (commonly referred to by the left as *los momios*, mummies).

In a moment, however, she sprung full-blown from a Marxist textbook on class warfare, complaining about her high taxes and the ruination of Chile by the UP.

"Why do you say that Chile is being ruined?" I ventured.

She looked at me as if I'd asked if she thought that the sun would rise in the morning. She didn't yet realize that I was one of THEM.

"Why, just look around!" she gasped. "Didn't you see in the first-class section there are three people sitting in two seats? I'm sure they all have friends in the government and haven't paid for those seats."

I didn't say anything, leaving her to imagine that I was pondering the wisdom and the significance of her remarks. The next moment she was into the "Socialism can't work in Chile because the people are ignorant, lazy and always drunk" routine. I thought of the several lushes who had said the same to me, barely able to get the words out.

"Why are they ignorant?" I asked. "Why have they been *kept* ignorant?"

This may have been the first time the question had been presented to her mind. She proceeded to turn the conversation to a different area without a trace of self-consciousness.

There's the classic Latin American story of the servant of a family of the oligarchy. He bought steak for his *patrón's* dog, but his own family ate scraps. He took the dog to the vet, but couldn't take his own children to a doctor. And complained not. In Chile now, those like my table companion had a terribly nagging fear that servants no longer knew their place.

Walden and I spent a couple of days on a farm at the invitation of a young woman he had met in Santiago. The first evening he and I and the family assembled in the back yard, where the father proceeded to hang a lamb from a tree by its legs, and then, much to my squeamish disgust, slit the animal's throat. With the poor beast still squealing, the father collected its blood in a bowl, added an ingredient or two, then passed it around. I only wet my lips while pretending to take a real swig. Lamb sacrifices were rare in my Brooklyn neighborhood. Giants fans were the victims of choice.

At one point in the evening, after a dinner of, yes, lamb, the father asked me what I was doing in Santiago. I replied: "*Soy periodista.*" (I'm a journalist.) His mouth fell open and he literally fell back a foot or two. It turned out that he thought I had said "*Soy socialista.*" I was sleeping in enemy territory.

Shortly after returning to Santiago, I became more certain of something I had only suspected earlier—I was being treated as if I were radioactive by a certain sub-group of the American colony, treated like a non-person in both social and political settings. I couldn't begin to imagine why. My ostracizers were half a dozen or so mainly Northern Californians whom Frank Teruggi hung around with.

Frank, short and slight of build, was a gentle soul, which is not to be confused with being naive. He called me and other men "brother," and today would be categorized as very politically correct. Back in Berkeley, he had had a passing knowledge of Willie Brandt and knew that I had lived with him. When I met Frank again in Chile, I told him of Willie's arrest. This, I eventually learned from Frank, was the source of my excommunication. He had made mention of Willie and Willie's favorite pastime to his friends—and it did what shouting the word "bomb" does at an airport.

Bill Blum was perhaps a "crazy," just the kind that the left in Chile didn't need and that the right would pounce upon with glee. I might go around planting bombs against conservative targets, tarring the UP with the "violent" brush, maybe even assassinate someone—who knows what a "crazy" might do, whether out of misplaced zeal or in the employment of the CIA?

It would of course have been nicer and fairer for me if the members of my jury had spoken to me about it before sticking a red "C" on my forehead. But putting myself in their shoes—what do you say to a "crazy"? He'd just deny any such intentions. Frank himself didn't know me all that well.

I was surely a veteran demonstrator, but I found some of the rallies in the center of Santiago very unnerving. Packed stuck in the midst of more than half a million people, crowds or brick walls as far as the eye could see in any direction, literally unable to move more than a few inches, if a stroke had suddenly hit me, my chin falling to my chest would have been the only indication. I was truly scared that a provocation—perhaps the sound of a single gunshot—would set off a panicked mob scene in which many people, like me, would be trampled to death. It is indeed surprising that the right wing didn't light such a fuse. They certainly wouldn't have been held back by moral considerations, having already shot at people marching in parades.

I was physically safer, but likely under observation, on January 20, 1973, when I and about a dozen other Americans paraded before the United States embassy. It was the day of Richard Nixon's second inauguration, and though the end of significant U.S. military involvement in Vietnam appeared to be imminent, our placards dealt primarily with the President's bloody record in Indochina. There was a certain added edge to be doing this in Chile because at some point in American history the guardians of the national image and defenders of the patriotic faith decreed that it was a greater sin for an American heathen to condemn the U.S. government in a foreign temple than in one at home. Witness one William Jefferson Clinton and all the flak he later received for having taken part in an anti-Vietnam protest while in England. (At the same time, however, it appears that young Bill was reporting to the CIA on his fellow activists, a story that his congressional and media critics found too painful and embarrassing to deal with, so they didn't.)

Another demonstration I remember with fondness was the protest against the American company, Kennecott Copper. Copper was Chile's export lifeblood, and in July 1971 its Congress had voted unanimously for nationalization of the industry. The UP subsequently moved to sharply limit compensation payments to Kennecott on the ground that over the years the multinational had reaped wildly excessive profits from its investment in Chile compared to what it had earned in other countries. In retaliation, Kennecott flexed its international legal muscles and succeeded in blocking payment to Chile for a shipment of copper to France. Thus it was that on a day in October 1972 our North American contingent marched over to join the assembled Chileans, carrying a large sign reading: "Norteamericanos Ayudamos [support] Chile Contra Kennecott." I will never forget how the face of a middle-aged Chilean woman lit up when she first spied us and read our sign. It was as if at that moment she knew that the revolution could not fail, that if even *Yanquis* could support the Unidad Popular against their own country, all was possible. In the years since the crushing of the revolution that woman's face has come back to me repeatedly, compelling me to wonder about her fate. Did she wind up rotting away in a prison? Was she executed? Even worse to contemplate: Was she tortured?

The congressional elections scheduled for March 4, 1973 were crucial. The

UP sought a majority in each of the two chambers to enable it to deal effectively with a host of economic and social issues, like agrarian reform, taxation, and the black market, the last being responsible for the bulk of the shortages (including cigarettes) and the oppressive waiting lines, which alienated so many Chileans from the government. The opposition Christian Democrats and the ultra-reactionary National Party hung their hopes on securing a two-thirds majority in each chamber, which would enable them to impeach Allende. Neither outcome was very probable. And there was still no "issue" separating the two sides capable of being resolved through dialogue, compromise, or any other artifact of civilization we like to think of as moving history. Most people saw it as a totally uncompromising fight to the death. Which is of course exactly how it turned out.

In the end, the Unidad Popular garnered a 44.1 percent plurality of the popular vote, a gain of more than seven percentage points over 1970, the first such gain in Chilean history for a government in power more than two years. The left was uplifted. The right devastated—getting rid of Allende through legal means appeared further out of reach then ever. In hindsight, it can be said that this was the last straw for the conservatives, the day that those who had not done so earlier washed their hands of the constitution.

I had been in Chile eight months, a year since I stepped foot in Mexico. It seemed like no big surprises were imminent, and walking the streets of Santiago had lost much of its novelty for me. I decided to return home, although I had nothing and no one special waiting for me, not even a place I could call "home." I had no pressing need to leave, other than maybe financial, but neither did I have a pressing need to stay. It was just time for another change of experience. . . I thought. . . Or so it seemed. . . I guess. Where would this all end? I was now 40 years old. When, oh when, was I going to make my old mother happy and settle down with a nice Jewish girl, children, and a regular job?

I actually had had a nice Jewish girlfriend in Santiago. Toya was her name, short for Victoria. I met her at one of Vince Santilli's frequent parties. She was a school psychologist, Chilean, but of European Jewish background. She spoke very little English and so our conversations were almost entirely in Spanish, which, although wonderful for my Español, frustrated me. My "real self" could never make his stage appearance. At my semi-fluent (at most) level, I could rarely be witty, or subtle, or profound, or smooth, or complex. Nor could I easily pick up the tints of lavender and blue and silver behind Toya's even grayness. After a dozen get-togethers, we didn't know each other awfully well. What we had going was smoking marijuana, followed by marvelous marijuana-enhanced sex. She said once that when the sex between a couple is good, the whole relationship is good. I don't hold that view. I think sex as a binding and bonding agent is highly overrated, certainly after the initial passion. The fact that Toya was not really a committed socialist, not quite a comrade, carried more weight with me than all the ecstasy.

CHAPTER FIFTEEN
CHAIN GANG, SOLEDAD
PRISON, AND *COUP D'ÉTAT*

Shortly after arriving back in Berkeley in May, following a month in New York and Washington, one of the first things I did was to call on Bill MacGilvray. I was taken aback, although not excessively so, to see Ol' Bill sitting in the same chair, in the same room, in the same house, doing exactly the same thing he was doing when I last saw him—reading a book. I didn't know if it was the same book or not.

One of the second things I did was to go to the police station to turn myself in. Oh yes, did I mention that while I was in Chile, a letter from the State of California was forwarded to me? I well knew the content of it before opening the envelope. They were asking me to explain the apparent contradiction between collecting unemployment and not reporting wages being earned simultaneously. I was informed that if I didn't respond by a certain date, long since passed, a warrant for my arrest would be issued. Logical. Fair.

But much to my surprise, the police treated me like—no sarcasm intended here. . . oh, maybe a little—a criminal! Instead of showing any gratitude—never mind admiration—for my voluntary surrender, they immediately arrested me and threw me in a cell for the night. The next morning, I and about six or seven other prisoners were all handcuffed to a long horizontal thing, and thus decked out, we had to march a couple of blocks through the streets of Berkeley from the jail to the courthouse. I and my fellow convicts kept our heads as far down as they could go, and I prayed (so to speak) that no one I knew, or would ever know, would see me. Didn't the fucking police own a fucking van? I didn't know about my chainmates, but it seemed to me that I, having turned myself in, should not have been regarded as a threat to escape. I had to remind myself that this was Berkeley 1973, not Mississippi 1933.

In court, after pleading guilty, I was fined $235, an amount a lot less than I had actually received in unemployment benefits, never mind penalty and interest. The accountant in me was very curious about how they had arrived at this figure, but something told me that I shouldn't ask.

At this time, however, surrendering $235 would have been fatal for my standard of living. Since arriving back in the States I had been living on small gifts from family, a payment of an old debt from a friend, and a fee still owed to me by Dispatch News Service in Washington, whose office I made it to just as they were closing up shop for good, and with just enough cash left to pay me the $65 I was owed.

The court gave me six months to pay the money.

I came to the conclusion that everyone should experience arrest at least once for its existential, political and social value: handcuffing, booking, fingerprinting, verbal abuse, humiliation, at least one night in jail, and the childish psychological games the police guards play with you—you make a simple request which the officer knows you're entitled to, but he refuses and walks away; half an hour later he's back and he complies, a tactic to demonstrate his seniority, as basic as a dog sniffing another's urine and covering it with his own.

There was no defense committee set up in my behalf, no rallies to "Free the Berkeley One!"

Soledad. . . in Spanish it's solitude, loneliness; in California it's a prison, some 150 miles southeast of San Francisco. The bus stops on highway 101 to allow the mothers, wives, children, and friends of the inmates to disembark and begin their walk. Set back from the highway almost half a mile, the prison stands in the absolute middle of nowhere in Monterey County, like a medieval fortress. I would not have been terribly surprised to see a moat and drawbridge.

Visiting Willie was my first time inside a prison; the jails I had been in, as visitor or inmate, were nothing of the sort. The prison imposed a way of life, a self-contained tight, little, scary world. As I made my way through the entrance process, each time I heard the sound of a heavy door slamming behind me, like a great brass ring thrown down on marble, I shuddered to think how it would be if I was actually confined there. I told myself I'd rather be dead.

But Willie was not even depressed. He still had his big life's-a-fucking-absurd-ironic-insane asylum laugh. Bizarre!

We sat in a large room where all visitors and inmates were meeting at the same time. No bars or windows separating people. A couple nearby were necking. Bizarre! Willie and I posed for a photo in front of a backdrop of trees and flowers. Bizarre! For inmates could not gaze upon any patch of the world from any window other than glimpsing some other part of the prison. Policethink: If they could see what the immediate surroundings were like, they could better plan and carry off an escape. Bizarre! The usual grain of rationality to it, but Bizarre!

On June 29 the inevitable confrontation became actual. A Chilean colonel led several hundred men and a few tanks in an attempt to seize the presidential palace, *La Moneda*. On this occasion, it was put down, quickly, by other armed forces. But the incident clearly could, and would, serve as a kind of dress rehearsal. Everyone was now waiting for the real thing.

I learned that my friend Frank Teruggi happened to be walking near *La Moneda* at the time and took a bullet in his foot. It was not a serious wound, but, as matters eventually turned out for Frank, this too was but a dress rehearsal.

I thought of the soldiers who blindly followed the colonel's command. What did they think they were doing, these sons of the poor? I had long thought that the only way to forestall the inevitable in Chile was for Allende to go before the soldiers—as many at a time as he could get to address, as often as he could push his way past shocked officers—and tell the soldiers, in no uncertain terms, that it was NOT a law of God or nature that they obey their officers under all circumstances, that the constitution came first, that programs for their poor families and old, destitute neighborhoods came before the wealthy who were egging the military on to a coup. This would perhaps have been unprecedented in history, and may have flopped miserably. But Salvador Allende had no better plan of action.

Two or three visits to Soledad earned me a visit from the FBI. I had never been amongst those many on the left who refused to speak to the FBI on principle. Willie had once told an agent at the door that he couldn't speak to him because they were not of the same race. "Why, what is your race?" asked the FBI man, perplexed. "The human race," replied Willie, shutting the door.

But I was too interested in the man and the process to say no. He and I sat in the living room of the beautiful, old Berkeley house on Dowling Place, where I was renting a room from the owners, Steve and Dulcy Brown, whom I had known in Washington. Steve, a physician, had founded the Washington Free Clinic, a much admired institution, which exists to this day.

The agent was interested primarily in the whereabouts of Wendy, Don Church and Kathleen Brooks. Of the latter two, I had not the slightest knowledge, but Willie was being kept informed about Wendy via some of his visitors, so I knew she was on the East Coast somewhere. I was also asked about Kathy Soliah, another of Willie's prison visitors, whom I had first met at Soledad and who gave me a lift back to the Bay Area. She and I had socialized a bit, and she, too, was to figure prominently in the Patty Hearst drama, still more than six months away from the headlines.

The FBI's visit had been thought out. The agent was in his late twenties, was dressed in jeans and T-shirt (sic), and informed me that in the '60s he had been an anti-war protestor at the University of Michigan. He further assured me at one point that he too had revolutionary leanings, although "not of the violent kind like Brandt."

I looked at him and listened to his words, and I was embarrassed that he would think me so stupid that he could thus win my confidence. But I didn't much doubt that he had been an anti-war protestor; as noted earlier, everyone and their cousin had jumped on that particular bandwagon.

He lingered on because he couldn't bring himself to leave without snaring a single juicy item of information for his report, and I finally told him that I had to go somewhere. I doubted very much that I had inadvertently revealed anything of importance.

As I watched him walk toward his car, I thought that I should have asked him to explain what he meant by his "revolutionary" leanings, just for the heck of it. But here was a guy who had gone, in the course of a few years—perhaps months—from taking part in a serious challenge to Authority's Divine Right to wage war. . . to applying to the FBI in order to become an integral, functioning part of The Authority Machine. What measure of enlightenment did such a confused individual have to offer me? On the other hand, there were those who had thought me confused because I had changed in the opposite direction, in perhaps an even shorter period of time. To which I would reply: Yeah, but. . . um. . . that's different.

I actually felt slighted that the agent had exhibited relatively little interest in me *per se* and didn't seem to know that I had just spent a year in Latin America. Was I a has been? Perhaps I never was what I used to be.

Once again, I really didn't know what road I should be walking. The only "careers" that made my pulse quicken, that grabbed me intellectually and "spiritually," were being a political activist in this world not of my making, and being a writer. In 1973, finding a position as the former which paid a livable wage was still virtually a lost cause; as to the latter, I was still making pocket money, with the occasional article for the *Barb* and for Alternative Features Service. I made more at office temp jobs, where my train of work thought was derailed repeatedly by "What the fuck am I doing here?"

September 11. When I heard the news that morning, I leapt back screeching like a scalded cat from a spilled cup of hot tea, staring horror stricken at the radio with open mouth.

In Chile, the military boots had marched, as they have always marched in Latin America.

Thus it was that they closed the country to the outside world for a week, while the tanks rolled and the soldiers broke down doors; the stadiums rang with the sounds of execution and the bodies piled up along the streets and floated in the river; the torture centers opened for business; dogs trained to sexually molest female prisoners were set loose; the subversive books were thrown to the bonfires; soldiers slit the trouser legs of women, shouting that "In Chile women wear dresses!"; the poor returned to their natural state; and the men of the world in Washington and in the halls of international finance opened up their checkbooks.

I had to be with others who felt equally sick at heart, enraged, helpless. At a rally in Washington Square Park in San Francisco, condemning the coup and the murder of Allende, I was shocked to see a band of about a dozen young people coming by, carrying signs supporting what had happened in Chile. Without a moment's forethought, I leapt at the guy in front and began to choke him, pushing him up against a wall. I don't know how far things would have gone if I hadn't been pulled off of him, but I certainly did not have murder in mind. He and his fellow Latinos, at least some of them Chilean, quickly dispersed. They were greatly outnumbered, and as foreigners were much more legally vulnerable than Americans.

I wasn't at all surprised by what I had done. To have just stood and passively watched these young *fascistas* was not an option open to me.

I was soon volunteering at Asian News Service, founded to report on Indochina. News of what was happening in Chile was coming into the office from Latin America and elsewhere, via wire services, telephone, and people arriving back from Chile. It was imperative to get the real story out, including the historical context, to counteract the mass media's totally predictable slants. One of the media's themes was that because the UP had not won a majority of the popular vote, it was not quite legitimate—Allende had fallen because "his socialist program had no electoral mandate," and therefore he had been wrong, fatally wrong, to try to impose socialist measures to the extent that he did. The News Service had to point out that while the UP had won only 44.1 percent of the popular vote in March, the man sitting in the White House had taken power in 1968 with but 43.4 percent of the vote. No, Salvador Allende was not overthrown because of what he did wrong. He was overthrown because of what he did right.

I was translating wire dispatches from Spanish to English, then summarizing them along with information from other sources, including myself, into press releases. One of our main consumers was the Pacifica Network radio station, KPFA, in Berkeley, where I was later to work.

I was so eager to learn about what was taking place in Chile, and the fate of people I'd known there, that I was latching onto anyone who walked into the office, reading over people's shoulders, firing questions at everyone, grabbing wire copy and other stuff as soon as it landed. I was making a nuisance of myself; not typical of me, I must say. After several days of this, the head of the news service, Banning Garrett, thought I was more than a nuisance. I believe he thought I was some kind of agent. He certainly hinted as much. I was shocked when he asked me to leave. I tried to reassure him and promised to change my behavior, but I had already crossed a line that he couldn't tolerate, and there was no one there who could vouch for me.

I was heartbroken, but could I blame the guy unequivocally? By late 1973, we in the movement had learned a few lessons about people who are not what they pretend to be, and the coup in Chile had raised the level of paranoia several notches because much of our warnings for three years about American subversion of the Chilean revolution had turned out to be prophetic.

Not too many years later, Banning Garrett could be found working as a consultant to the Pentagon.

About two weeks after the coup, I received a call from Frank Teruggi's sister, Janis. Frank had been arrested in Santiago several days earlier, she said, and she and her family in Chicago were very worried.

In early October, Janis called me again. Frank was dead. The story which eventually emerged was that on September 20, paramilitary policemen had raided the apartment Frank shared with David Hathaway, seized a number of Frank's "Marxist" books, roughed him up, and took both him and David to the infamous National Stadium, being used as a giant prison. The next day, Frank was called out of his cell. He was seen at one point later by other prisoners after being terribly beaten. He moaned to them that he could no longer resist. They never saw him alive again.

When Frank's father later went to Chile to learn how his son had died, he was told by Frank Manitzas, a CBS correspondent, what Manitzas had learned from Paul Sigmund, a Princeton professor. Sigmund had been informed by a high Chilean military officer that when Frank and David were in the stadium, the U.S. Consul, Frederick Purdy, had been phoned, told about the two men, and asked what he would like done with them. Purdy told his caller to do as he pleased.

What chance happenings, what bureaucratic vagary, what capricious god, had decided that Frank Teruggi should be called to die, and not David Hathaway, or some other American, or none of them, will never be known.

One other American was actually killed by the new military junta, but not in the stadium. This was Charles Horman, whom I also knew. In Valparaiso, where the coup began, U.S. military officers were meeting with their Chilean counterparts. Horman, who was stranded in that city by the coup, happened to engage in conversation with several Americans, civilian and military. A retired naval engineer told him: "We came down to do a job and it's done." One or two American military men also gave away clues to Charles they shouldn't have. A few days later, Horman was arrested in his Santiago residence, and never seen again. The 1982 film, *Missing*, with Jack Lemmon as Charles' father, deals with Horman's death, and to a lesser extent with Frank's. As would be expected from a Constantin Costa-Gavras film, it pulls no punches in pointing a finger at American complicity in the two deaths, which U.S. government documents released in 1999 and 2000 make even clearer concerning Horman.[39]

They also came for Marc Cooper, who for some time had been working for the government press office as a translator for Allende. He had already made a very lucky escape via a special air flight to Argentina arranged by the United Nations High Commissioner on Refugees when the boots blew the door off his apartment and marched in on a search-and-destroy mission. They then held your traditional and much beloved fascist book-burning in front of his house, and Marc—who's now a regular contributor to *The Nation*—would like to think that this included some of the books snatched from his apartment.[40]

CHAPTER SIXTEEN
DOWN AND OUT
IN COPENHAGEN,
LONDON, AND BERLIN

For months my old friend Pat Cawood had been writing me to join him in Copenhagen. He had been living in Europe since 1966, and was married to a Danish woman, Lis, whom I had met when she and Pat had visited Washington and again in Berkeley. They had a daughter, now aged about four. I was sorry to hear that Pat and Lis were now separated and sharing custody of Sara.

Pat had a big, old apartment, plenty of room for me, he said, and a job too. He worked as a computer programmer for the European Space Agency's center in Copenhagen, and he was sure I could work there too at a good salary.

I didn't know. A whole new country again so soon, whole new esoteric language, not knowing a soul there save Pat and Lis, programming with hardware and software totally new to me. And I was lacking the genes to deal with a Scandinavian winter.

So I went. Besides the fact that there was nothing in particular in the Bay Area holding me close to its bosom, I think what happened inside my head, not entirely conscious, was a basic, primitive revulsion toward those men in Washington who had given life to the thugs in Chile, whose monstrosities against their people were becoming known more graphically with each passing day. It was like I didn't want to live in the same country with such men.

The thing called Watergate, then at its peak of publicity, with daily disclosures of long-hidden FBI and CIA ugliness, was not designed to give me any more of a warm fuzzy feeling about the men in Washington, although the spectacle was certainly entertaining. Indeed, more than one person I knew rebuked me for taking so much pleasure in all the revelations and the disgracing of the White House. (A *Barb* front page: "Don't tell my mother I work at the White House. She thinks I'm playing piano in a whore house.") My critics viewed it as tragedy, an embarrassment for the country, whatever they personally thought of Richard M. Nixon. But that was a bit too abstract for me—"the country," "the presidency," "the White House." I didn't know then, nor do I know now, how to morally judge a person or an institution by other than the harm or the good they do.

In late October, without having yet paid the money owed to the court, and with money lent to me by Pat, I bought a one-way ticket to Europe. Landing in Luxembourg, I took a train to Paris to see Sal Ferrera.

While in Chile I had corresponded with Sal, sending him a couple of my articles at his request, one of which he may have gotten into *Politique Hebdo*, a weekly publication (yes, I know, that's what *hebdo* means); or failing that, sent it off to his CIA handler to help justify his fee. Before settling in Paris two years earlier, Sal had stayed for awhile with Pat Cawood in Copenhagen, at my suggestion. I was to learn eventually that while in Copenhagen, Sal had spied on peace activists who were involved in an underground railroad for American GIs who had deserted because of qualms over Vietnam.[44] I was like a goddamn Typhoid Mary, and Sal was my infectious agent!

In Paris, Sal was still maintaining his invaluable journalistic cover, sending back articles to College Press Service and my former news agency, Alternative Features Service. At the same time, he had been leading another life for the CIA—befriending, and spying upon, former CIA officer Philip Agee, who was spending time in Paris and London writing what was to become the most sensational exposé of the Agency ever written.

During the two days I spent with Sal, I knew nothing of this of course, which, in hindsight, made me feel rather foolish about my displaying the pleasure I did at seeing him for the first time in three and a half years and laughing about the good ol' days in Washington. He must have had more important things on his mind, perhaps even wondering if I really knew about his secret life—Why, after all, had I suddenly turned up in Paris with scarcely any warning?

But I left Paris as innocent as I had arrived, and made my way to Copenhagen via Amsterdam. In Amsterdam, as in Paris, I squeezed in a bit of sight-seeing, but I didn't really have the carefree attitude necessary for good touristy enjoyment. I was anxious to get to Copenhagen, get settled, and see how my newest new life looked.

Pat had a large rambling flat in the working class Vesterbro district, lots of space, but not much warmth. The heating system depended on oil, and the world was in the throes of a so-called "oil crisis," the result of Mideast oil nations using substantial price increases and an oil boycott in an attempt to force Washington to influence Israel into withdrawing from its recently occupied territories. The price of oil in Denmark was prohibitively expensive. To keep the flat comfortably warm all the time would have consumed the lion's share of Pat's earnings. And so we were uncomfortable most of the time. Getting out from under the quilt in the morning and taking a shower in the unheated bathroom was the worst. And it was only early November. The California weather was never far from my thoughts.

But being with Pat was a pleasure. He had one of the best minds I'd ever interacted with, applying his intelligence with equal impressiveness in technical areas and the social sciences, as well as being extremely handy with carpentry and all the fix-it skills. Pat, raised in a small town in Oregon, loved my depraved New York humor. We relished our laughing conversations.

True to his word, he got me a job at the Space Agency at a pretty good salary, and I spent a couple of weeks there reading through computer, programming, and operating manuals. My fear of being in over my head after seven years away from such material gradually eased, although I still was rather insecure about the space stuff. I was not, it must be remembered, a scientist, nor a mathematician like Pat.

It was amazing. I hardly had a real interview. I don't even think I was asked for a resumé. And there wasn't any kind of security check done on me. Just like in the States—not!

The head of the Space Agency was Dr. Bernard Peters, a physicist who had worked on the atom bomb in the U.S., but after the war had been hounded by McCarthyism because in his native Germany he had fought against the Nazis on (gasp) the same side as the Communists, and MAY even have been a member of said group, which he denied, for those who care about such things. The House Un-American Activities Committee was of the opinion that Peters was trying—in the words made famous by the committee—"to overthrow the United States by force and violence." This is what physicists like to call "spherically senseless"—nonsensical from whatever direction you look at it. I'd like to think that it was Peters' distasteful experience with McCarthyism that gave rise to the Space Agency's relaxed hiring procedures.

As a foreigner, though, I did have to apply to the government for a work permit. After finding the right building, and naturally being ping-ponged from office to office, I landed in the room where I was presented with all the required forms to fill out. I was then called into the office of a Danish bureaucrat, a man who looked extremely solemn, if not actually deceased. Much to my surprise, after looking over my documents, he sprung to life, scorn hissing out like a broken gas main. Here was a man I had never met before, but he was relating to me, in good English, with what I can only call hatred. What the hell was going on here?

What was going on was the oil crisis. Governments all over the world were cutting back on expenditures. Civil servants were being axed left and right. And this man sitting across the desk from me, now standing to better manifest his outrage, this man thought that I was displaying nerve and arrogance verily beyond his ken to think that the Danish government would give a foreigner a work permit when Danes were being laid off. The possibility that I had no knowledge at all of this policy and attitude was apparently not one of the options entertained by his mind.

In short, I was refused a work permit and had to leave my job at the Space Agency. Immediately.

The stereotype of Scandinavians held by Americans, at least at that time, was one of relaxed, mellow, sophisticated people. I think this image stemmed primarily from the tolerant attitude toward sex supposedly practiced by them, as exemplified by the celebrated 1967 Swedish film *I Am Curious—Yellow*, which had been banned for awhile in the United States. But I did not find such to be the case at all. I found Danes and Swedes to be very uptight, needing to get drunk to really loosen up, something they did with some regularity, not infrequently to the point of obnoxiousness.

On Sundays during the oil crisis, when driving was prohibited, I was repeatedly astonished by the scene: not a car in sight as far as the eye could see, nor could there be one, but the good burghers still waited patiently on the corner for the light to change before crossing, and would not do otherwise, I surmised, unless you threatened to take their first born. On another occasion, during normal traffic, I was standing on a curb with a red light facing me and ventured a step or two into the street. When I saw a car coming, although some distance away yet, I stepped back on the curb. But that wasn't enough punishment for my crime—the driver left his lane and came directly at the spot my feet had just vacated, running over my spirit.

At one point I spent several days in Stockholm, which greatly impressed me with its seamless blending of glass and steel skyscrapers and twisting medieval streets. Then it was on to Uppsala, a city about 50 miles further north in Sweden. I went to there to visit Hannes Frischknecht, my former roommate in Chile. Hannes, a chemist from Switzerland, was working in a laboratory at the 15th-century university and living in a modern apartment building for students. He showed me how everything had been thought of: every room or floor had all the amenities, from washing machines and ironing board to study areas, kitchen, and vending machines, all new, shiny and spotless. And a great view overlooking a large wooded area. But there was one thing missing, he said. Any human warmth. Socializing of more than a perfunctory nature was rare, he told me, and based on the few hours I spent there in the common areas, I couldn't dispute that. It was enough to make one cry. Perhaps this explains at last the hilarity and zaniness we've all come to love in the films of Ingmar Bergman, who was from Uppsala.

But the Swedish ambassador in Chile, Harald Edelstam, repeatedly risking his life in the extreme, had saved well over a thousand Chileans, the entire Cuban embassy, and others from torture and death, and seen to their relocation in Sweden and elsewhere. While I was in Stockholm, he was being honored as the hero he was. In his courageous efforts in Chile, he had had the indispensable support of Swedish Premier Olaf Palme, a socialist, as was Edelstam. When Edelstam was finally forced out of Chile by the junta three months after the coup, the Chilean right-wing newspaper (the only kind still free to publish), *La Tercera,* named him as "the most degenerate" of the year, while proclaiming General Pinochet and Henry Kissinger as "the most outstanding." So if Swedes were less spontaneous, open, and "crazy" than some—only some—Americans, and their students didn't have wild spring breaks in Daytona Beach, they could still produce leaders that filled my American heart with envy.

And in their land, they can now measure children of a certain age—their height, weight, and various health measurements—and are then not able to tell which social class the child is from; i.e., they have ended class warfare against children.

A month after the coup, the Nobel Peace Prize was awarded to Kissinger, this to a man who could now add Chile to Cambodia and Vietnam on his list of crimes-against-humanity achievements. Soon he would be adding Angola.

Two years later, the Peace Prize was awarded to the celebrated Soviet dissident Andrei Sakharov, who, when asked shortly after the Chilean coup what he thought of the junta, had declined to take a stand for or against it on the ground that "Chile is too far away." This is what anti-communism can do to the mind and soul, and why I was an anti-anti-communist.

One of the occasional flights of fancy I entertain myself with in idle moments is to picture myself winning the Peace Prize so that I could announce to the world media flocking about me that I was not proud to be the recipient of an honor also bestowed upon Henry Kissinger. Then I'd take the money and run.

Speaking of money—a nice segue, that—I, job free, needed to warm my cold hands with some. Off the Danish books of course. Under the Danish table. Thus it was that our hero wound up with an outdoors job—standing in one of "the walking streets" (no cars ever permitted), wearing. . . costumes. . . "*Stort*

Tøjmarked, gamel sjovt tøj," said the sign I held, "Large clothing store, old funny clothing." Sometimes I was one of the three musketeers; other days I played Hamlet, with full-length cape, and crown atop my regal head; at other times I was an American Civil War soldier. We're talking here of January, February, serious winter stuff in that part of the world, not merely their basic freezing autumn. And these costumes I wore were not exactly designed for crossing the Arctic tundra. Standing outside for hours at a time. . . how shall I put this?. . . I was cold. . . especially my hands and feet. I took to standing on a thick piece of cardboard, which was but of minimal improvement over the pavement.

For those of you who doubt that I had fallen so low, photos of me in my various costumes exist, for one Don Hinrichsen came by and took them. Don was a freelance print and radio journalist from Iowa whom I had met through Pat, and with whom I had gone to Stockholm. We had stayed there with his "wife," a Swedish woman he'd earlier married in the States to make her legal. Don was submitting tapes regularly to NBC and writing for a couple of European publications, on political and other topics. This of course made me somewhat envious. But, as I rationalized to myself, and as Pat agreed, although Don liked to hang around leftists, and perhaps fancied himself as one, he didn't have much of a radical perspective. If he had, he probably wouldn't have been acceptable to the likes of NBC.

Don and I shared many a glass of wine in pubs, commiserating with each other about our lack of women. The women of Denmark's highly homogenized population, Pat advised me after awhile, did not go for men who regularly tried to be humorous. So Don and I entertained each other.

One morning in early February, a front page story in a Danish newspaper caught my eye, something about a kidnapping in dear old Berkeley. I sought out the *International Herald Tribune* and learned that it had taken place on a block I knew well, and that the victim was a young woman named Patty Hearst, whose name I didn't know. Should I have? There were so many famous people in America, I hadn't heard of half of them. However, the young woman's grandfather, William Randolph Hearst, the Hearst newspapers, and Hearst Castle, were all of marquee stature. Some group calling itself the Symbionese Liberation Army had claimed credit. If I hadn't been receiving letters from Willie in Soledad, I might have thought that this was a spinoff of his Revolutionary Army, snatching Patty Hearst instead of the more problematical Robert McNamara.

I had another reminder of Berkeley one day as I stood in my spot on the walking street, holding my sign. An older guy with a bushy beard happened by and stopped. We stared at each other for several moments, unable to believe our eyes. "Max?" I tentatively inquired. "Bill?" he said. It was Max Scherr of the *Berkeley Barb*. He was traveling around Europe with a lady friend, who at the moment was off visiting relatives in Copenhagen. My first reaction following the surprise was some embarrassment, about what Max might think about seeing his star reporter reduced to a mannequin. But ol' Max was a bit long in the tooth for such judgements; too many beatniks, hippies and lefties under the bridge. We had a nice dinner together that evening.

Nonetheless, I was prompted into my own fresh evaluation of my situation. Although the size and the pace of Copenhagen were utterly human, the city had a provincial soul, with little in the way of outstanding views, and I had no real job, no money, no love life, precious little warmth, inside or outside, an abundance of darkness (the sun rose at 9:30 am and set about 3:30 pm), and though everyone liked to say how all Danes spoke English, at the very best that applied only to younger people (the older ones generally spoke German), and only to one-on-one situations. When I was with two or more Danes, they spoke Danish, and that left me out. A few classes I attended had scarcely advanced the frontiers of my knowledge. I just didn't have the incentive to throw myself into a language that I knew did not have a starring role in my future, or anyone's future except a Dane.

In other words—deep breath here—it was time to move on, again. Those who believe that life is a journey rather than a destination could use me as a poster boy.

I managed to dig up at some library a directory that listed firms all over the world which made substantial use of computers, and sent out resumés to about two dozen of them, in about seven or eight countries, not including the United States. My computer experience was much more impressive and unique abroad than at home. Even more important, to return to the States so soon would have depressed me, putting a decidedly premature end to Bill's Excellent European Adventure.

It was a long shot, given the complications of me being in Denmark, and the other countries being where they were, and the expense of getting there, and interviews, and work permits, and all that jazz. But I got back two very positive replies—one from London and one from Bombay. Bombay certainly sounded like the more exotic setting, but I didn't think I'd take to Indian women, and vice versa. Being a member of Stereotypes R Us, I pictured them as being inordinately tradition bound, tied to their families, religious, sexually repressed; you get the picture. So I informed the London firm that I'd be in town in a couple of weeks if they wanted to interview me.

In London I spent a week at the home of my Brooklyn cousin, Barbara, who lived in posh Sloane Square with her American husband and their two children. Her spouse's engineering profession had for many years allowed Barbara the luxury of pursuing a career as an artist, turning out these very large, wholly abstract, thickly applied, multi-colored blob. . . things. She informed her obviously less-than-enchanted cousin standing in her studio that she was a hundred years ahead of her time.

How did it begin, this practice of inculcating the population with the idea that to be thought of as sophisticated, worldly, refined, educated and/or—the word that makes me reach for my gun—"cultured," one must acquire a certain measure of "art appreciation"? One must be enthused, or at least appear to be so, about walking into an art museum or art gallery, or any place where the paintings gave off the sanctified odor of Serious Art, and no matter what your instincts tell you to think or feel about what your eyes are seeing, you can not say—even about a canvas of pure whiteness with a solitary dot of black in the lower right-hand corner—that a particular painting has no meaning for you, or that it moves you aesthetically not at all, and certainly not that it's pretentious or phony. If such words should actually cross your lips, those within hearing distance would stamp you immediately as a Philistine. And one knows that only too well.

To be a "successful" painter, one does not necessarily need to feel passionate about anything in particular except the wish to be a successful painter. John Cage, whose minimal compositions, including absolute silence, are the musical equivalent of the white canvas with the black dot, said, in response to questions about his music and his musical philosophy: "I have nothing to say and I am saying it."

Meanwhile, back at the Computer Information Centre in Kings Cross, I was being interviewed for a position, but this, it seemed, was only a formality. Impressed with my four years at IBM, an uncommon commodity in Europe 1974, I was hired on the spot and advised to return to Denmark to await the British work permit they would send me.

April 20, Adolf Hitler's birthday. Der Fuehrer would have been 85 today if he'd stuck to painting, coulda made a fortune with minimalist kitsch. (Hmmm, is this of any significance to my story? Absolutely none, except that it was the day I arrived in London.) By the next day I had found a place to live. My new location in the universe was on Fountayne Road, N16, in Stoke Newington. It was not Sloane Square, it was not even Camden, but it was a relatively short bus commute to Kings Cross, and it was cheap. The bad part was that I got what I paid for—a "bed sitter," a British institution that means a room with the bare-bones furniture pieces, mini-fridge, hot plate, and sink; toilet and bath outside in the hallway, in my case two flights up, shared with about ten other tenants. But it was all mine! The first (sort-of) apartment of my own in almost three years. I was so broke, however, my first day on the job I had to ask for an advance on my salary, which did not sit at all well with my boss. This very conservative (in more ways than one) man gave me a withering look, and was clearly wondering whether he'd made a big mistake in hiring this (ugh) American, who, to boot, was a decade or so older than the rest of his staff.

My first Saturday morning I left the house to do a big shopping for apartment stuff and food. I began to walk up the street and suddenly stopped, my jaw falling open. In front of me was a veritable sea of long black coats, wide-brimmed black hats, yarmulkes, long beards, *peyes* (hair curls running down the side of the face), *tzitzis* hanging out of shirts. . . dozens of people going to a synagogue just down the street. In the sprawling 625 square miles of London, I had moved into the single most Orthodox Jewish block in the entire city—Chassidim Central! Even in my Brooklyn youth, they hadn't been right on my block. Had I done something in a previous life to deserve this? It was more than just a personal, emotional reaction to unpleasant memories. What produced my mental nausea was the display of ignorance of people who believed that the garments they wore on their body and the way they kept their hair, and whether they fasted on certain designated days, and four dozen other trivial and arbitrary do's and don't's, were somehow forces for good in the world—even determined what took place! Literally! "You're feeling sick now because God is punishing you for turning on the TV on *shabbes*."

I want to cry out at people reduced to so much less than they could be.

My computer firm soon assigned me to a client in The City, London's financial center. It was a commodities brokerage, and my task was to convert their manual system of keeping track of the operations to a computer system, the kind of systems analysis and programming I'd done many times at IBM. But this was to prove exasperatingly complicated. When I sat down with someone to find out exactly what he did, and how, I was confronted with 10 or 20 years of a highly personalized system. He would open one drawer to show me a list he kept by hand of one thing, then another drawer to show me a second list he kept, then he'd reach under his desk blotter for a few scraps of paper, which contained other information vital to the workings of the system. To all this had to be added other critical details that existed only in the man's head, or which he got, verbally, from so-and-so each month, whose system was just as personalized, only very different.

As anxious as I was to make a great impression on my boss and justify his faith in hiring me at sight, after a while I was foundering, in deep, deep doo-doo. I began to spend hours working at home, trying to come up with flow charts that made sense and data which could be quantified. My sensitive little stomach was not happy.

All this effort and stress devoted to an enterprise I had scant sympathy for, a place where grown men and women spent their days doing no more than speculating and hedging on the market price of various grains, meats, metals, wood, and other materials, trying to guess whether prices would be going up or down. A single transaction in copper could net a profit far in excess of what a Chilean copper miner earned in a year under the earth. And typically, the seller did not as much as lay eyes or hand upon the copper which enriched him.

Many a moment did I long for my carefree, impoverished days, which is not to say I was becoming affluent. Though my salary of 3,500 pounds a year put me in the 90th percentile amongst English wages, this said a great deal more about English wages than about my purchasing power.

One evening two visitors, a man and a woman, both in their thirties, came to my apartment. They were from the Workers Revolutionary Party (WRP), and had come by in response to my having signed a petition of some kind. The woman, whose name I forget, was rather pushy in trying to persuade me to contribute money and to join the party, which, like the SWP and YSA in the States, was "Trotskyist." I politely declined to join, but gave her a 10 pound donation. A few weeks later she was back, asking for another contribution and again pressing me to become one of the comrades. I gave her 15 pounds this time, to which she responded: "Is that all the money you have?"

"Of course it's not all the money I have," I said, "but I have to save something, don't I?"

"Why?" she replied. "After the revolution, the money you have won't be worth anything. We're going to do away with money altogether."

I looked at her, grinning, certain she must be kidding. She didn't return my grin.

But not all WRP members were of this mold. I became friendly with a young married couple on my block who were in the party, but were not under the impression they were living in Petrograd 1917. They were a working-class couple with a young child, neither of them particularly educated or intellectual, but they understood well enough the basic political and economic facts of life of British class society, even under a Labour government.

Eventually, after all the years, and all the doubts, I took the plunge. I joined the party, as much for social reasons as a desire to commit myself politically. So I was now in the same party as Vanessa Redgrave, whom I saw at city-wide party meetings. She was a prime financial supporter of WRP, and over the ensuing years stuck with it through one public scandal and internal controversy after another, often expressing herself ideologically in terms much too dogmatic for my tastes. At the first city-wide meeting I attended, in a large hall in Shepherds Bush, the head of the party, Gerry Healey, spoke to the assembled comrades.

I had never seen him before. When he walked out on the stage I could scarcely believe my eyes. It was George F. Babbitt, fresh from Minnesota. A short, chubby, balding middle-aged man, white shirt, tie, dark suit, the whole bit. . . I was half expecting him to start pitching life insurance policies. So this was our leader, The Lord High Almighty Poobah, The Grand Ayatollah of thousands of militant revolutionaries? If any doubt remained about the notion that women are attracted to men of power, it must have been dispelled a while later when the story broke that Healey had had sex with 26 female members of the party.

As a speaker, he had an impressive voice, but he immediately plunged ahead at length about complex and technical Marxian economic and dialectical matters that left me gasping for breath by the side of the road. I was certain that many, probably most, of the young people in the audience had gotten exceedingly little out of the talk. Local branches of the party were in the habit of grabbing warm bodies off the street in the competition to increase membership figures. I had met several new members who were not even socialists, who hardly knew what the word meant, and there was no formal educational process set up for them. The whole policy vis-à-vis new members left a bad taste in my mouth.

As did the campaigning for WRP's parliamentary candidates. They of course had as much chance as an ice cube on a Calcutta street in July, but such campaigns were used to spread the gospel. One way was door-to-door. In the company of another party worker, or alone, I would ring a doorbell, interrupting god-knew-what—eating, sleeping, defecating, fucking, masturbating, a heated marital argument, sickness. . . I had maybe 30 seconds to rip their attention from whatever they had been doing and make them focus on my words—the party, the candidate, the opposition, the neighborhood, the issues. . . pause, catch my breath. . . so what do you think Sir/Madam? Would you consider casting your ballot for our woman?

"Who'd ya say ya with?"

That's if I was lucky and they opened the door. With those reluctant to do so to a stranger, I had to stand in the hall and shout my spiel.

This was not my style at all. But the party was remarkably insistent that I go through the shit again and again, evenings, weekends, right up to the day before election day. At times I could swear they actually thought our candidate could win the fucking election! My 1960s instincts about joining a militant leftist political party had been on the mark. Before long I stopped going to meetings, and they called me once or twice to inquire. I don't remember now what I said to them, but that was that. Let the record show that I was an official Trotskyist for four months.

At one point I did join another group, one with a much more modest sounding name: Concerned Americans Abroad—Yanks who were veterans of struggles from McCarthyism to Vietnam. We often met at the charming Primrose Hill home of Bernard Vorhaus, who had been a prominent film director in the 1930s and 40s in both the United States and Britain. In 1951, he was named as a member of the Communist Party by a witness before the House Un-

American Activities Committee, which was investigating "communist influence" in Hollywood. Bernard had been shooting a film in Italy starring John Wayne when his name came up in the hearing. Then, at the request of the United States, the Cold-War-obedient Italians arrested him and summarily threw him out. Fighting communism was serious business. Vorhaus settled in London, went on the Hollywood blacklist, and never made another picture.[42] I wonder what good ol' anti-commie John Wayne thought of all this.

Our expatriate (expatriot?) group took part in several protests against U.S. foreign policy, including one concerning Chile in front of the American embassy. In England, as in Denmark and Sweden, and in every country of Europe, even a year after the coup, outrage was still being vented against the Pinochet junta and their American *éminence grise*. At these rallies, seeing Chilean refugees never failed to choke me up.

Concerned Americans Abroad also staged its own unique week-long event: the "CIA Stately Homes Tour—A mis-guided tour". . . "Take a useful tour: Blow the cover off your friendly CIA operative". . . "Special prizes if you spot the CIA operatives who might infiltrate your tour". . . said our slick red, white and blue flyer. Each tour went to the homes of known CIA officers stationed in London, with the express purpose of exposing and embarrassing them in front of their neighbors and whatever media showed up. As we stood chanting in front of the town house of the CIA Station Chief, Cord Meyer, with an American troupe performing guerrilla theater in the street, Meyer's neighbor came out and began to berate us. "The United States is our ally," she yelled. "They saved us in the war."

It was futile asking her what one thing had to do with the other, whether World War II gave the U.S. the right to do whatever it wanted anywhere in the world. Her anger had bypassed her cerebellum and gone directly to her vocal chords.

My work at the commodities brokerage was not my first experience with this particular irony—working on something that I felt was socially useless, even parasitical, but getting so involved in it that I wanted it to function well. By late fall, however, not only I, but my superior at the Computer Information Centre had concluded that the task I had been assigned to do at the brokerage was simply undoable; some things just can't be put on a computer, or at least shouldn't; conceivably the old employees of the brokerage planned it that way. It was depressing to have surrendered six months of my life with nothing to show for it, not even anything of transferable educational or hiring value.

The whole episode left me with a strong desire to make a fresh start, without any cloud of suspicion about my work hanging over my head. Thus it was that I soon took leave of CIC and wound up working for the American multinational, RCA, near Oxford Street. Unlike at CIC and the Danish Space Agency, my new employer subjected me to a fairly rigorous interview, and I had all I could do to paper over the fact that my knowledge of certain key technical things was lacking or very dated.

For some time I had been taking part in an Extra Sensory Perception (ESP) group, in which we experimented with reading each other's mind. I had long been curious about such things and had read a good selection of the literature, both the believing and the skeptical varieties. Deep relaxation exercises were followed by one person focusing mentally on someone whom they knew well, but who was unknown to the "mind reader." The latter was told—seemingly arbitrarily—only the first name, gender, and city of residence of the person thought of. From this the mind reader had to try and divine other pertinent information about the person from his partner's head. The results, I must say, often seemed extraordinary, certainly beyond what chance would dictate. Yet I instinctively shied away from flatly accepting the process as valid, as an amazing discovery.

I eventually decided that the members of the group, myself included, were so anxious to make the experiment work that we put the best possible spin on everyone's mind-reading guesses—if it was possible, it became probable; if it was probable, it became virtually certain; and if it was actually accurate, albeit mundane and applicable to a third of London's population, it was WOW! There is of course a lesson to be learned from this which pertains to the credibility of much more than psychic phenomena.

One of my ESPmates, a fellow from St. Louis named Richard Deutsch, was the editor of a magazine which was one of several being published by the same company. These magazines were—how can I put this delicately?—Men's magazines. And the company was Warner Brothers; yes, like in Barbara Stanwyck and Humphrey Bogart; published out of the Warner House on Wardour Street. I soon was one of their stable of authors, appearing in *Symposium* and *Parade*. Besides a few pornographic stories, I did some serious ones, like the nude-group psychotherapy described earlier herein, and a study of "confession" magazines which were aimed at young women. The latter I wrote from a decidedly feminist perspective, which, circa 1974, was no mean accomplishment in a men's magazine. I also wrote erotic letters to the editor from "readers," which has led me to cast a skeptical eye at letters to various magazines ever since. The articles, however, were under my real name; my writer's ego would not have it otherwise.

I never ceased to be amazed at the idea that one human being can put words on paper which sexually excite other human beings to a high degree simply by their reading those words, without any physical or even visual contact with another human being, and even when the reader is fully aware that the writer is consciously trying to manipulate his libido. I must have been good at it because I couldn't write any of the porno stuff without it arousing myself. And it was some of the easiest money I ever made—50 pounds per not-very-long piece.

I remember thinking during the last few days of 1974 that I had spent New Years Eve '71 in California, '72 in Chile, '73 in Denmark, and this year, England. Should I be concerned about this, I wondered. What did the clinical textbooks on the pathology of alienation and rootlessness say? The only book that interested me that week was a paperback I chanced upon in a bookstore, *Inside the Company: CIA Diary*, by someone named Philip Agee, who had spent 12 years as a CIA officer. I had never heard of him or the book, but clearly that had to change. It was an eye-opener. I thought I knew something about how the CIA operated, but not in such detail, not in such daily dirty-tricks minutia all over Latin America. The Agency, it appeared, was much more diabolical in every way than its most severe, "paranoid" critics had imagined.

A scene etched in my memory forever: I'm sitting in my kitchen—now to be found in the more upscale neighborhood of Maida Vale, albeit still with the bathroom in the hall—eating dinner, Agee's book propped open before me. I'm near the end, and he writes of how he's been befriended in Paris by two Americans who "display excessive curiosity and other indications that suggest they may be CIA agents trying to get close to me for different purposes. One of these, a supposed freelance journalist named Sal Ferrera. . ."

Instantaneous sucked-in breath, a heart-rending cry of horror, I am literally propelled out of my seat and backwards two full meters. . . I stand there, staring at the book on the table like a man finding out that the wife he's lived with for 20 years is actually a man. . .

The cover of Agee's book featured a photo of a portable typewriter with the inside lining of the carrying case pulled back, revealing an electronic panel. The typewriter and its CIA-altered case had been foisted upon Agee by Sal and his girlfriend, the electronic panel being a transmitter to enable the Agency to find out where in Paris its wayward son and his manuscript-in-progress were actually residing.

I had to meet and speak to Agee, to compare notes about Sal, and just to meet the man. But where in the world was he living? By lucky happenstance a former *Washington Free Press* colleague and friend, Elaine Fuller, was just visiting England. She was working for the National Action Research on the Military Industrial Complex (NARMIC), part of American Friends Service Committee, and was in the UK that January to attend a peace and disarmament conference in Kent. The war in Vietnam was not yet over, and NARMIC was still focused on it, and they thought that Phil Agee might know something about CIA activities there. Of all things, Agee was living in Cornwall and Elaine had his phone number. I was soon on the phone to him—I eagerly, he clearly cautious—and we arranged to meet in London in a few days at the home of Robin Blackburn, one of the editors at *New Left Review*.

When we met, we discussed the tremendous ordeal he had gone through to complete the book and find a publisher. Agee had mentioned in his book about how an unnamed American publisher had been on the verge of publishing his book and then, at the last minute, had backed out, perhaps under CIA pressure. I asked him if he had tried Grove Press in New York.

"How'd you know it was Grove?" he fired at me, almost angry.

I didn't. Agee hadn't been back in the U.S. for several years and didn't know that Grove was the only major publisher with a leftist bent, and thus that it was only natural for me to have thought of them. I tried not to let the incident ruin the conversation. After 12 years in the CIA, and then pursued by the Agency with venom, he was entitled to be a little suspicious of strangers. And, after all, I had been a close friend of Sal.

Neither one of us could imagine why, if Sal were working with the CIA, he had suggested and carried out with me the exposure of all those CIA employees. He may have been "turned" by the Agency afterwards; perhaps they had something to blackmail him with; or he could have pulled off the caper to establish his *bona fides*, although that certainly seemed like overkill. Years later, I was to give the published list to Daniel Brandt who had created a computer database on the CIA and related subjects. He entered all 215 names and saw that 34 of them were already in his database, a surprisingly high percentage of matches. That meant that the list must have included many actual operatives, not just support and service personnel.

Agee's last meeting with Sal had taken place in London early in 1974, while Phil was still working on the book. Sal had come from Paris to plead his case. He knew that Phil thought he was a spy, but Sal insisted that it simply wasn't so. He was going back to the States soon, he said, and would be ruined as a journalist if his name appeared in Phil's book. Sitting in a pub, Phil pressed Sal to answer long-standing questions concerning the bugged typewriter and other matters. Sal still couldn't give anything approaching satisfactory answers. When Phil told him at last that he didn't believe him, Sal jumped to his feet, picked up his pint of beer, and threw it on the table, splashing it all over the place. Phil instinctively hurried out to avoid a scene involving the police. He never saw Sal again.

Two members of Concerned Americans Abroad, Louis Wolf and Steve Weissman, were working with Agee on a campaign to uncover and publicize the names of CIA officers secretly operating under political cover at U.S. embassies throughout the world. Using the State Department's *Biographic Register* and *Foreign Service List*, found at the British Library, they could spot the CIA people by analyzing employment histories and cover assignments. Another valuable tool in this endeavor was to have the embassy directory, with which to collate office and phone extensions, to see who was working with whom in which offices. Steve asked me to try and get a copy of the directory at the American embassy.

In the embassy's library, I spied a copy on the librarian's desk as I asked her a made-up question. I then sat at a nearby table, pretending to be working on something, waiting for her to leave her desk. When she did, I nonchalantly strolled by her desk, placed the directory on top of my papers, and walked out. It hit the jackpot. Agee's team was able to identify only six or seven CIA officers without the directory. With it they found no fewer than 62. Publication of the names in the weekly magazine *Time Out* caused a mild sensation in England and Western Europe, with of course unknown consequences for the CIA.

I meanwhile had written a review of Agee's book and sent it to the *New Republic* in Washington. The magazine was, at that time, still in the liberal camp. Much to my great surprise and elation the review was accepted for publication by the magazine's literary editor, Doris Grumbach, later a well-known author. The book had not yet appeared in the United States and the New Republic was pleased to have what would be one of the first reviews. At last my writing resumé would list something other than the alternative press. (No, I was not planning to add the Warner magazines to it.) Who knew where this might lead?

A couple of weeks later, another letter arrived from Grumbach. She was sorry to inform me that the *New Republic's* Editor-in-Chief, Gilbert Harrison, had vetoed publication of my review at the last moment. The article was returned to me, already edited for publication, even with an issue date marked on it. Some years later, I came to appreciate that Harrison was a typical liberal, or at least a typical Cold-War, anti-communist liberal—no matter how progressive their views concerning the individual and society, the basic tenets, assumptions, and objectives of American foreign policy were held sacrosanct. Harrison had been a friend of John F. Kennedy, and in 1961, when his magazine had obtained a comprehensive account of the preparations for the Bay of Pigs invasion of Cuba, he dutifully submitted the planned article to the White House for advice. When Kennedy asked that it not be printed, Harrison complied.[43]

My review cited a number of the odious covert crimes carried out by the CIA—some of them of the type which could be found mentioned in the establishment press of that time as well—but I had failed to insert or imply any of the *de rigueur* euphemisms and qualifications, like: "all nations spy," "we're at war with an even more unprincipled adversary," "there's a few bad apples in every barrel. . . ."

The *Barb* later printed my review. Max's ties to the White House and CIA were not very extensive.

After but two months on the job, I was fired by RCA. There had been too many occasions when my ignorance of the current state of the computer art could not be concealed. I had been found out.

The firing was completely unexpected, but I was not crushed. Working at a "permanent" career job had not been my natural state for eight years and I was not anxious to go back to that. Still, I was a month shy of 42, and I had no idea what to do next. The next day, Saturday, I went to a public social gathering sponsored by an organization called Women and Psychiatry (to have contact with the former, not the latter), held in a room over a pub on Tottenham Court Road. It was there that I met a woman who was to become very important in my life. She was a 28-year-old German named Adelheid Zöfel, who was visiting from West Berlin, where she taught German, Greek and Latin language and literature.

These were not subjects I was very well versed in, but she and I, we found out soon enough, shared much: an absence of religious belief and a revolutionary political outlook; both of us very much products of The Sixties, we despised the power the police and military had over us all, and we questioned all manner of tradition and authority; we carried around a highly refined sense of injustice and absurdity; we embraced protest, feminism, Bob Dylan, Phil Ochs, Joan Baez, the Beatles, and Tom Paxton, although at the same time we were both more word-idea-issue people than music-dance-visual people; we also hit it off sexually like it had been invented just for us; and her mother had not painted a smile on her face at an early age and taught her that the most important thing in life is to be liked.

Being unemployed and with a month's severance pay in my pocket, I was able to go off with Adelheid on a week-long auto trip through Western England and Wales. By the time we returned to London, we had developed a certain attachment to each other, although not to be mistaken for lovesick teenagers. I think that I, as a New York Jew, carried a certain exotic appeal for a gentile raised in a small town in Germany. She had to return to Berlin shortly afterward, but we knew/hoped that that was not the end of the attachment.

May Day 1975: A serendipity day to celebrate the final American withdrawal from Vietnam the day before as North Vietnamese tanks rolled into Saigon. I joined an overflow crowd in Conway Hall in Holborn, the site of so many anti-Vietnam War and other progressive rallies. I choked up more than once during the speeches. So now, finally, the 30-year horror was over. Or was it? Amidst all the cheering and self-congratulatory speeches, there were also the cautionary notes, reflecting that Vietnam had been destroyed to its core, the cream of its youth lay dead, the earth, the air, the water, and the gene pool poisoned for generations to come, the psychological trauma immeasurable. Anticommunists the world over were now poised to pounce on every defect and shortcoming of the unified Vietnam and cry with glee: "See? We told you so!" No allowance would be made for the devastation.

Almost everyone believes that the United States lost the war, but Washington had in fact achieved its primary purpose: by turning Vietnam into a basket case, it had prevented what might have been the rise of a good development option for Asia, an alternative to the capitalist model.

I had to hurry home from the rally because Adelheid was arriving any minute from Germany for a 10-day visit. The next evening we went to hear a talk by Phil Agee before a very large crowd. Agee was clearly the genuine article, not just some liberal who was upset at the CIA's "overzealousness" and who called for some wrist-slapping reforms. I tried to speak to him afterwards but he was surrounded by admirers, mainly South Americans in exile from the anticommunist holocaust that had engulfed Brazil, Uruguay, and Chile. I did get his attention long enough for him to promise to come by my apartment the next day.

He did in fact phone me the next morning to tell me that he was being delayed, but that he'd get back to me as soon as he knew when he could make it over. About half an hour later, the bell rang. It was Agee, without any warning. I was sure this was a trick he'd learned in the CIA—to catch someone off guard and see if there was anything lying around that would indicate that the person was not what he said he was. Years later, Elaine Fuller told me that he had done the exact same thing with her. Again, I couldn't blame him.

After we chatted for awhile about our favorite subjects, Sal Ferrera and the CIA, Agee said he had to leave. He accepted my offer of a lift to wherever he was going, but wouldn't say exactly where that was. I was simply directed to drive where he told me to. At some point in Swiss Cottage, he asked to be left off. Adelheid and I watched him walking away for only a moment before I drove off.

Subsequently, the UK government, spurred on by Washington, deported Agee, citing every "espionage" and "national security" cliché in the book. A dear old Labour Party government it was.

In late June, I drove to Berlin, picked up Adelheid, and we took off for Spain and Portugal, via the Côte d'Azur, living cheaply, even sleeping in the car a couple of times. Portugal was our primary destination, for in April of the previous year there had been a military coup which overthrew 48 years of fascism. Military officers in a Western nation who spoke like socialists was science fiction to the American mind, but it had become a reality in Portugal—nationalization of major industries, workers' control, a minimum wage, land reform, and more, were in the offing. The center of Lisbon was crowded from morning till evening with people discussing the changes, just as in Chile.

The visual symbol of the Portuguese revolution had become the picture of a child sticking a rose into the muzzle of a rifle held by a friendly soldier, and we got caught up in demonstrations and parades full of people, including ourselves, standing on tanks and throwing roses, with the crowds cheering the soldiers. It was pretty heady stuff, and I would dearly have loved to believe, but I and most people I spoke to there had little doubt that The American Empire could not let such a breath of fresh air last very long. The overthrow of the Chilean government had raised not only the level of paranoia, but the world's collective political consciousness. The CIA's fingerprints were already evident in Portugal, and before the year was out, the CIA-heavily-financed "Socialist" Party had come to power. The Portuguese revolution was dead, stillborn.[44]

In August, Adelheid and I went our separate ways for the third time in six months, but the following month I decided to move to Berlin to live with her. Yes, I asked her first. After selling what little furniture I owned, all my belongings could fit into my compact Austin Mini and it was off to my next European home.

Adelheid (whose name means "nobility" in German) lived in a *Wohngemeinschaft* (literally "living community"), in one of the huge old apartments that Berlin was known for—six or seven bedrooms, each one occupied by an individual or couple, mostly German, but including one French-American couple. Adelheid's room was immense; it probably had been the living room at one time; the large kitchen served that purpose now. Her room also had a large balcony attached, looking over one of the main streets of the Schoneberg section of the city. We were not cramped.

I was soon busy teaching English, at a school and with private students as well. The school was just off the Kufürstendamm, the main boulevard of the city that went on and on, and was the West's showcase. Being surrounded on all four sides by East Germany and the Cold War lent an aura of intrigue to living in West Berlin. I imagined that everyone I passed on the Kufürstendamm was a spy, Eastern or Western, when in fact probably only half of them were.

Under the Allied agreement on the status of Berlin, Americans could cross the checkpoints and go into East Berlin whenever they wanted, a privilege denied to German residents of West Berlin. What always struck me first in the East was the absence of advertising. The only public signs were the occasional announcements of cultural or sporting events and the like. It's hard to realize to what extent your consciousness and senses have been hijacked by advertising until you enter into such a land. It's as if you had been trapped in a small room with a large heavy-metal band performing non-stop for hours and then suddenly you walked into a completely sound-proofed room and shut the door behind you. Of course, some people can't get enough of heavy-metal music.

I never had any problems with the authorities in East Berlin, but once on a train trip to Copenhagen to visit Pat, an East German guard picked up a magazine I was reading. It was something put out by the Socialist Workers Party in the U.S. and was full of anti-Stalinist and pro-Trotskyist material. It was really stupid of me to be carrying such a publication passing through East Germany. I sat there wondering how much English the guard understood and how well he had learned his lessons about the official heroes and villains. He left my car with the magazine, returning it a while later without comment.

The urge to put words to paper never strayed far from my desires. It was time to activate the old-boy network. Don Hinrichsen, my American friend in Copenhagen, put in a good word for me with the editor of an English-language newsweekly he wrote for. Soon I was contributing to *To the Point International,* published in Antwerp and distributed in much of Western Europe. I was like their Berlin correspondent, filling a need they didn't know they had before. I wrote about my *Wohngemeinschaft* and others, about a new police computer system in Berlin, and a couple of other things lost to my memory. Oddly enough, I never saw an issue of the magazine during the short period I wrote for it. Several years later I learned that the publication was covertly owned by the government of South Africa for the purpose of improving the apartheid regime's world image. This was readily apparent in its coverage of the civil war in Angola, the magazine supporting the side on whose behalf South Africa was intervening militarily.

In January 1976, I decided to return to London. Though Adelheid and I had many good times, our difficulties were taking their toll. My lack of money (I'd been forced to sell my car) was one major source of friction. And my poor German hampered things socially too often; countless times, at the kitchen table or in a restaurant, I'd be sitting with her and other Germans, knowing what they were talking about, but unable to pick up most of the details and nuances, unable to take part or really be myself. I vowed that I would never again put myself in such a position. But I had made the same vow in Denmark.

We parted once again, with the usual expectation that it would not be permanent.

My hate/hate affair with customs and immigration people was about to reach a new high/low. The Australian woman in front of me had just come back from Morocco, which, at that time at least, rang the drug bell. This naturally inspired the customs officer to empty the woman's purse out and look through her address book. Neither she nor I will ever know what they hoped to find.

Then it was my turn. The customs officer—a woman, which made me apprehensive because women in such positions often feel compelled to prove that they're as tough as the men—was immediately suspicious that someone who had had a work permit for the UK and had left was returning only four months later. With two large pieces of luggage. Now, it's not illegal to enter the UK on a tourist visa and look for a job while you're there. I had done just that two years earlier. But you can't tell them that. The immigration mind thinks: If he doesn't find a job, he'll stay anyway, illegally. That formulation is not without some logic, but it didn't happen to apply to me. I could not stomach living there illegally, for several reasons: poverty and paranoia being near the top of the list. So I insisted that I was just visiting, giving my cousin's address as my destination.

The first thing they found in my luggage was a letter from a London computer firm that was in reply to a letter I had sent from Berlin inquiring about employment. Hmmm.

Then they found a clipping from an American newspaper someone had sent me concerning Wendy Yoshimura and her arrest with Patty Hearst a few months earlier. Why in the world was I carrying such a thing, they wondered. Hmmmmm.

They then found a letter from Willie to me, clearly marked as emanating from world-famous Soledad prison. Hmmmmmmm.

They read Willie's letter. *Of course!* they would say. *Why not? What are letters for if not to be read? Are they any more sacrosanct than an address book?*

I was kept waiting for hours, while they checked with Scotland Yard, who then checked with their partners in crime, the FBI, who then reported on both my transgressions: the anti-war demonstration arrest and the unemployment fraud; no mention of the fact that I hadn't yet paid the fine.

I was taken to a building at the airport used for detention. To be locked up pending my return to Germany. Depressing.

There were a dozen or so other men there, and I soon noticed that some of them seemed to be staring at me a lot. Why was that? We were all stuck in the same sinking boat. Then I realized that the others were all Asian or African. I was the only white person. I allowed myself to fancy that they were thinking that I must be one hell of a dangerous dude—If they do this to a *white man!*

The next morning I was taken by a police officer, to whom I just happened to be handcuffed, aboard a plane. After speaking to a steward, the officer uncuffed me and left the plane. I did not make much eye contact with my fellow passengers on the trip to Berlin.

And all the civil servants who had functioned together to humiliate me for no good purpose that they could substantiate—all of them, they were all just doing their job.

Adelheid received me back with amused resignation. Our relationship had evolved to the point where she couldn't in good conscience just leave me lying outside, particularly in the winter. I returned to the routine I had just left, but a few months later I decided to return to the United States, being driven by my longing for an English-speaking country and relief from fucking poverty. I had been away almost three years. Adelheid and I parted again with our usual implied understanding. We had some difficulties living together, but we actually liked each other a lot.

CHAPTER SEVENTEEN
PATTY HEARST AND THE GANG

I wound up in San Francisco, my third time in the Bay Area. It was July 1976, but thankfully after the fourth so I missed the worst of the Bicentennial orgy celebrating the state religion, patriotism. I had been worried that my outstanding court debt might cause complications in entering the country, but thanks to my older sister Toby, who lived on Long Island, the money had been paid.

I was sharing the lower half of a duplex in the Mission district with two other men I had not known before. Very close by was the local office of the Socialist Workers Party, the leading Trotskyist party in the United States. I began attending lectures there, talking to party members, and before I knew it I was once again a "Trot." I must have been lonely.

Although I certainly ascribed to Marx's materialist/class-based method of analyzing history—now widely utilized by historians of various political stripes—I didn't usually refer to myself as a Marxist because of the heavy baggage attached to the word by Americans and others. All of Stalin's sins, real and imagined, crammed the suitcase, though the Marxist analysis had nothing to do with what happened in Russia; it's like blaming Jesus Christ for the Spanish Inquisition. I was further reluctant to adopt the label because I had read much more by Marxists than by Marx himself.

But even if I had called myself a Marxist, I would still have found the dogmatism I encountered in the SWP stifling—uncritical belief in the historical, dialectical destiny of the American working class to overthrow capitalism. The actual political state of mind of the American worker, particularly of the blue-collar type which the party idealized—often reactionary, racist, supportive of American imperialism, and caught up in playing the lottery of rising to be a CEO—was accorded scant weight. Without reservation I embraced the attempt to raise the political consciousness of as many benighted American souls as possible, but I couldn't bring myself to really believe that anything could propel a critical mass of the American working class into the vanguard of a revolution.

One day I crossed the Bay to Oakland to surprise Bill MacGilvray, whom I hadn't seen in three years. I was actually expecting to find him in the same house, same room, reading a book, etc., etc. But he no longer lived there and no one had any idea of where he could be found. Years later, in the 1990s, I learned of his fate. At some point he had returned to his hometown of Portland, Maine, and at some point after that—shocking to say—he had fallen to a terribly low level; he had become a street person. On October 13, 1990, his body was found floating in a river. It was called an accident on the certificate of death. There was a nice tribute to him in a local paper, with a photo of him dressed in the type of clothing that associates itself with the homeless, with unkempt hair and beard to match. It was only because I knew it was him that I was able to make out Bill's face. A local art dealer, the article said, had known Bill well—Willie, he called him—and had taken him in for a winter. "That was the winter of 1986-87. Willie spent a lot of time reading Will Durant's *History of Civilization.*"

Before long, I was working as the business manager cum office manager for Radio Station KPFA, a listener-supported, non-commercial station in Berkeley, where I once again moved to. KPFA was the flagship of Pacifica Radio, the sole progressive radio network in the United States. I soon began to help write the daily newscast from wire copy and other sources, feeling much more in my element than I did as financial watchdog. The newswriting was technically as a volunteer, after five o'clock and occasionally Sunday, but often I was asked to do so during my regular business-manager hours.

Unlike many of the other news writers, I was able to bring to the news writing some sense that the world had not begun that morning. When a U.S. official made a statement which contradicted a previous government statement or policy, or was otherwise deceptive, I would add such observation to the news copy. Most of the young people who volunteered to help write the news—indeed, most of the people who worked at the station—were not any kind of radical, contrary to what most listeners and critics assumed. They were fuzzy-minded liberals or apolitical, even a few politically conservative, working at the station because they were in love with the idea of being in "show biz," particularly those who went on the air; they relished being part of the station's charisma, as KPFA was a venerable institution in the Bay Area; some hoped to use the station as a stepping stone to greater media fame and fortune (a number in fact did wind up with National Public Radio and other news outlets).

During the four years I worked at the station in a variety of off-air capacities, there were several different station managers. The last of them was David Salniker, a white attorney who had been active in the civil rights movement. When it came to African-Americans, he was nothing if not "politically correct," his office walls being covered with framed photos of well-known black men and women. At one point, the Pacifica national office in Los Angeles sent their bookkeeper to Berkeley for a few days for some educational purpose, and I spent some time with her. When I later mentioned to Salniker that I thought the (black) woman didn't know even the basics of bookkeeping, it was clear that my remark did not sit well with him. (I later heard that the woman was discharged for incompetence.) And when, on several occasions, I pointed out how Pacifica executives were wasting significant amounts of money, which we could ill afford, he was likewise annoyed with me. David was not a person inclined to rock the boat. When he decided to fire me, he was unable to muster the courage to tell me this directly. He simply cut back on my duties, one by one, assigning them to other people, until I saw no point in remaining. I didn't stage any confrontation with him on this because I no longer cared about remaining at the station under him.

Wendy Yoshimura's trial took place in Oakland during November 1976 to January 1977. She was charged with several counts of illegal possession of explosives, bomb parts and an automatic weapon, all stemming from the 1972 arrests at the Berkeley garage. Oddly enough, no charges to do with helping hide Patty Hearst for over a year; perhaps this had to do with Wendy being a fugitive herself. However, Wendy's attorney was of the opinion that it was her association with Hearst that lay behind this trial, that otherwise her case might have been dismissed or she might have gotten straight probation.[45]

When Wendy was on the stand, she was asked repeatedly who it was that had telephoned her about Willie Brandt's arrest. She refused to answer the question. The judge ordered her to answer, upon threat of contempt of court. She still refused, declaring that to do so might cause harm to the people who had helped her, which was not only against her moral principles but was also contrary to traditional Japanese concepts she had learned as a child. The judge cited her for contempt several times.[46]

I've never understood why the prosecution was so interested in knowing who had called Wendy that night. Was it a crime what I had done? Ditto for helping her to vacate her apartment and take her somewhere else—she was not yet wanted for anything. But I was grateful for her silence. If I had been named, it might have induced the district attorney to set his legal pit bulls on me. Because he could.

Wendy's attorney emphasized to the jury that she had been dominated by Willie, that without his influence she would never have had any association with bombs and guns and the like. I'm sure this is correct. Patty Hearst later wrote in her book that "It was difficult to keep in mind that this quiet, cheerful young woman was a revolutionary." Wendy was nonetheless found guilty. The presence in the garage of guerrilla-war-type manuals, all the documents and photos about McNamara and his home, in addition to the weapons and explosives, were just too much for a jury of respectable citizens. Wendy couldn't pass the smell test. But she served only six months in prison.

Shortly before her trial began, Willie had been released to a halfway house in Oakland after four and a half years in prison, during which time he had taught basic adult education and was a leader of the prisoners union. He and Wendy had a brief reunion, including screwing in her attorney's office closet, Willie laughingly informed me, but that was more for old times sake than anything else; too many major life changes had occurred; their relationship was not destined to be reincarnated.

Jack and Micki Scott, who had lived near our house in Oakland, and had been part of the "gang," played key roles in the entire Patty Hearst saga. It was they who had brought Wendy and Patty together and who had rented the Pennsylvania farmhouse where Wendy, Patty and Symbionese Liberation Army fugitives Emily and William Harris had hidden out for a considerable period of time. Jack—well known as a radical sports activist—also drove various of the above individuals back and forth across the country in the face of a major FBI manhunt for Hearst. I don't know how he managed to escape any kind of indictment. He told me years later that at one point he had driven Patty Hearst to her parents' home south of San Francisco, parked the car opposite the house, and told Patty that she was free to get out of the car and go into the house. She declined.

Jack died in 2000 of throat cancer at age 57, as attorneys for Kathy Soliah were asking a court to take his death-bed testimony in her behalf. Kathy, whom I'd met when we were both visiting Willie at Soledad, was charged with placing a bomb under a police car in 1975, allegedly as an act of revenge for the police killing-cum-execution of Symbionese Liberation Army members in Los Angeles. She had been caught in 1999 after 24 years on the run, during which time she had created and led an entirely new life as doctor's wife, mother of three, and esteemed community activist in St. Paul under the name of Sara Jane Olson. Her friends and neighbors in St. Paul raised a million dollars in bail for her.

To me the strangest outcome of all the gang members is that of Willie. In

1984 he moved to Portland, Oregon, where he still lives with his wife and two teenage daughters. Although he does do some battle with local bureaucracy on self-involved issues, he has zero sympathy or interest in radical politics, regards the Vietnam era as having been "mostly a misadventure" for himself, and is mainly preoccupied with the home he owns, tending his garden, and following his stock investments (sic), this worldly wealth deriving from an inheritance from his much maligned parents. Where did I go wrong? Bizarre!

Oh, did I mention that in March of 1977 Adelheid came to live with me in Berkeley? And that two years later we got married so that she could get a green card and work legally? And that three years after that the good Lord decided to bless us two non-believers with a son? Well, the good Lord did have some vindictive fun. We had planned a home birth and the midwife was there. . . and there. . . and there. . . for two days the creature inside Adelheid's swollen belly refused to come out. We finally had to drive to the hospital in one of the worst rainstorms in Bay Area history. Six hours later the creature still refused to lower its standard of living by entering this tired old world. Alexander Simon Blum was finally born by a Caesarean 54 hours after his mother's water had broken; born in Oakland instead of the more hip-sounding Berkeley as we had planned.

At the time of his birth, I was general manager of *The Daily Californian*, the newspaper of the University of California at Berkeley, and two months shy of my 49th birthday. If you wonder how I took to fatherhood for the first time at that advanced age, the answer is *marvelously*. I found that I loved babies. And didn't even mind being remarked to repeatedly by strangers that I had a "lovely grandchild." The editor of *The Daily Californian* at the time, Margaret Talbot, daughter of old-time Hollywood actor Lyle Talbot, told me that her father was 59 when she was born.

From day one, Adelheid spoke to Alexander only in German and I spoke to him only in English. It was so simple, and it worked perfectly. He grew up impeccably bilingual. I've often thought that I would love to have had insight into his young mind at the precise moment when it finally came home to his consciousness—Hey! These two people who are always talking to me, they're not speaking the same "language"!

Adelheid and I both worked at People's Translation Service in Oakland (everything was for the people in those days). PTS put out a magazine called *Newsfront International,* which contained translations into English of selected articles from the foreign press. Adelheid did translations from German of course; others worked in Italian, French, Arabic, and Spanish. I did some Spanish, but mainly I edited the English of some of the translations. The aim was to provide a foreign—usually Third World—perspective on major issues of the day, like how it felt to be on the receiving end of Western policies, which would not usually find its way to the American media.

In August 1982, when Alexander was seven months old, and I had saved up a fair amount from my job at *The Daily Californian,* we moved to London. After five and a half years in the States, Adelheid was anxious to return to Europe and show Alexander off to her family. It had been enlightening to me to see the United States and Americans through her foreign eyes. When she remarked one day about the "optimism" she observed in most Americans, more so than in the Old World, I was struck by how something so seemingly obvious had escaped me. "I wish I had grown up with it," she said, "instead of with this stupid German guilt. I envy all Americans for their national innocence." She loved the "great poetry" of the Declaration of Independence, something my hardened political views had not encouraged me to dwell upon.

We wound up in the lower-middle class Crouch End neighborhood of North London, a nice top-floor apartment with balconies front and rear, the latter offering a grand view of Alexandra Palace. After I found a used car of hopeful condition, we took off on a trip to Germany via France to visit Adelheid's mother and some of her seven siblings in the south. It went well with the family, no noticeable awkwardness; my German performed sufficient to rise above the moron level (my German accent is actually pretty good due to regularly hearing Yiddish for so many years).

Back in London I set to work on a book that I had done some preliminary work on in Berkeley. It had begun as an article, cataloguing U.S. government interventions since the Second World War and the damage they had done, à la Chile. I had planned to include the 10 or 12 that were most famous, pretty much all I knew of. But as I began to research it I soon realized that there was more to this than I had imagined, a lot more. My government, I discovered, had easily been the intervention king of all history. There was scarcely any place in the known world where the CIA and/or the U.S. military had not been doing its dirty work. This was not a magazine article, I decided. This was a book. And I was excited.

In October I took a trip alone to Russia after coming upon an irresistible bargain trip offered by a group with some connection to the Communist Party of Great Britain—10 days in Moscow, Leningrad and Novgorod, airfare, all internal transportation, all hotels, all meals, guided tours, all for $300. If not for the baby, Adelheid would have come along as well. (So why didn't she go and leave me with the baby? I knew you'd ask that. Because it was all my idea and my initiative.)

I was impressed most with the beauty and history of Leningrad, the Moscow subway, and the omnipresent, monumental banners and photos heralding the Glorious October parade for the 65th anniversary of the Russian Revolution, which I freezingly stood watching for hours. And Lenin's mausoleum. I had to remind myself that I was not looking at a lifelike photo of Lenin, not a wax dummy of him, but Lenin himself. Think of some historical person you'd like to see in the same manner.

Some of my traveling companions from the UK were either Communist Party members or fellow travelers and comported themselves in a defensive manner. When a young boy approached us in the street and asked for some gum, one of them remarked: "Well, if all he asks for is gum, things can't be too bad here, can they?" And when we passed by what might have been a store that was now closed and empty, this moved one them to declare that in the UK, ha-ha, the windows would all be broken by now, boarded up, covered with graffiti, homeless people living inside, ha-ha. I found their remarks annoying, even embarrassing, yet I understood that their attitude was a reaction to a lifetime of living in the West, where their beliefs about an alternative kind of society were ridiculed and distorted wherever they turned in the media or schoolbooks. Had I not been raised in a similar environment?

One day our Russian guide asked me what I wrote about, and I told her that I was now writing a book very critical of American foreign policy. She was taken aback. She told me, in all seriousness, that I shouldn't be writing books against my own government; she didn't mean because of any danger, but simply that it just wasn't right. When I asked her if she would have objected to a German in Nazi Germany writing a book that was derogatory of the government, a light bulb instantly lit above her head and she said she understood my point. If only I could have dissolved American conditionings so easily.

For four years I worked on the book at the equivalent of more than a full time job. Though my subject dealt with the United States, I was at an advantage being in London with its remarkable libraries and singular institutions. For my chapter on Australia I had The Australia House to consult, run by the government of Australia and containing a library full of material I'd have had a very difficult time finding in the States. There was also the University of London with its huge specialized libraries like the one on Oriental and African Studies, the London School of Economics library, the British Newspaper Library, and of course the grandaddy of them all, the British Library, in whose awesome Reading Room Mahatma Gandhi, George Bernard Shaw, W.B. Yeats, Karl Marx and V.I. Lenin had sat and studied, which I would enter and feel as some people feel upon entering a cathedral.

I was putting together a book that no one had ever come close to doing before. Can it be imagined that the Nazi Holocaust could have taken place without anyone knowing of it? With growing astonishment, I was discovering that the American holocaust had.

From Alexander's age of one to two, I was a househusband. Adelheid had a job with a publisher doing English to German translation, for which she was gone ten hours a day. I watched Alexander for six of those hours, and he was with a "child minder" for four, during which I worked on my book, as I did part of most evenings. When Adelheid's employer decided to move the German department to Germany, employees were given a choice of moving there or getting more than a year's severance pay. This was thanks to the National Union of Journalists, which Adelheid belonged to. Her severance pay allowed her to stay home and me to frequent the libraries. I felt very privileged, being able to spend my days doing important and fascinating research at one splendid institution or another.

We lived within walking distance of Highgate Cemetery and Waterlow Park which adjoined it. Many a time we'd push Alexander through the charming little park in his stroller or let him run about. Then we'd go into the cemetery to look upon the famous and unfamous dead, usually winding up at the oversize tomb of Karl Marx. I liked to see the crowd of tourists that was invariably there, many from China, the Soviet Union and Eastern Europe, dropping flowers at the foot of their idol. On the centennial of Marx's death, March 14, 1983, there was an especially large crowd there, along with the media. Adelheid's sister Nine was visiting from Germany and in front of the TV cameras the two women broke out into a moving rendition of "The Internationale" in German. I don't know if it appeared on the evening news. On one visit to the site, when Alexander was about four, he suddenly shouted out in front of the crowd: "No Marx!" I didn't know whether I was more amused or embarrassed. What that little child could possibly have meant will remain one of life's enduring mysteries.

With the book about half done, I found a publisher in London. Zed Books, a scholarly, academic-oriented press, agreed to publish it only a few hours after I left a partial manuscript at their office. I would have been at this stage sooner, but like the vast majority of Britain, or even the U.S. at that time, I didn't have a computer. The British Library was only just beginning to automate its catalog. In the end, I estimated that I could have knocked a full year off my efforts by not having to retype large portions of chapters again and again to incorporate my continuous findings of new information. And to be able to do instant searches through the immense files of data I was building up daily would have bordered on magic. In the end the 428-page book chronicled serious U.S. interventions into about 65 countries, most with multiple incidents.

The day before the printer was to send the first copies of my book to Zed, I was shown a copy of the cover, and I became instantly agitated. The title, we had agreed, was to be *The CIA, A Forgotten History: U.S. Global Interventions Since World War II*. But the entire subtitle—which captured the essence of the book—though it appeared on the title page, was left off the cover. The book was

NOT a history of the CIA—"CIA" had been stuck in for sales purposes—but that's how it now appeared to be, because the Artistic Director decided that so many words on the cover was injurious to the aesthetic appearance. Once again, the triumph of style over substance. I stormed about Zed's office, angry, talking loudly, shaking my head, moaning. . . until I realized that no one was responding at all, no one was even looking at me. Typical Brits! Repressing their own emotions and embarrassed by seeing them hanging loose from anyone else.

In my years in London, I was constantly encountering this stoney embarrassment. Everything embarrassed the natives; they were always apologizing for one thing or another.

A neighbor came to the door one evening, a young woman, and told Adelheid that she was very sorry to bother her, she didn't mean to intrude, but. . . well. . . it seemed that we had left our car lights on and. . . well. . . she thought that under the circumstances. . . she. . . well. . . should tell us. Adelheid felt a bit silly, but she had to reassure the woman, more than once, that it was perfectly okay, that she was indeed glad that she had told her.

The other side of the embarrassment coin is privacy. The English chuckle about the Americans they've met who, before half an hour has passed, are telling them of their marital problems, their psychoanalysis, and their delvings into all manner of growth-movement inner exploration, if not their financial situation and sex life. Those English people who are not simply turned off by this display find it amusing, much like their forefathers who built the Empire found certain ways of the natives amusing, perhaps even charming, but certainly not for them, and certainly not "proper." Not only is England an island, every Englishman is.

The consequence for myself of the English obsession with privacy was the extreme difficulty of getting to know people there, getting close to them, simply making friends. I never knew where I stood with them, or where *we* stood, and there was no process of evolution—the tenth time I met with someone the nature and depth of our conversation was scarcely different from that of out first meeting. No, I was not a masochist. I met some of them so often because they were parents of children at Alexander's school and also lived in the same neighborhood.

Typically, in a social situation, I had to initiate conversation if there was to be any at all, or if there was to be any contact beyond the introductory banalities. If the conversation lagged, it was I who had to refuel it or it petered out. If I didn't maneuver the conversation to more "interesting" areas, we stood mired in the mud of polite, safe, small talk which the English never seem to tire of. They can small-talk you to death; it's their social glue that tells them that all is well with the world. Someone I once read asked "Do children ever make small talk with each other? The idea sounds ridiculous."

It's all quite ironic. The image of the British that has captured the American imagination is that of "charming"—David Niven, Cary Grant, Alec Guinness and the like leap to mind; the accent alone sells the image. But those of course are roles they play. In real life I found the British rather boring; most of our friends were other foreigners. The British, in turn, did not know what to do with me. I often was made to feel that I was the awful American child. I learned to—was compelled to—tone down my act, but not enough to alter the simple fact of my life there: I was a bull, and all of England was a china shop.

Following a serious train crash in London in 1999, the Washington Post stated: "But despite the horror of the moment, the famous British stiff upper lip was firmly in place at the accident scene." One of the survivors, novelist Jilly Cooper, said: "I was proud to be British. Everyone was so calm. The rescue teams went about their business, and those of us who could do just walked quietly away." The *Times* of London boasted in a large headline that the British had displayed "grace under pressure."[47]

Contrast this with the observations of the Japanese-British novelist Kazuo Ishiguro: "In British and Japanese society, the ability to control emotions is considered dignified and elegant.". . . British restraint is based on "a fear of revealing how human you actually are." Japanese formality derives from "a fear of offending.". . . Often what appears to be the exercise of dignity and restraint "is merely a kind of alibi for cowardice."

My book came out in October 1986. I was soon introduced to the treacherous world of book reviewers. Much to my surprise and delight, Jonathan Steele, the chief foreign correspondent for my favorite British newspaper, *The Guardian,* phoned me at home. But he was disturbed, it turned out, that I had written that Andreas Papandreou was reported to have worked with the CIA in the early 1960s. Papandreou, the then-prime-minister of Greece, and Steele were friends. I told Steele that I was simply repeating what the *New York Times* had reported in 1974 and that Papandreou had criticized the report but had not denied the charge. This was all documented in my book and seemed as plain as could be. But not to the eminent foreign correspondent. I repeated what the book said, but he was still not satisfied. To this day I don't understand why he called or what he expected me to do about the story, either in the *New York Times* or in my book. Our conversation ended inconclusively.

About a month later Steele reviewed my book along with two others in *The Guardian.* Only two column inches of the total of 18 1/2 were devoted to my opus, but he managed to find space to state that the events in the book were dealt with "not always accurately."[48] Like a kick to my stomach it was.

I wrote to Steele asking him to tell me exactly what the "inaccuracies" were. Six months later he replied, giving two (2) examples. One was a judgment call about how revolutionary the MPLA of Angola was or was not, and I think that subsequent events definitely proved me correct that they were not the answer to a radical's prayer. The second example was in my chapter on Grenada, where I wrote that "US forces killed hundreds of people." Upon further examination, I decided that I couldn't be certain of my statement, and in the next edition of the book it was changed to "killed or wounded hundreds of people."

And that was it. Those were the sum total of my transgressions that had caused Mr. Steele to throw a blanket of doubt over my entire book on the pages of the daily newspaper most likely in the entire world to win me readers.

Many authors have similar tales of severe review-heartburn to relate of course. Soon thereafter, I was to experience an even worse example of this occupational hazard.

There were as well positive reviews in the *Times* and smaller publications, and a negative one by a Tory MP of all people in the *Times Literary Supplement*. He cited some paragraphs from my book to illustrate what a self-evident dastardly work this was, but I was pleased with those passages and I would think that most readers of the review were not turned away.

When the book was about to make its appearance in the States, in early 1987, I was hit by an irrepressible desire to be there and enjoy whatever fruits there were to be enjoyed by the "famous author." That plus my having had enough of the Brits, thank you, made me decide to return "home." Unfortunately, very unfortunately, Adelheid didn't want to. I was faced with an awful decision.

I decided to return alone, not just for a visit—commuting back and forth indefinitely was not a practical option—but I actually moved back, shipping my books and stuff ahead of me. In hindsight, on countless occasions I've rued the fact that we did not find a better option and even more often have I wondered how I was able to leave that darling little boy, just two months past his fifth birthday. I must have been awfully hungry for those literary fruits. I was 54 and for all I knew this was my fifteen minutes.

CHAPTER EIGHTEEN
THE AUTHOR VS. HOLLYWOOD.
HOLLYWOOD WINS.

I wound up again in the Bay Area, the fourth time I had moved there, this time renting a furnished room in a beautiful house in the Berkeley Hills from a man who heard me being interviewed on KPFA, which I had closed with an appeal for a place to rent. That was Pacifica Radio and that was Berkeley.

Another listener to my interview was Larry Bensky, former manager of the station, who had hired me ten years earlier, and was now Pacifica's chief national affairs correspondent. He phoned me at the station and asked me to leave a copy of the book for him in his box. He wanted to include it in a review of similar books he was doing for a local weekly called *Express*.

When it came out I was stunned. Bensky wrote that the book was not "worth the effort of either writing it or reading it" and that it would "be forgotten as soon as the next book comes along."[49] The review, as short as it was, also contained several factual inaccuracies about what I had supposedly left out, when in fact they were plainly there. The *Express* published my letter refuting the review and then Bensky's letter in return. It was clear to me that he had not read the book as much as he had perused the index, and even that he had not done very well, criticizing me for not touching upon the CIA and its airlines, when the index stated: "CIA: airlines" with reference to six pages. Another of his criticisms was that I had not discussed the CIA's domestic activities. I pointed out that I had not gone into this because the book dealt only with *foreign* interventions, a fact obvious from even a cursory glance. His counter letter stated: "Not dealing with the CIA's domestic incursions in a book subtitled 'The Untold Story' is irresponsible and absurd." What book, or what index, I wondered, had the man read? My subtitle was U.S. Global Interventions Since World War II. None of the books he reviewed was subtitled "The Untold Story."

As to the book being soon forgotten—as I write this in the year 2001, the book, including its updated versions, has been in print without a break for more than 14 years and has had seven printings.

What had motivated an intelligent and politically aware person like Larry Bensky to trash the book in such an obviously silly manner? (Its full silliness can't be appreciated without my risking boring the reader with yet more details of "he said-I said.") I can think of no reason except personal jealousy. He had writing aspirations of his own, had written for *Paris Review,* and based on a few things of his I had seen, I'd say he in fact wrote well. But he had not produced a book, and here was his former flunky, whom he had yelled at on occasion, who had worked under him as a (ugh) numbers cruncher, not an on-air showbiz celebrity, here was this virtual non-person coming out of nowhere with a voluminous, serious book dealing with U.S. foreign policy, an area Bensky himself often ventured into as a news commentator.

If, at this point, the reader is thinking that the above has been written just to get back at Bensky, all I can say is: "You're damned right."

Well, no, it's not *just* that. It's to provide another lesson about how a hidden agenda can lie behind the comments of a book reviewer who wields his pen like a machete. Editors who assign books to be reviewed should question the potential reviewers carefully to weed out any serious personal biases, in fairness to both the author and the reader.

In September I went back to London for a visit. The way Alexander gleefully ran into my arms at the airport dispelled my grave worries that he might have forgotten me in the six months I had been gone. The three of us had a nice two-week visit, albeit not without some soul-searching late-night dialogues between Adelheid and I.

Back in Berkeley, I continued speaking in bookstores and doing radio interviews, slowly acquiring much-needed polishing of these skills as I went along. I also sent out free copies of my book to well-known liberals, not knowing what might blossom from these seeds. Suddenly there was a beautiful sprouting. Oliver Stone sent me a thank-you letter from Hollywood, saying "I bought several more copies to circulate to friends with the hope of shedding new light and understanding on their political outlooks." I eventually learned from the owner of Midnight Special Bookstore in Santa Monica that Oliver had bought some 20 copies.

I was intent upon finding an American publisher to put out an American edition of the book, so I could make a number of additions and changes, including to the botched cover, which Zed was not willing to pay for. Moreover, having my publisher in England caused all kinds of complications, not the least of which was that they shipped books to the States on a slow boat to the East Coast, and then there was another slow trek across country via some other means of transportation. I wrote back to Stone, asking him if he knew of a literary agent who could help me find a publisher. A few days later, his secretary called me and told me that Oliver would like to meet me and wanted me to come down to Los Angeles.

Well, if he thought that I would jump at his beckoning just like that. . .

Having no car, I took a Greyhound bus to L.A. I stayed with my dear old friend Pat Cawood, who was now living there with his third wife, Susan Smith, and their newborn twins. Pat was almost 49, same age as I was when Alexander was born, although the two girls weren't his first children of course. He and Susan had a growing computer consulting firm, specializing in hydrological applications (don't ask me to explain). It was a source of great pleasure how Pat and I had managed to stay in touch for over 20 years from several continents. He had even lived for awhile with Adelheid and I in Berkeley before Alexander was born, and I had helped to arrange for him to meet Susan.

I took a city bus to within a few blocks of the Twentieth Century Fox lot and walked the rest of the way to the Pico Boulevard entrance. When I went up to the guard's booth to ask him where Stone's office was, he just stared at me. Finally, he got the words out: "Where'd you park?" When I told him that I didn't have a car, I might as well have told him that I didn't have a liver or a pancreas. Welcome to La-La land.

I found my way to the temporary office set up for Oliver while he was making *Wall Street*, and introduced myself to his gal Friday, Elisabeth Seldes, granddaughter of the eminent journalist George Seldes. Soon Oliver appeared and invited me for lunch at the studio commissary. As we walked there, he told me that the agent he had in mind for me—one of the Seldes family—hadn't panned out and he had been unable to find another.

So what the hell am I doing here? I thought. He just wanted to buy me lunch? But while we were eating, Oliver told me that he'd like to make a documentary film based on my book.

My immediate reaction was of course great surprise. My second reaction was that this was a foolhardy undertaking and could never succeed. I was not thrilled. The beauty of my book was its documentation—what the United States had done in and to the world, presented in such vast and careful detail that even those people who found it painful to believe what the book was saying would be left with no choice but to believe it. How could any film provide such detail? How could we find film footage of pertinent events, so much of which had occurred covertly? It was not a story made for the screen. It was a story made for my favorite medium, a book. I did not take him seriously.

But then Oliver suggested that we drive over to his producer's office on Sunset Boulevard, a block from Beverly Hills. John Daly, Britisher, head of Hemdale Films, had helped to launch the first of Stone's Vietnam sagas, *Platoon*. I sat in his office while he and Oliver discussed the documentary film. I looked from one to the other. . . so this is Hollywood. . . this guy Daly, straight out of Central Casting to play the part of a film mogul, what the fuck does he care about American imperialism? He just wants to keep his fair-haired boy, Oliver, happy. I interjected that I could not see any way to make a film based on my book that would not come out looking, sounding, and smelling anti-American.

It was like I hadn't said a word. Daly mentioned to Oliver that Bernardo Bartolucci had loved his last film, and Oliver looked as pleased as a kid getting a report card covered with "A"s. The meeting came to an end, Stone drove back to the studio, I walked over to a bus stop to go the other way. . . nothing at all concrete had been resolved, no other meeting scheduled. . . so that was Hollywood; it would make a funny story to tell.

A few days later, back in Berkeley, the phone rang. It was John Daly, asking me how much I'd need in the way of salary.

All thoughts of the unworkableness of the film disappeared immediately, as my true, greedy capitalist nature came to the fore. Until that moment, the most I had ever earned on any job in my entire life was $2,000 a month, at *The Daily Californian* five years earlier. My mind raced. Do I dare ask for $5,000 a month? That would be fantastic. I could live like a king. But I couldn't bring the words across my lips. If I was too greedy, I thought, I might kill the whole thing. (Yeah, right, being too concerned with money is a real no-no in Hollywood.) Finally, I said, "Gee, I don't know. How much would someone in my position [whatever *that* was] usually be paid?"

"How about $2,000 a week," said John.

"Oh, uh, um. . . yeah, that would be okay. . . yeah."

Obviously, I could have asked for and gotten more.

I returned to Los Angeles and signed a contract with Hemdale Film Corporation guaranteeing me a minimum of four months employment at the above salary as well as another $2,000 for relocation expenses. Hemdale also paid $7,000 for the film rights to the book, of which Zed got half. I was glad they could share a little in my good luck because I remained grateful to them for rescuing me from the literary netherworld.

I quickly found an apartment in Hollywood (i.e., the section of L.A. of that name, not on a studio lot). Los Angeles is the only city I know of where you can, at least at that time, choose where you want to live, often down to the exact block. There were "For Rent" signs all over the place, supposedly due to a period of great overbuilding.

I had a very spacious one-bedroom apartment—living room almost 20 feet long, bedroom large enough to hold two king-size beds without crowding; a palm tree right outside my living room window in a central court that was part overgrown jungle; a swimming pool about 20 yards away; free parking, all for $550 a month, what I'd be earning in less than a day and a half.

I began working at the start of the new year of 1988, spending most of my time at the UCLA Film and Television Archives looking through their vast index for pertinent film footage. I didn't know what I was specifically looking for so much as seeing what was available and letting my imagination play around with it. Oliver had not asked me whether I had any experience or talent in making a documentary film. In effect, he had simply told me to make the film and told John Daly to pay for it, then walked away. Fine by me.

In the meantime, I was furnishing my apartment, buying my first computer, and buying a car. I bought the cheapest new car I could find, a Ford Escort. The fact that it was new and that I didn't have to spend time taking care of it or worrying about problems was everything. I had virtually no other concern about the kind of car I drove as long as it started, took me to where I wanted to go, and stopped.

Adelheid and Alexander had moved to Freiburg, Germany, near the Black Forest, an hour or so from France and Switzerland. Adelheid had gone to university there and still had friends in the city. She felt that if she was going to be a single mother, she'd rather it was where she had family close by. I was not happy about the move; it would make visiting a lot more difficult.

In April they came to visit me for about two weeks. One morning as we left my house, I checked my mailbox and took out a check from Hemdale for the past five weeks, $10,000. Adelheid gasped. "Oh my god," she said, and we just stood there looking at the check and at each other. We had never experienced each other in the context of no worries about money. I was able to greatly increase the monthly payment I sent for Alexander's upkeep.

The admission price for the three of us to enter Disneyland was about $100, and I was fully aware that it was an outrageous price, which I normally would be opposed to paying—How can a poor family ever take their kids to Disneyland?—but I wasn't going to deny Alexander, now six, the thrill of his young life when I could so easily afford it. Ditto Knotts Berry Farm and other places. It came as a surprise to me, however, to realize that appreciation of scenic beauty was not somehow inborn. Alexander, like almost all children, was not moved by the feast for the eyes that was California outdoors. This was to remain the case into his teens.

The thought came to me that I needed to learn more about making documentary films. Of course. Thus it was that I joined the International Documentary Association and began attending their seminars. I was meeting lots of people to whom filmmaking was as important as writing was to me. They almost all had the same intractable problem—lack of funding for their cherished projects, films they had been working on for years, having to stop to raise financing, starting and stopping again. For awhile I would tell my story—unlimited funding, for whatever I wanted to do, no grant proposals to write, no questions asked, complete editorial control. . . and then I stopped telling my story. It distressed them too much; the envy was palpable. I switched to a scaled-down version.

After several months of research, I was beginning to become somewhat of a believer. I had accumulated many old newsreels showing scenes surrounding various government overthrows, civil wars, bombing damage, assassinations, important speeches, parliaments in debate, press conferences, parades and other celebrations, and much more, most of it in that melodramatic voice and music style of 1950s and '60s Hearst and Fox newsreels, which can be very effective; and which, if judiciously juxtaposed with appropriate interviewees saying the appropriate things, and further enhanced by voice-over narration, which I would write, *might—just might*—in sum total, capture a decent measure of the impact I liked to think my book had upon a reader.

At one point, the UCLA Archives gave me a form to have filled out by Hemdale, simply guaranteeing payment of the fees for all the film footage I was receiving. I handed it in to the Hemdale office, but I was unable to get it signed. Weeks went by. UCLA kept after me and I kept calling Hemdale, unable to get the right party or a clear answer, and Oliver was away on a shoot. What the heck was going on?

I eventually found out that Daly and Oliver had had a falling out a while back. Over money for *Platoon*. The way of all flesh in Hollywood. Every day. Daly and his assistant, Dorian, with whom I mainly dealt, being British, were too embarrassed to tell me that the project was dead. They allowed me to keep on working, without signing the form, without telling me anything, but still paying me.

It reached the point where I—still not knowing about the fall out—went to Hemdale's office, asked the receptionist to call Daly or Dorian and sat down in a room adjacent to her. I was not leaving until I saw one of them.

I sat there and waited, and waited. The door to the room was slightly ajar, just enough to see. . . I could hardly believe my eyes. . . John Daly, a man of fifty, was *tiptoeing* down the stairs and was on his way out of the office when I flung the door open and called out: "John! Where are you going?" I really would not be shocked to learn that he pissed in his pants at that moment. This was major league embarrassment—9th inning of the 7th game of the World Series embarrassment.

"Oh, I'll be right back," he stammered, turned his back on his tormenter, and left.

I waited another short while before I went home. A couple of hours or so later, Dorian called me to inform me—as if nothing had transpired—that "For the time being, we've. . . uh. . . we've decided to. . . uh. . . put the project on hold."

I forget now how I found out about the Stone-Daly fallout, although when I finally got to speak to Oliver he opined that Daly was "lower than whale shit," an expression new to my ears. I later read that Daly was being sued by several people in Hollywood for one reason or another.

So that was that. I would never find out if there was a film living inside the voluminous material I had gathered during six and a half months. Oliver made a passing reference to perhaps finding some other financing, but nothing came of that. On my own, to have as a selling point, if needed, I put together a 15-minute video composed of some of the newsreel material, other intriguing footage I had collected, some special effects, and narration. It cost me about a thousand dollars, which I could well afford, my short-lived career at Hemdale having netted me $62,000. The editing was done at the Empowerment Project in Santa Monica, where the Academy-Award-winning *Panama Deception* was later done. Now that's a film that's more effective than a written version of what the United States did; dealing with only a single American intervention, and a recent one, it could explore the events in sufficient detail and capture the visual horror and the victims' testimony more compellingly.

My little video was not made entirely in vain. A few years later it became part of a CD-ROM that was made of my book by a company in Boston, which paid me $10,000. My fortunes certainly had changed. Would success spoil Bill Blum?

So there I was, living in Los Angeles, having learned a few things about the film industry, having made a few contacts, and with writing still my first love. What to do next? But of course! I joined the mob of aspiring screenwriters.

The first of the three screenplays I hammered out over the next few years was based on the life of a former CIA officer, Verne Lyon, whom I had met when I became an honorary member of the Association for Responsible Dissent, a group set up by former national security personnel, including Philip Agee, Daniel Ellsberg, and John Stockwell. The group's ultra bland name was soon changed to the more apt Association of National Security Alumni. They held several public forums in Southern California and elsewhere on "the national security state" the United States had turned into while the citizenry had been preoccupied with living their lives.

Their forums were enthusiastically attended; for such men and women— former CIA, FBI, Defense Department, U.S. military—to go public and critically expose and analyze covert, sometimes diabolic, government operations was a unique spectacle indeed. Though many of the events they spoke about were in my book and elsewhere, there was nothing like the audience hearing it from their lips, in the context of their own personal involvement and eventual disillusionment. It was exhilarating to be associated with them and take part in question and answer sessions at the end of a couple of the talks.

Public forums like these are the kind people are inclined to put down as "preaching to the converted." That expression bothers me. Based on the questions asked by audiences and the discussions I've had with people there, it's been made plain to me on numerous occasions that the great majority of those attending may (or may not) have their heart in the right place, but their gaps in knowledge of both the details and the big picture of U.S. foreign policy goals leave them only about one notch above that of the average American. They are so in need of the education that they're vulnerable to being moved in one of several directions.

This is not to say that they're terribly aware of their gaps. Most people would not presume to argue an esoteric point of quantum mechanics with a physics professor if they had not even taken Physics 101. But when it comes to political questions, so many think that they not only have the right to express their opinion, but that their opinion is just as valid as anyone else's. Like it's in the Constitution.

Verne Lyon's story was particularly dramatic and might have made a great movie, if I knew how to write a screenplay. With but a cursory look at some screenwriting guides and a couple of actual scripts, I plowed ahead. After I finished it, I showed it to a friend of mine, David George, who was much more savvy about the art of screenwriting. He said it needed a lot of work. But I was too excited to wait, or even to place much credence in David's verdict. I left it at Oliver Stone's office for The Great Man to read and sat back and waited for his ardent plaudits, fantasizing about my glorious new career and the fame and fortune that everyone in L.A over the age of 10 and not residing in a religious retreat was busily striving for. I figured if the script needed work, it could be done by one of Stone's script doctors, or by me with some guidance. That's what often happens when they really want a script.

Oliver called me. He had read the script. The bottom line of what he had to tell me was this: "Bill, it's lacking the *human touch!*" He didn't go into any further detail. When you tell an applicant for a basketball team that he's not suitable because he only has one leg, you don't feel any need to go into further detail.

What Oliver had tried to tell me so succinctly was that "ideas" weren't enough, not even close. I had to learn the art of manipulating an audience to achieve the kind of emotional effects that Hollywood cherishes.

I write these words in hindsight. The concept didn't fully sink in for some time. Something in me resented the idea of consciously manipulating people's emotions, although when I now think of it, much of my non-fiction writing is an attempt to manipulate people's intellects, in order to pry them loose from a lifetime of emotional attachment to "country" and other gods. And can not the fundamental musical experience be seen as the transformation of sound into emotion?

David and I as co-authors did a major rewrite of that script—which I called *Plausible Denial*—and various permutations of it actually still float around the offices of Hollywood agents and producers, or line the bottoms of Los Angeles bird cages, a decade later. David occasionally sends me an email about someone new who has "expressed some interest" in it. I tell him not to bother me until he has a contract for me to sign. Hollywood can express-interest you to death. I was excited the first time I went to a party there and met a film or TV person who, upon hearing about my book, told me that he was thinking of doing something on the CIA—or, in fact, it was actually in progress right then—and would be in touch with me. The second time was still exciting. By the tenth time, I handed the person my card with about as much enthusiasm as if he had told me that he cleaned carpets and would like to come by to give me an estimate. They all like to think they're players.

My second screenplay started out as a satire about Hollywood—how quickly I had reached that level!—and soon expanded to satirizing and parodying all of American society with pokes and jabs at every pet peeve of mine. This mishmash, which also suffered from EMD (emotion-manipulation deficiency), was fun for me to write, but I was soon made to realize that it would have been a film rated "N"—suitable for no one.

Okay, enough fooling around. I began to read the guidebooks seriously, attended a screenwriting class everyone said was THE class, and spent many hours at the Writers Guild of America reading scripts of actual films while simultaneously watching the films on a VCR. All of this study was based on Hollywood conventional wisdom that there is a right way to write a film: rules laid down about plot and character; the setup within the first 15 pages, the first turning point by around page 35, the second turning point by page 90, finally the climax and the resolution, one script page equaling one minute on screen; rules honored much more in the breech than the observance, which may be just as well.

Much better than following the rules is having names attached—a name actor, name director, or at least a name writer. Get Clint Eastwood and Tom Cruise to agree to spend two hours sitting on toilet seats talking about the weather, and producers will be knocking your door down.

"Stars are essentially meaningless," wrote dean of screenwriters, William Goldman. "Studio executives know this—they know that *the picture is the star* . . . They absolutely, positively, one hundred percent in their heart of hearts, in the dark nights of their souls, they *know* it. They just don't believe it, that's all."

But still believing that if I built it they would come, I plodded ahead and eventually turned out "Soon to be a major motion picture" Number 3. . .

The president of the United States is dying of a rare blood disease, aplastic anemia. He needs a bone marrow transplant and the only suitable match that can be found is a very liberal social worker in Santa Monica. And she refuses to be a donor unless the government makes some striking concessions because many of the president's policies have inflicted great suffering on her clients and many other people. As a result, she becomes a target of attack, from the White House, the media, the American public, her neighbors, her father, her own husband and daughter. . . Well, that's enough. I don't want to spoil it for you when you see the film.

The few film people I heard from were upset by what I had written. They insisted that no American in that position would refuse to help the president. The reader at the firm Oliver farmed out my script to, wrote: "The premise is just too much to take seriously. . . the premise is so far out in left field that one can hardly take it with any sense of credibility making this a quick and easy PASS." The one-line Comment Summary on the first page of the report (called "coverage" in Hollywood, and which the screenwriter normally does not get to see) read: "Incredulous premise likely to be laughed off every screen it plays on."

Standing in contrast to these coverage comments we of course have the 90 percent of the films actually made which have incredulous premises.

I, in fact, had asked people I knew and every one of them had agreed with me that they would act the same as my heroine. Of course that's the people I associated with, as opposed to the people who make the evaluations and decisions in Hollywood, who would not allow themselves to believe that reasonable and sane Americans could be so turned-off by the kind of society the president's policies were fostering that they would not be willing to trouble themselves to protect his well being.

One agent, however, actually found a fairly well-known Canadian TV-film director—whose name I forget, although I did look up his credits—who wanted to use it for a film-of-the-week series. "I just have to raise the money," the director assured me in a phone conversation; words fit for a filmmaker's tombstone. I think he's still trying to raise the money and I may just hear from him any decade now.

Best of all was Geraldine, the development director of a British-French film company. She told me she loved it; my main character was one of the strongest female roles she had ever come across. Great, I thought. I met with her and her boss, Mr. Pitts of the London office, and the two of them covered me with bouquets. They sat there quoting their favorite scenes and lines from my script. Pitts even mentioned a director he had in mind for the film, and Kathy Bates for the lead role. I was not easily impressed, but this succeeded. Our meeting ended on a highly encouraging level.

Neither one ever called me again. I eventually called Geraldine, but she couldn't—or didn't wish to—give me anything approaching a clear explanation of what had happened. Presumably, whatever had happened was the film industry; i.e., something to do with money.

It all seemed so arbitrary to me, which scripts became films and which were not even read; whether the textbook rules were followed or not; whether some banker type decided to throw money at it or not. They notice serious flaws in a script when the writer has no credits and there's no star attached; but other scripts, the ones made into films, are full of identical flaws. I frequently saw films or read reviews of them which made me think that if I had submitted the exact same script, word for word, to one of the gatekeepers, it would, in all likelihood, have been rejected out of hand, for reasons I would never clearly learn.

All those executives making more money than they ever dreamed of, knowing that they're eminently replaceable, that their bubble might burst with one big mistake, one failure. This has got to lead to great insecurities, unrelenting stress, a mind-set of take no unnecessary chances; more and more films being made are remakes or virtual remakes of old ones (*Dracula 2000* was announced a while ago—Is that the year or the sequence number?). If you use big names and it flops, you can at least point to Robert Redford in the lead as evidence of your good judgment. They don't necessarily know a "good" film from a "bad" one. They don't necessarily care. What they care about is protecting their ass and their job.

The time had come for the madly-sought-after screenwriting sensation of Hollywood to hang up his computer and his script software. Were there any worlds left to conquer?

The principal international development of the early 1990s was of course the end of the Cold War and the dissolution of the Soviet Union. All over the former Soviet bloc, and even in the West, Communist Parties changed their name and individuals changed their tune; many others simply curled up and cringed in despair; personal relationships metamorphosed.

But this extraordinary historical event had no effect upon my own political beliefs or activities, for the simple reason that I had not come to the world of radical politics because of the Soviet Union or any Communist Party. Not even a fellow traveler had I been. There was nothing for me to change in head or heart, although the anti-communists gloated as if people like me had now, in some way, been proven "wrong" and exposed as frauds.

Inasmuch as U.S. interventionism, NATO, the bloated military budget, and a host of other cold-war relics have not disappeared at all, it appears that what's been proven fraudulent is the doctrine that the Cold War had been a moral struggle to contain an evil, expansionist Communist Soviet Union, when in fact—as skeptics like myself had maintained—it had been about American imperialism all along, with "communist" merely the name given to those who stood in the way.

It has been an advantage to me that I was not raised by leftist parents; as a red-diaper baby I wouldn't have experienced what it felt like to be an anti-communist true believer, but having experienced it I've been much better equipped to write and speak to the many Cold Warriors.

The end of the Cold War actually made political activity easier for those like me, for "red baiting" became pretty much *passé,* and in the mainstream media, much more than ever before, one could come upon serious questioning of past and present U.S. foreign policies, as well as frequent criticism of the way we collectively organize our economic lives—"capitalism" became almost a dirty word.

With the Soviet Union out of the way, the United States was free to pursue its hegemonic ambitions without restraint. We thus were treated to the bombing of Iraq. For 40 days and nights in January and February 1991 the bombs fell on the virtually defenseless people of Iraq, destroying their ancient/modern capital, incinerating men, women, and children alive in firestorms of napalm, depleted uranium, and other chemical compounds concocted by America's best and brightest. It revolted me. I kept waking up at night. I didn't dare turn on the TV, not just to keep my eyes averted from the slaughter, but to keep out of earshot of the chorus of newscasters all singing the same song of homage to cruise missiles. When I bought the morning paper, I attempted the difficult task of not reading the page-one headlines.

There was a protest movement of sorts in Los Angeles as elsewhere, which paled in comparison to Vietnam and the '60s, but how could it not? I took part in some of the repeated demonstrations outside the Federal Building in West L.A. The building was the nearest thing to a surrogate Washington, DC, but the whole setup was pathetic. We were allowed to assemble there only after all the employees had gone home at five o'clock. At that secluded corner of Wilshire Boulevard and Veteran Avenue, in the cold and dark of those winter evenings, there were no pedestrians passing by. Only motorists. We cheered when a driver blew his horn. That was our audience. It was all so impotent, bordering on desperate, but I had to be with others who shared my feelings, who were sickened by the carnage.

Demonstrations like ours are traditionally cited as evidence of a "healthy democracy." But, truth be said—on that occasion, as on virtually all others—I and my fellow dissenters had no more influence over our government's foreign slaughter than a peasant in China, a sheep herder in Nigeria, or a tin miner in Bolivia have over their own governments. Contrary to popular belief, we hadn't even been responsible for ending the war in Vietnam, though we probably succeeded in keeping the massacre a level or two below what it would otherwise have been and giving the American public one hell of an education.

When the Gulf War servicemen came home, they were given "heroes" welcomes all over the country, American versions of Nuremberg torchlight rallies. There was one along Hollywood Boulevard, right near where I lived. The night before, I walked along the parade route surreptitiously posting dozens of little signs saying: "Welcome Home Mass Murderers." Yes, I felt self-conscious, perhaps even a bit silly. Was this any way for a 58-year old man to behave? It was the way I had to behave. I pictured some people at the parade, their eyes falling upon one of the signs—"What kind of sick, twisted bastard would put up shit like this?" With others though. . . Who knows?. . . It might be the first instruction code of a deprogramming process. . .

Unhappy the land that has no heroes.
No. Unhappy the land that *needs* heroes.
—*Bertolt Brecht*

I devoted a long chapter to Iraq in the greatly enlarged and revised version of my book, that was published by Common Courage Press of Maine in 1995, and entitled *Killing Hope: U.S. Military and CIA Interventions Since World War II.* It took the equivalent of two years to complete the 460 pages of small type, in addition to the four years I had spent on the first version in London.

When it was finished, I decided I wanted to leave Los Angeles and move back to Washington, DC. With my no longer having any kind of involvement in the film industry, the city had lost much of its appeal for me. I would miss California and the West, the spectacular National Parks, the haunting deserts, my beloved mountains; the Hollywood Hills, only a ten-minute walk from my house, just standing there posing for postcards; the ocean, the weather. But I would not miss the city itself particularly. What bothered me most about LA was the absence of any real parks or woods. I'm judging by London standards here: a place where you can go for a long walk—horizontally, not hiking up a mountain—where parents can push a child in a stroller, sit on a bench in the shade, leave the city behind, and escape the sight, the sound, and the smell of cars. There was no such place that I could find in the vast city. All the real parks in Los Angeles had long ago been hijacked for golf courses.

And I would not miss my neighbors from hell—right-wing, racist, anti-gay Russian peasants who hung their wash over the balconies; American white trash, with whom I came very close to physical fights; young, narcissistic, Hollywood wannabes next door, with whom I did have a shoving match because of their frequent all-night partying, whose door I smashed a hole in with a heavy iron rod (not to worry about me); the building manager who verbally abused her two young children in the most terrible way, as loud as her lungs would allow, without, apparently, any sense of shame for the neighbors. When, after two years of being forced to listen to this depressing tyranny, I finally reported her to the city's child-abuse office, her husband rewarded me by slashing three tires on my car. Charming. I slashed one of his in return. (It was an educational experience: I learned from his technique to slash the tire on the side, rather than on the tread; this places the tire beyond repair.) Farewell, all you lovely people.

And bye-bye to the city with fifteen (15) metaphysical bookstores, a place where you could get your car repaired through "Astral Mechanix," which would do a full astrological profile of your car based on the time it left the manufacturer (using the engine block number). You could also get a set of instructions on psychic healing exercises for your car.

Girolamo Cardano would have been at home in L.A., he being the 16th century Italian mathematician, doctor and astrologer, whose faith in astrology reputedly led him to commit suicide so that he might die on the very day predicted by his horoscope.

Washington held out two great attractions for me: the research facilities, in particular the Library of Congress, National Archives, State Department, etc., as well as the multitude of Non-Governmental Organizations; secondly, being there would cut by about 40 percent the time and cost of flights for exchanging visits with Alexander and Adelheid. He had come each of the seven years I lived in LA, most of the time with Adelheid, with whom I remained on very good terms, and I had spent time with them in Europe almost every one of those years. It was not the ideal way to have a family life, but it was the best we could do under the circumstances, and it was a joy for each of us.

CHAPTER NINETEEN
FAREWELL CRUEL WORLD

Alexander was 13 when I returned to Washington in 1995. If my mother were still alive, I would not have heard the end of it that he hadn't been bar mitzvahed. She had died four years earlier, not long before her 91st birthday. Her death had not saddened me particularly since both her eyesight and hearing were almost at the vanishing point and for several years she had expressed a wish to die. Although she wouldn't have admitted it, I had been a large disappointment to her, or at best a great mystery. She had spent the entire period of my youth and adult life vexing over where she had gone wrong; it's painful to think of how that bent and shriveled wisp of a woman agonized over her only son.

Yet, she must have done something right by me. I will leave it to the reader to judge the veracity of that statement.

It was great fun that summer showing Alexander and Adelheid around the marvelous sights of Washington, one of the most beautiful cities in the world.

I began to write on a fairly regular basis for *Covert Action Quarterly* (CAQ), a slick and professional looking 64-page magazine, the most consistently radical magazine in the United States, which regularly paid all its writers and graphic artists a halfway decent fee. It had been publishing since 1978, with a circulation of about 12,000, a national and international reputation, and a readership of the very loyal kind.

Though I was getting articles on foreign policy published in various progressive magazines more than ever, to keep from digging excessively into my savings I still had to work in the CAQ office a few days a month, taking care of their accounting and taxes. Would I ever be able to earn my living solely from my writing? Probably not. Very few writers can.

But *Killing Hope* was taking on a following; email and snailmail came in from people all over the world thanking me for having opened their eyes to what the United States had done to other countries, for having articulated so much of what they believed and felt but couldn't put into words or document it as I had. Students of international relations informed me that they had learned more about their subject from my book than from four years at university; sections of the book could be found on many hundreds, quite possibly thousands, of Internet webpages; in the first three years I had over a hundred radio interviews; in the mainstream print media and TV neither I nor my book existed.

In 1998, CAQ imploded. There had been increasingly vituperative feelings between—on the one hand—the editor, Terry Allen, and the office manager, Barbara Neuwirth, and—on the other hand—two of the magazine's founders/owners: Bill Schaap in New York and Lou Wolf (whom I'd met in London, as mentioned above) in Washington. The reasons for the acrimony and the triggering events are not important to my story. Suffice it to say that Schaap sent Barbara a letter warning her of her possible firing if things continued in the same vein. Barbara and Terry, joined by the assistant editor Sanho Tree, who was new and had been only marginally involved in the acrimony, sent a letter back saying that the three of them were a team and that if one were fired, all three would have to be fired.

The three of them were fired. Letters informing them of this were slipped under their apartment doors; at the same time, the office locks were changed. This is what brought down the wrath upon the owners from many in the progressive community. The Great E-mail War began. The Internet was flooded with shock, hurt, disappointment, and anger from all over the country and even abroad attacking the magazine owners. The image was striking: the BOSSES sneaking notes of discharge under doors at the break of dawn, locking the WORKERS out, and even posting a rent-a-guard in the office. Lou, Schaap and Ellen Ray, the third owner, and I sent out many emails giving the other side.

One of the stories making the rounds and receiving great currency was that Terry had been fired because of political reasons, some kind of ideological clash with the owners—a "purge," with all the Stalinist connotations that that word carries. It was claimed that Schaap tried to force Terry to print certain stories and it was her refusal to do so that led to her dismissal. These assertions were clearly false since only Barbara—not directly involved in editorial matters at all—was the target of the original move to fire anyone. Terry and Sanho had in effect quit, an honorable gesture but still their choice.

The manner of the firing was vehemently attacked. Surely, it was argued again and again, a more principled and civilized manner of firing people could have been found. This seemed as plain as day to all the critics. But they were wrong. The degree of acrimony had reached the level of deep contempt and there was no way to give the employees the usual week or two of notice, thus allowing them sufficient time to sabotage the magazine. As it is, Terry happened to have her office computer at home with her and when it was finally retrieved from her it was as bare as a newborn babe. There was no telling for sure how many years of articles had been deleted, along with the address book which was our main listing of writers and sources of information, as well as the templates used for the layout (which she did). If the subscription database had been on the same computer, it would have spelled the end of the magazine. She subsequently sent out letters to CAQ's printer and a software association falsely charging the magazine with violations of law.

Even though I had no involvement whatsoever in the firings, and learned of them only after they were *faits accomplis,* the fact that I had sent out emails defending the action and continued to write and work for the magazine made me the object of hostility and ostracism in certain quarters of Washington. Some of this has survived to the present day, more than a year after I decided to leave the magazine.

What I found most remarkable about the whole incident was how so many otherwise intelligent and sophisticated people had gone directly to conclusions, without stopping at inquiry, and taken sides passionately against the magazine, knowing no more than what one side was telling them.

In the midst of the reorganization of the magazine, I took off for a two-week stay in Cuba that had been planned earlier—my first visit to the island in 40 years, the first since the revolution. I went as part of a Radical Philosophy Association delegation, which was holding a conference in Havana with similar Cuban academics. I was not a member of the Association, and attending the conference was not my reason for the trip, although I did agree to present a paper. There were about 63 of us in the group and, like good "free" Americans, we had to apply to the Treasury Department's Office of Foreign Assets Control (OFAC), the office concerned with sanctions, for "permission" to travel to Cuba, technically permission to spend money there. The Association cautioned us to apply well in advance because the public servants at OFAC liked to let applicants twist in the wind for any excuse they could think of.

I booked a flight to Nassau, whence I would catch a flight to Havana. Then I sat back and waited to hear from OFAC. And I waited. I began to call them to try and learn the status of the processing. I must have called ten times and gotten nowhere. I finally went there in person, not only in my own behalf, but in behalf of all the others in the group since I was the only one who lived in

Washington. The others would be flying out from many different cities. There was still no approval forthcoming.

The day before the departure date arrived. I had a decision to make. If I were caught on the way back from Cuba without a license, I could be fined some insane figure like $250,000. But I decided to go. If it wasn't now I might never make it there again. I flew to Nassau and boarded the flight to Havana. I'd worry about my return when I returned.

A few days after my arrival, our group leader arrived with the news that OFAC—two days after the departure date, which the Treasury office was fully aware of—had approved 60 of the 63 applicants. Everyone had been greatly inconvenienced; some had canceled; most had been forced to miss the first few days in Cuba. But the Treasury Department had shown who was boss—If you insist upon visiting one of your country's many Officially Designated Enemies (ODE), it's only right that you suffer a little punishment.

I was one of the three not approved, perhaps because I was one of the very few non-academics in the group, and had applied as a journalist, or perhaps because of some not-nice thing from my past that had come across OFAC's desk. Whatever, I was in Cuba after all these years.

I stayed with a family in a large apartment that had seen better days, but I had my own room and was comfortable enough. I alternated between attending sessions of the conference at the University of Havana and walking around the city. At the conference I delivered a paper entitled: "The United States, Cuba, And This Thing Called Democracy," which analyzed the Clinton administration's oft-repeated declaration that Cuba was the only non-democracy in the Western Hemisphere. The paper sought to demonstrate that Cuba, during the 40-year period since its revolution, had had one of the very best human-rights records in the hemisphere, a proposition that might be received by the American mind as the idea of the world being round was once received by an earlier mind.

My observation of Havana was that life is not easy for many of the city's residents. I came upon numerous buildings that clearly had been lovely at one time but now were in various states of neglect; blocks of run-down houses which had never been lovely, unpaved or torn-up streets, large mounds of uncollected garbage, a marked shortage of stores enticing one to enter, air conditioning at a premium on hot June days, the water turned off at various times; even at the university there was one day or so a week without any functioning bathrooms, (a particular inconvenience for me because the change of diet was having its usual effect upon my sensitive innards).

But these conditions certainly did not define the city for me, and there was a lot to feast one's eyes upon, including the many buildings and plazas of aesthetic and historical interest, the Hemingway-vintage hotels, the long walking path along the embankment looking out at the Caribbean, the vibrant street life. The absence of virtually any apparent homelessness, hunger, or begging could not but enhance the picture.

Our group was taken on visits to medical and educational institutions, a Communist Party office, a woman's organization, etc. What struck me most was that the people who spoke to us and answered our questions invariably made no attempt at all to hide or minimize the problems in Cuban society, including the fact that it was now a two-tier economy, with those being paid in dollars having a definitely superior purchasing power over those paid in pesos; the latter included the doctors and other professionals we met with. It seemed to me that the huge influx of tourist dollars was not reaching the mass of Cubans or their standard of living very effectively. This continues to bother me.

Something else that bothered me—in a country that boasts of having wiped out illiteracy, I walked into a medical clinic, counted 80 people sitting in the waiting room, and not one of them was reading anything. Others in my group I mentioned this to placed little weight upon it—"Oh, they were probably all just feeling ill."—shades of my Communist traveling companions in Moscow. In the long lines of people sitting or standing as they waited patiently for a bus, which I observed several times each day, it was scarcely any different. Teaching people how to read and instilling in them a love of reading are of course not the same; and it's no different in the United States amongst the poor.

We left Havana after about 10 days and split up into various tours. My group went first to the city of Matanzas, where we bunked at the university and I again presented my paper. We then made brief stops at several new resort sites of the fledgling touristy Cuba, and paid a visit to the Bay of Pigs and its intriguing museum, which focuses on the 1961 CIA invasion. The exhibits just oozed with the duplicity of American foreign policy. Since the invasion, the Cuban government has seen the CIA as being behind every problem, when in fact the CIA has been behind only half of the problems. The problem is, the Cuban government can't tell which half.

On my return flight to Nassau (Head of state: Queen Elizabeth II) I had to pass through United States (sic) immigration. How many countries in the world are able to bully other countries into allowing them to establish their own customs or immigration checkpoints on foreign territory? There were five others from my group passing through at the same time. One by one I watched as they were asked for their license, and produced it. I then walked through and saw for the first time that the immigration officer was a woman; uh oh, bad news. . . With but a glance at my passport, she smiled and nodded me through. Deep sigh.

All these years Sal Ferrera was not far from my mind. I wanted very much to get together with him, not for any angry confrontation—at least I would endeavor to keep my cool—but simply to try to understand. Was he an agent at the time we met, and thus for the entire period of our "friendship," or had he been recruited by the CIA after I moved to California? In either case—with all he knew about what the CIA did, with all that he said about the Agency, with all that he wrote about them—how could he have been their willing servant?

In 1997, a book was published posthumously called *Secrets: The CIA's War at Home*, in which the author, Angus Mackenzie, wrote that Sal had been recruited by the Agency while studying political science at Loyola University in Chicago, before moving to Washington. But Mackenzie does not indicate how he knew this and inasmuch as he died in 1994, I may never find out. From the information revealed in the book about Sal, which Mackenzie uncovered from CIA documents and CIA court testimony, it seems probable that Sal was already an agent when we met. Yet, my CIA file does not indicate any report on me emanating from Sal until October 1970, 21 months after our first meeting, while I was living in California and Sal was still in Washington.

Mackenzie wrote that Sal's master's thesis at Loyola had been entitled "Regis Debray and Revolution," a treatise "on Marxism, with particular emphasis on the conflict between orthodox Marxists and the upstarts Fidel Castro, Che Guevara, and Regis Debray, who had advocated a leap into guerrilla struggle."

How, I wondered when I read that, could anyone who had pursued such studies work for the CIA? But that was a *non sequitur* on my part. In doing research for various of my writings, I'd read the memoirs and speeches of dozens of American presidents, secretaries of state, diplomats, CIA officers, etc. without being swayed to their side.

Many years before his book came out, Angus had revealed to me and others that Sal had legally changed his name, but he refused to divulge what Sal's new name was, apparently because for a long time he harbored the hope of selling a story about Sal to *Playboy* magazine. It wasn't until the 1990s that I got the idea of calling the city of Chicago, Sal's home town. After winding my way through the bureaucracy with a dozen phone calls, I finally reached a clerk who—wonder of wonders—told me on the phone, right then and there, that Sal had changed his name on June 16, 1975, about a year after his beer-splattering showdown scene with Phil Agee in London.

Salvatore Ferrera was now Allen Vincent Carter. I spent countless hours using search engines on the Internet to locate someone of that name, but with no luck. The first and last names are too common, and middle names seldom show up in the databases. So, the search continues.

Mackenzie actually located Sal in 1980, in Costa Mesa, southern California and traveled to his apartment. Sal was "visibly discomfited" when he came to the door, Angus wrote, and denied that he had worked for the CIA. But when Angus showed him copies of the informant reports which Sal had sent to the CIA, "his face registered shock. He flipped up his middle finger and slammed the door."[51]

If Sal were any kind of dedicated or professional government agent, brimming over with hostility toward the left, would he be so embarrassed at having been found out? Would he have reacted so emotionally in response to Phil Agee's suspicions of him? Would he have legally changed his name? It was not, after all, the Mafia that he had betrayed and thus had to fear for his life. Sal reported to the CIA about how tightly bound and introspective the *Quicksilver Times* collective was, how all the in-house sex was causing problems. He told the Agency that he could not imagine living so close to the people he was spying on, day in and day out. "He wouldn't even consider staying there," said a CIA report.[52]

All of this is to suggest that Sal Ferrera was a rather torn person. What the forces were that were pulling on him, or who or what he really was, I don't know. And I probably never will unless he and I sit down someday and have a long heartfelt talk.

As a member of the group, I was embarrassed. The group I speak of is the human race. As a member of the human race, I was embarrassed that the 20th century was ending the same way it began, with wars and violence.

Periodically, American leaders convene to decide a question: Which mothers' sons in a faraway land who've done us no harm shall we kill today? In the spring of 1999, they selected the mothers' sons of Yugoslavia. Like with the bombing of Iraq, it disturbed my peace of mind and my sleep, and made me avert my eyes from much of the media. Only now it was twice as long, 78 days. I forced myself to read at least parts of some articles—noting, for example, that one of the missile attacks successfully killed those dangerous reporters and makeup girls at Serbian TV—but I clipped many more after reading little more than the headline. When the bombing was over, I'd be able to stomach them a bit easier.

> We never see the smoke and the fire, we never smell the blood,
> We never see the terror in the eyes of the children.
> Children whose nightmares will now feature screaming missiles
> from unseen terrorists known only as Americans.
> Children whose dreams will be the taste of revenge.[53]

It was for "humanitarian" reasons, we were told, as our leaders glued black hats on the pictures of one side and white hats on the other. We had to bomb to put an end to the Serbian "ethnic cleansing," they said. I could see that this was a lie even with only a cursory reading of the news. But the vast majority of Americans, including so many on the Left who should have known better, swallowed the story whole without gagging.

It was for all these true believers that I began to work on a new book, a book in response to the claim of "humanitarian intervention," the newest gimmick trotted out by the imperial court to replace "communism" as the excuse for interventions. My book would be a mini-encyclopedia of all the *un*-humanitarian actions of the U.S. government in the modern era, from the bombings and torture to subverting elections and supporting terrorism. The book, entitled *Rogue State: a Guide to the World's Only Superpower,* came out in May of 2000. It immediately turned U.S. foreign policy on its head—all of Washington's support for repressive regimes was halted, popular movements rebelling against such regimes were embraced as allies by the CIA, all bombings and sanctions ceased, the military budget was cut 90 percent, manipulations of elections were confined to Florida, assassinations of political leaders were confined to Dallas, and the deed of ownership of the world held by Globalization Incorporated was declared invalid for having been obtained through extortion.

I write this in the aftermath of the elections of 2000, which led to my being rebuked both before and after election day by real-life and Internet friends and acquaintances because of my support for Ralph Nader. As with William Goldman speaking above of Hollywood executives, these people know that there's no difference between a Democrat in the White House and a Republican in the White House significant enough to command the loyalty of a person firmly committed to domestic justice and international human rights. . . "They absolutely, positively, one hundred percent in their heart of hearts, in the dark nights of their souls, they know it. They just don't believe it, that's all."

The remarkable closeness of the vote was a reflection of the public's inability to distinguish between the two men and their parties, which caused the voters to lose their bearings and reduced the election to the mathematical probability of 50-50 chance. On every issue closest to my heart, I could not expect any difference between Al Gore in power and George W. Bush in power—the draconian War on Drugs, national health insurance, globalization, slashing the military budget, bombing foreign peoples, police and prison horrors, affordable housing, a humane welfare system, a livable minimum wage, hunger in America, and civil liberties. (How many of the Democratic voters were aware of the Clinton-Gore administration's police-state record in this last area?).

Abortion was the only question mark, but even there the long-term difference is highly unpredictable if one looks at the Republicans' record as well as Gore's record in Congress.

"You call this a two-party system?" asked columnist Barbara Ehrenreich. "I demand a recount."

The vituperation unleashed against Nader by loyal Gore supporters, and even his lesser-of-two-evils supporters, was disheartening, at times almost bizarre. The *New York Times, Washington Post,* et al attacked the man for being solely ego-motivated and questioning even his sanity, literally. None of the Nader Haters could admit that he was acting out of principle because they'd then be faced with the unenviable task of elucidating just what Albert Gore's non-negotiable principles were.

Slandering by the establishment of people who are trying to unite the disenchanted has a long history, such as practiced by the southern segregationists against anyone intent upon bringing poor whites and poor blacks together based on their common class interests, or the FBI against Martin Luther King because of the danger he represented in trying to link the civil rights and anti-war movements.

Can there be hope for a society that prices its products at $.99, $9.99, and $999.99? And, when you're not looking, changes egg-size labels from small, medium and large to medium, large and extra large? And raises the prices for basic necessities, including rent, following natural disasters like floods and earthquakes?

Ralph Nader is not a socialist, and presumably he would not think along these lines, but—since you're dying to know—if I were president, I would nationalize (or if anti-communist indoctrination has made that a word you can't deal with, try "deprivatize") those enterprises which are too important to be left to the whims of the profit motive: health care, air travel, insurance, banking, mass housing, university education (i.e., making it free), energy, automobile manufacture... The military budget could pay for all this and much more without the officers even losing their Happy Hour. And that would be only Phase I, to ease the shock in gradually. Phase II, however, would never see the light of day because I would already have been assassinated (by some "lone nut") or overthrown by a military coup.

My being a socialist has nothing to do with any other country, any model so to speak. I'm a socialist because of having lived all my life under capitalism— a system operating on the theory that the worst people, acting from their worst motives, will somehow produce the most good—and having enough intelligence, imagination and compassion to think in terms of a better society. When I think in such terms, only a form of socialism comes to mind. By whatever name. Try it yourself—think of your ideal society... think of the premises upon which it would rest, think of the working details, think of how people would relate to each other... is it taking on the form of a capitalist society?

Workers, consumers, and environmentalists of the world, unite! You have nothing to lose but a decaying world. Down with the dictatorship of the marketplace!

Unlike Candide, and Willie Brandt, I don't intend to resign myself to cultivating my garden, even if I had one. I'm not resigned to much of anything. Many of us have read this, in one form or another: "A man who is not a Socialist at twenty has no heart; a man who is still a Socialist at forty has no head." I don't know how many times I've read those words cited by conservatives, and each time I think that the author believes he's really scored a point against people like me, perhaps embarrassed me into thinking that I should act my age.

As readers will have noted, I did it backwards. I had my sober, law-abiding, patriotic, responsible-corporate-government-employee career first, till past the age of 30, and only after that did I lose my head. I've yet to find it.

Has following this path made me happy? Well, not following it would have made me pretty miserable, albeit well-to-do perhaps. If my happiness were based on only the objective conditions of my particular life—work, social relations, health, adventure, material comfort, etc.—I could say without qualification that I have had and continue to have a happy life. But I'm cursed with a social conscience that attacks my tranquility. Reading the daily horrors in my morning newspaper: the cruelty of man, the cruelty of nature, the cruelty of chance... I'm frozen in despair and anger. No, it's press exaggeration, it couldn't have happened, I try to convince myself... The Good News fairy tries to rescue me, reminding me it's only on paper, I didn't see it happen, it didn't happen to me or to my child or anyone I know—remarkable the psychology there—just turn the page and it's not even on paper, turn the page and it's gone forever.

I know I'm going to turn the page and forget about it soon enough, but I don't think I'm getting away with anything. Even as I turn the page, I'm afraid that I'm losing something, that something in me is diminished, and that it's cumulative. Often, what makes it hardest to take is that my own government, and its operatives and clients without number at home and abroad, are responsible for more of the misery than any other human agent. I would have been incredulous, during the first half of my life, to hear that one day my own government would scare me.

How did this world become so excruciatingly cruel, corrupt, unjust, and stupid? Can it have reached this level by chance, or was it planned? It's enough to make one believe in some kind of deity. Or devil.

On a more encouraging side is the development in the past couple of years of a new "movement," which cannot fail to remind me of my beloved Sixties—the sundry wings of the anti-globalization campaign, the actions on so many campuses against the likes of sweatshops, poverty wages, and the prison-industrial complex, the drive to end sanctions against Iraq, and more. I couldn't begin to predict whether the size of this movement will reach critical mass, but I don't think today's protestors will be as easily derailed as their parents were, for there's no single, simple war whose end can mollify them and return them none the wiser to pledging allegiance to the flag and Wall Street. It's nothing less than "the system" they're directly fighting: the secret, anti-democratic global corporate system, which—while we were all sleeping comfortably—quietly purchased the world, then had the contract signed and notarized while we were still rubbing our eyes, and is now intent upon exercising the full rights and privileges of ownership.

As I get older, as my thoughts turn to death more often, the absence of any kind of religious belief, particularly a belief in some kind of life after death, imposes an increasing discomfort. I used to think that religious people, whatever I thought of them individually or en masse, could face death with more serenity than I could. But I've come to think now that the religious don't have any such advantage; they fight a life-threatening illness as desperately as any atheist; they're as confused and uncertain about what, if anything, lies on the other side, their devout declarations notwithstanding. And on the subject of death, they have no advice to give, no wisdom to impart, necessarily more profound than my own, which is of no value.

Many religious folk like to believe that atheist folk can not live lives as morally imbued as the religious can. I would ask: Who is the more virtuous—the person who lives righteously because he is afraid of god's wrath or hopes for god's rewards, or the individual who lives thusly because it disturbs him to act cruelly and it's in keeping with the kind of world he wants to live in?

Farewell, dear reader. Inasmuch as this book is, to the best of my knowledge, not being published posthumously, there's a good chance our paths will cross again.

PHOTOGRAPHS

the author at 21

A Socialist Party rally, Santiago, Chile, 1972
photograph by Gary Crystal

the author at work, Copenhagen, 1974

Bill and Adelheid,
San Francisco,
around 1980

Adelheid Zöfel with
Alexander, 1982

The author and
Willie Brandt at
Soledad Prison,
1976

Alexander Blum and
his friend Karl in
London, 1990

Alexander Blum, age 18

The author, 2000

NOTES

1. "Quicksilver spies on CIA," *Washington Daily News*, September 3, 1969, p.5

2. The person was Mr. D. B. Bhosle, age 24, Killari, India, *Los Angeles Times*, October 3, 1993

3. Orwell, George. *1984* (New American Library, New York, 1961) pp.174-5

4. "Spying on U.S. Travelers by embassies Assailed," *Washington Post*, March 24, 1966

5. Pincus, Walter. "Russian Spy Chief Calls Ames Dignified, Discusses Agency's Current Challenges," *Washington Post*, December 21, 1995, p.26

6. Schlesinger, Arthur, Jr. *Robert Kennedy and His Times* (Ballantine Books, NY, 1979) p.789

7. *Los Angeles Times*, December 12, 1994, p.B3

8. Kelley, Ken. "Blissed Out, Hissed Out," *Berkeley Barb*, April 20-26, 1973

9. *U.S. News & World Report*, (Washington), January 19, 1981, p.41

10. Ibid., February 21, 1966, p.112

11. *The Progressive* (Madison, WI), February 1997, interview of Hitchens by Sasha Abramsky, pp. 32-6.

12. Mackenzie, Angus. "Sabotaging the Dissident Press," *Columbia Journalism Review*, March-April 1981, pp.57-63, based on FBI documents.

13. Hersh, Seymour. "Break-In by F.B.I. Alleged Before 1969 Inauguration," *New York Times*, May 31, 1973

14. Ibid.

15. Lewis, Sinclair. *Main Street* (1920), preface

16. Mailer, Norman. *The Armies of the Night* (The New American Library, New York, 1968), used in several parts of the book.

17. Remarks made by Rubin during a debate with a Socialist Workers Party representative on the question: "What policy next for the anti-war movement?" December 29, 1967, reported in the *Washington Free Press*, January 1968.

18. Ibid.

19. Ibid.

20. Mungo, Raymond. *Famous Long Ago: My Life and Hard Times With Liberation News Service* (Beacon Press, Boston, 1970), p.24

21. Mungo, p.150

22. Mungo, p.156

23. Mackenzie, Angus. *Secrets: The CIA's War at Home* (University of California Press, Berkeley, 1997) p.33

24. *Washington Post,* November 19, 1969

25. Zaroulis, Nancy and Gerald Sullivan. *Who Spoke Up? American Protest Against the War in Vietnam 1963-1975* (Doubleday & Co., New York, 1984), p.210

26. Levine, Mark, et al, eds. *The Tales of Hoffman* (Bantam Books, NY, 1970) p. 81; Hayden, Tom. *Reunion: A Memoir* (Collier Books, NY, 1989), pp. 31-2

27. "Extent of Subversion in Campus Disorders: Testimony of Max Philip Friedman," Hearings Before the Subcommittee to Investigate the Administration of the Internal Security Act and Other Internal Security Laws, of the Committee on the Judiciary, United States Senate, Part 2, August 12, 1969, p.101

28. Ibid., p. 92

29. Ibid., p. 138

30. Philby, Kim. *My Silent War,* (Panther Books, UK, 1969) p.170

31. Mackenzie, *Secrets,* p.32

32. *Atlanta Journal,* September 25, 1965

33. *San Francisco Chronicle,* January 9, 1971; see also Taylor, Telford. *Nuremberg and Vietnam: An American Tragedy* (New York, 1970)

34. Hearst, Patricia Campbell, with Alvin Moscow. *Every Secret Thing* (Doubleday & Co., Garden City, N.Y., 1982), p. 281.

35. *San Francisco Chronicle,* October 16, 1971, p.1

36. Steiner, Claude, et al. *Readings in Radical Psychiatry* (Grove Press, NY, 1975) excerpts from "Manifesto" and Chapter 1 ("Principles"), both by Steiner.

37. Ibid., p.13

38. Dinges, John and Saul Landau. *Assassination on Embassy Row* (London, 1981) p.43.

39. Many of these documents can be found at the National Security Archive in Washington, DC or on their website; some are in the author's possession.

40. See Coope's account in his book *Pinochet and Me: a Chilean anti-memoir* (Verso, 2001)

41. Mackenzie, *Secrets*, p.55

42. Agee, Philip. (Lyle Stuart, NJ, 1987) p.162; *Washington Post*, November 28, 2000, p.B6 (obituary)

43. Marchetti, Victor and John Marks. *The CIA and the Cult of Intelligence* (New York, 1975), p.307; Wyden, Peter. *Bay of Pigs: The Untold Story* (New York, 1979), p.142-3

44. See Blum, William. *Rogue State: A Guide to the World's Only Superpower*, (Common Courage Press, Maine, 2000), pp.146, 174, for further information.

45. *San Francisco Chronicle*, March 5, 1977, p.2

46. Ibid., January 6, 1977, p.1

47. *Washington Post*, October 7, 1999

48. *The Guardian* (London), January 16, 1987

49. *Express* (Berkeley, CA), June 12, 1987; also see my letter and Bensky's reply in two subsequent issues.

50. Goldman, William. *Adventures in the Screen Trade* (Warner Books, New York, 1983), pp.28-9

51. Mackenzie, *Secrets*, passim

52. Ibid., p.34

53. Kelly, Martin. *NonviolenceWeb*, written following the U.S. missile attacks on Afghanistan and Sudan, but even more applicable to the bombing of Yugoslavia

INDEX

abortion issue, 94-5

Agee, Philip, 172, 184-6, 188, 211

Alternative Features Service, 130, 142

Asian News Service, 167-8

Association of National Security
Alumni, 211

Bello, Walden, 158-9

Bensky, Larry, 205-6

Berkeley Barb (newspaper), 106-8,
120-1, 172, 187

Berkeley Tribe (newspaper), 120-1

Bernstein, Carl, 101

Blum, Alexander, 197, 200, 209-10, 219

Blum, William, and inglorious
Hollywood career, 206-15; and LSD,
62-4; and religion, 22-4, 26-7, 148,
179, 229; observations of the British,
200-2; observations of the
Scandinavians, 173-5; observations
of Los Angeles 217-8

Bock, Irwin, 97, 98

Bortin, Michael, 134

Brandt, Willie, 108-13, 116-20, 132-6,
159, 195-7

Brasco, Frank (Congressman), 72-3

Brooks, Kathleen, 121-2, 165-6

Brussell, Mae, 97, 101

Cawood, Pat, 35-6, 38, 45-8, 171-3, 207

Chile, socialism and *coup d'état* in, 131,
140, 147, 149, 151-62, 165, 167, 175,
182

Church, Don, 121-2, 165-6

CIA, and author's exposure of employees'
names, 1-10; exposure of diplomatic
covers of, 185-6; sending agent to
seduce author, 7-10

communism/Communist Party/anti-
communism, 85-6, 98, 140, 175,
199, 215-6

Concerned Americans Abroad

(London), 181-2, 185-6

Cooper, Marc, 156, 169

Covert Action Quarterly, 219-21

Cuba, study group, 36-8; visits to, 36,
221-3

Daily Californian, The, 197

Daly, John 208-11

Davis, Rennie, 55

Dispatch News Service, 156-7

Dominican Republic, US invasion of, 32

extrasensory perception experiments,
183

FBI, 13, 83-5, 88, 199, 100, 102-3, 165

Ferrera, Sal, 1-4, 10, 99-102, 105, 116,
172, 184-5, 224-5

Fields, Suzanne, 76-78

Food for Peace program, 50

Freedom of Information Act, files
received under, 2, 6, 14, 18, 46-8, 53,
67, 116, 224

Friedman, Max Philip, 98

Frischknecht, Hannes, 174-5

Fuller, Elaine, 184-5, 188

Garrett, Banning, 168

George, David, 212-3

Ginsberg, Allen, 76-7

Goldberg, Sam, 136

Greenberg, Allen, 44-5

Grosman, Art, 84

Grossman, Michael, 79

Harrison, Gilbert, *(New Republic)*, 186-7

Hearst, Patty, 119, 176, 196

Hess, Karl, 100

Hinrichsen, Don 176, 190,

Horman, Charles, 169

Hughes, H. Stuart, 41

hypnosis, 90

IBM, employment at, 57-61

informers, government, (see Bock,
Ferrera, Friedman, Tangen)

Printed in the United States
By Bookmasters

Printed in the United States
By Bookmasters